HOMELESS ADVOCACY

Homeless Advocacy

Laura Riley

Director of the Clinical Program
University of California, Berkeley, School of Law

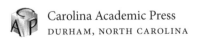
Carolina Academic Press
DURHAM, NORTH CAROLINA

LIBRARY OF CONGRESS CATALOGING-IN-PUBLICATION DATA

Names: Riley, Laura (Law teacher), editor.
Title: Homeless advocacy / by Laura Riley.
Description: Durham, North Carolina : Carolina Academic Press, LLC, [2022]
Identifiers: LCCN 2022035437 (print) | LCCN 2022035438 (ebook) |
    ISBN 9781531021917 (paperback) | ISBN 9781531021924 (ebook)
Subjects: LCSH: Legal assistance to the poor—United States. | Homeless persons—Legal status,
    laws, etc.—United States. | Homeless persons—Services for—United States.
Classification: LCC KF336 .H66 2022 (print) | LCC KF336 (ebook) |
    DDC 344.7303/258--dc23/eng/20220914
LC record available at https://lccn.loc.gov/2022035437
LC ebook record available at https://lccn.loc.gov/2022035438

Cover art by Jared Edgar McKnight, from *Criminalized for their very existence:
The Spatial Politics of Homelessness.*

Carolina Academic Press
700 Kent Street
Durham, North Carolina 27701
(919) 489-7486
www.cap-press.com

Printed in the United States of America

Summary of Contents

Contents

LIVED EXPERIENCE NARRATIVE

PRACTITIONER NARRATIVE   195

Table of Narratives

Acknowledgments

The idea for this book sparked just weeks before the COVID-19 pandemic began in Spring 2020. In the following couple of years, the project came together with significant support and work from many people. All of them deserve my plentiful and sincere thanks:

The publishing team at Carolina Academic Press, for believing that it is worth developing a book in order to create a pipeline of advocates to work with the unhoused population, in particular David Herzig.

The author contributors, Maria Foscarinis (Chapter 1), James Gilliam (contributed to Chapters 2–8), Sara Rankin, and Nantiya Ruan (Appendix) for sharing their expertise in this book.

The University of Southern California Gould School of Law Research Assistants who spent hours on substantive research, drafting, and cite checking. Bichnga Do, Angela Hwang, Junghoon Kim, Tammi Matsukiyo, Ryan Mellino, Sarah Taranto, and Cristian Torres all made the process of writing this book easier, more inspirational, and just plain fun; you helped make the content of the book insightful, and I cannot wait to see the work you all do as attorneys in this field.

The advocates and persons with lived experience of being unhoused who shared their stories so that readers could better understand how to work on homeless advocacy matters: Larae Cantley, Deborah Diamant, Robert Henderson, George Hill, Janet Kelly, and Adele Nicholas.

I would like to thank Stanley Chen, who—beyond being an empathetic, funny, and handsome husband—navigated childcare challenges and family crises together with love (during a pandemic!) so that I could carve out time for this book; Otis Chen who is my biggest little love; Mari Chen my littlest love; and Mummy who I owe so much, including my compass for social justice.

About the Author

Laura Riley is Director of the Clinical Program at University of California, Berkeley School of Law. Previously, she was Associate Professor of Lawyering Skills at the University of Southern California Gould School of Law where she taught a veteran's law practicum in which students assisted veterans, many of whom were unhoused, with discharge upgrades. Previously, she directed the experiential learning program and oversaw externships at Gould. Before joining Gould, Laura Riley practiced public interest law in Los Angeles working in the disability rights, gender justice, health, and veterans law fields. She has published many consumer and legal articles, including a Rutter Guide chapter on disability rights discrimination, a textbook chapter on Fetal Alcohol Spectrum disorders, and two amicus briefs to the United States Supreme Court. With two small children, she has no hobbies to speak of, but on occasion enjoys making hot sauce, practicing yoga, and spending time in the high desert.

About the Contributors

Maria Foscarinis has advocated for solutions to homelessness in the United States since 1985. She is a primary architect of the landmark McKinney-Vento Act, the first major federal legislation addressing homelessness, and has led groundbreaking litigation to secure the legal rights of homeless persons. Ms. Foscarinis has published dozens of articles, book chapters, and opinion pieces; lectured widely; and been frequently quoted in the media. In 1989, Ms. Foscarinis founded the National Homelessness Law Center (formerly known as the National Law Center on Homelessness & Poverty) and served as Executive Director until March 2021. She is a graduate of Columbia Law School, where she holds an adjunct appointment, teaching homelessness law and policy. In 2019, she was named a "Human Rights Hero" by the American Bar Association's Human Rights Magazine. In 2021, she was a Rockefeller Foundation Practitioner Resident in Bellagio, Italy.

James Gilliam is Director of Career Development and Public Interest Programs at Western State College of Law and is an Adjunct Professor at Loyola Law School in Los Angeles, where he teaches a homeless rights advocacy practicum he designed. Previously, he led homeless prevention and legal services at the Los Angeles Homeless Services Authority (LAHSA). He is the founding director emeritus for the Lawyers Preventing and Ending Homelessness Project, a first-of-its kind publicly funded legal services program for unhoused people. Prior, Professor Gilliam was the Deputy Executive Director for the ACLU of Southern California, where he founded and led an LGBTQ Student Rights Project. Professor Gilliam has received numerous commendations and awards for his impactful public interest advocacy, including the National LGBT Bar Association's "Top 40 Lawyers Under 40" and the President's Award from the Lesbian and Gay Lawyers Association of Los Angeles.

Jared Edgar McKnight, Assoc. ASLA and Assoc. AIA, is a Senior Associate and Designer at WRT (Wallace Roberts & Todd, LLC), and lives in Los Angeles, California. He holds a B.Arch with Honors from the Pennsylvania State University ('11), an M.Arch from the University of Pennsylvania ('12), and a Master of Landscape Architecture + Urbanism from the University of Southern California ('21). Captivated by the landscape's potential as a system to support environmental and social resilience, Jared's design-research, funded through the Landscape Architecture Foundation, USC's Landscape Justice Initiative, and Pando Populus, focuses on policy and design interventions that challenge the structures that isolate, exclude, and oppress communities and ecosystems. His research on the criminalization of unhoused individuals in Los Angeles seeks to amplify the voices of those least represented through an empathic lens that considers those voices, and identities, that are not often heard, or designed for in our civic spaces. Jared's research has been recognized as a 2021 LAF National Olmsted Scholar Finalist and with the 2021 ASLA National Award of Excellence in Research.

Sara Rankin teaches lawyering skills and homeless rights advocacy at Seattle University School of Law. She is also the founder and Director of the Homeless Rights Advocacy Project (HRAP) in the Fred T. Korematsu Center for Law and Equality at the Seattle University School of Law. HRAP regularly releases new reports that continue its groundbreaking research into laws that unfairly target the visibly poor. She also provides pro bono assistance and consultation on a variety of legal and policy matters concerning housing instability. She consults for and learns from cities, non-profits, legal aid organizations, and other advocates across the country about progressive, non-punitive, and effective means of addressing homelessness. Aside from teaching, community service, and advocacy, Professor Rankin's scholarship also concerns the criminalization of homelessness, including *Hiding Homelessness: The Transcarceration of Homelessness,* 109 Cal. L. Rev. 559 (2021); *Civilly Criminalizing Homelessness,* 56 Harv. C.R.-C.L. L. Rev. 368 (2021); and *A Homeless Bill of Rights (Revolution),* 45 Seton Hall L. Rev. 383 (2015); excerpt reproduced in Juliet Brodie, Clare Pastore, Ezra Rosser & Jeffrey Selbin, Poverty Law, Policy, and Practice (2d ed. 2021).

Nantiya Ruan is a Professor of the Practice of Law at the University of Denver Sturm College of Law and Counsel at Outten & Golden LLP, New York, NY. At Denver Law, Professor Ruan teaches first-year lawyering, poverty law, and advanced workplace law. She is the faculty director of the Workplace Law Program, as well as the Homeless Advocacy Policy Project, in which law students research and draft policy reports on the criminalization of homelessness. Professor Ruan writes in the areas of low-wage work, class and collective actions, poverty and homelessness, and social justice teaching. As part of her advocacy, Professor Ruan represents workers in national employment discrimination and wage and hour class actions.

Introduction

Equal Justice Under Law. Carved onto the marble entrance of the Supreme Court of the United States of America, these four words encapsulate the central commitment of the American judicial system. Despite this promise being set in stone, the legal and judicial systems in the United States consistently fail to uphold their vow, and today there are many groups of people for whom equal justice under law is but an aspiration. Among the most overlooked of these groups are unhoused people.[1] The temporal status of being unhoused, caused or confronted by historical systems of oppression and discrimination, is often misperceived as an identity—a stigmatized one of "homeless"—in the U.S. For the nation's societal commitment to equal justice to mean anything, institutions of higher education must provide students the tools necessary to effectively advocate for and with these individuals to attain economic equality with dignity. This book aims to provide individual activists, students, and faculty with one such tool so they may develop expertise in advocating for and beside unhoused people.

When the nation's founders drafted the Articles of Confederation, they specifically excluded unhoused people from the privileges and immunities of

---

1. In this book, the term "unhoused people" is used to emphasize the impermanent state of being unhoused as an unjust outcome of broken systems, as opposed to a marker or characteristic of a person. Others use the term "houseless," "people experiencing homelessness," while some research still refers to "the homeless." When including quotes or citing studies, the book uses the terms of the original authors and researchers. Terms change over time; the intent in this book is to use language that recognizes the dignity of all people, particularly those who are unhoused.

citizenship. While the U.S. Constitution does not explicitly exclude unhoused people, it continued to reflect strong hostility towards poor and unhoused people, as evidenced by property requirements for enfranchisement present throughout early America. The history of advocacy for unhoused people reflects a continuous struggle to enjoin courts and legislatures in our collective mission to ensure equal justice under law.

Advocacy for unhoused people brings to the forefront the conflict between a guarantee of equal justice and the primacy of negative property rights over positive human rights in American society. Effective advocacy for unhoused people therefore requires both a deep understanding of rights in the American legal system, as well as the ability to make creative legal and policy arguments to convince courts, legislators at all levels, and others within our capitalist and democratic power structures that the current system is failing in its central mission to provide equal justice under law for unhoused people.

Unhoused people represent one of the most disadvantaged groups, legally and politically, in the United States. Not only are unhoused people extremely disadvantaged by virtue of experiencing homelessness, other historically marginalized groups in America are overrepresented within unhoused populations. Thus, homeless advocacy sits at the confluence of, and must incorporate lessons from, advocacy for nearly every disadvantaged class in America. An effective advocate must understand the legal and policy issues affecting unhoused people, and also the unique socioeconomic factors affecting different groups within the unhoused population.

This textbook has two main goals. First, to provide advocates with a broad understanding of important legal and policy issues relating to homelessness in America today. Second, to share examples of creative legal advocacy models affecting a range of individuals who are overrepresented, or experience unique issues, in the context of homelessness so that students can evolve models going forward. The textbook provides advocates with the context necessary to understand the history of homeless advocacy in the United States (Chapter 1 by Maria Foscarinis) and to effectively assist diverse communities within the unhoused population, such as youth, BIPOC and LGBTQ individuals, or veterans, with compassion and dignity (Chapter 3). By reading the textbook, advocates will be exposed to the most important issues at the intersection of law and homelessness, including the foundational principles of homeless advocacy (Chapter 2); the criminalization of homelessness (Chapter 4); prevention as primary housing solution (Chapter 5); and hurdles to housing (Chapter 6–8), of which there are many kinds, including employment barriers arising from a lack of mental health treatment services, lack of access to affordable housing, shelter, and a need for legal representation. Readers will hear from advocates in the field and from those who have the experience of being unhoused. These narratives, woven throughout the book, provide a deeper understanding of how students and advocates might continue building on current models and solutions, including by reading in-depth on a current innovative initiative—Accessory Dwelling Units (Appendix, a report by Sara Rankin and Nantiya Ruan). While Chapters 5–8 present a range of ways that society can serve unhoused people by focusing on prevention programs and expanding existing interim solutions. One such current innovative initiative, Accessory Dwelling Units (ADUs), is presented through an in-depth report by Sara Rankin and Nantiya Ruan (Appendix). Having this full report on ADUs in the Appendix is a way to learn how logistics, policy, and multiple sectors can work together, and in doing so to examine what roles advocates can play in addressing homelessness.

Prospective advocates for unhoused people today face a daunting challenge, as many state and local governments across the country continue to show open hostility to the plights of unhoused people. However, this makes it even more necessary to ensure that advocates for unhoused people are equipped with the tools, both practical and theoretical, to ensure that unhoused people are afforded the same dignity, respect, and justice given to all residents of the United States. The hope is that anyone using this textbook will benefit from an effective learning aid in a collective mission to ensure the American legal and judicial system continues to make progress in its ultimate commitment: to do "Equal Justice Under Law," particularly for those who are unhoused and at high risk for unequal treatment.

PART I

The State of Homelessness and Working with Unhoused Populations

ONE

Historic and Societal Underpinnings of Homelessness Today

MARIA FOSCARINIS, CONTRIBUTOR

The current crisis of American houselessness began exploding across the country in the early 1980s. Seemingly suddenly, houselessness was no longer limited to single, white, male, older alcoholics living on the skid rows of big cities. Families with children, working men and women, members of minoritized racial and ethnic groups, and younger people in general, were now becoming houseless—and not just in urban centers, but also in suburban and rural communities. Massive cuts in social programs added to trends that had been building but largely hidden to trigger a crisis that was broadly visible across sectors of the public.

Charities, including some that were religiously based, responded by offering emergency shelter and food. Scattered around the country, they sounded an alarm for the need for government resources, often acting as advocates as well as providers of first response. Also playing a critical early role in advocacy were lawyers and legal advocacy more generally. These early advocates shaped much of the initial government response to houselessness, leaving a lasting impact.

A powerful tool for social justice, legal advocacy can take many forms. The term legal advocacy is used here broadly, to encompass not only litigation, but also legislative advocacy—work to create new laws at all levels of government—as well as administrative advocacy to influence how government agencies implement enacted laws. Also included, as a critical part of legal advocacy, are know-your-rights education efforts to ensure that the intended beneficiaries of laws and court rulings know about and can claim rights and resources, outreach, and public education more broadly.

Partnering with people with lived experience and grassroots advocates is critical to all forms of legal advocacy. These partnerships fuel and anchor advocacy, providing its content and the direct, on-the-ground connections that guide its content, priorities, and scope. They are also how advocacy measures its success or failure, and the need for and shape of further advocacy. In addition to grounding the work in lived experience, unhoused people have key roles as plaintiffs in litigation, witnesses in legislative hearings, and spokespersons. Partnering with people engaged in daily survival work and the organizations directly supporting them is an ongoing challenge for advocacy.

As typically carried out in the United States, legal advocacy reflects the current limitations of the U.S. legal system, which generally does not recognize economic rights as human rights for all. Instead, our system protects property rights, making legal advocacy especially challenging for those who, by definition, lack property. Legal advocacy has thus proceeded in makeshift, albeit creative, fashion. Sometimes and often most effectively, in coordination with community organizing and other forms of advocacy, it has yielded important victories and created a patchwork of rights and policies that provide important aid and protection, but that are insufficient to end or reverse houselessness.

This chapter summarizes the growth and causes of contemporary houselessness and highlights legal and policy advocacy and government responses to it. Moving broadly chronologically but also thematically, the chapter is not strictly linear in its progression. It starts with early efforts focused primarily on emergency relief first at the local level, then expands to the national level. It reviews legal advocacy to enforce newly created rights, to move beyond emergency relief, and to remove barriers to existing anti-poverty programs. It discusses the growing trend to criminalize houselessness, legal advocacy to fight it, and efforts to push for housing instead. It summarizes decades-long advocacy for the human right to housing, now gaining traction, and previews potential future directions. It ends with a look at current developments and their implications for the future.

I. Growth of Modern American Houselessness: A Brief Overview

During the Great Depression, millions of people lost their homes; many lived outdoors in makeshift shacks and tent-cities. When he came into office, President Roosevelt responded with a "New Deal," a package of social welfare programs to address the enormous needs the country was facing. Among them was the first federal housing program; over the coming years and decades, this led to the development of a series of federal low-income housing programs, with the two main ones being a program to directly build low-income housing—public housing—and a program to provide subsidies to low-income people to help them afford housing in the private market, now called "Housing Choice Vouchers."[2]

In 1981, the Reagan Administration came into office, with a commitment to shrink the footprint of the federal government.[3] Reagan promoted and signed legislation that cut and tightened eligibility requirements for many social programs,[4] and federal housing programs took an enormous hit. In 1979, the federal government funded 347,600 new units of low-income housing each year; in 1982, that was only 2,630, an astonishing drop.[5] The dramatic cuts initiated in the Reagan era have yet to be reversed; currently, only one in four of those eligible for low-income housing assistance receives it.[6]

These cuts came on the heels of the loss of inexpensive housing in the private market, including an estimated loss of some one million units of Single Room Occupancy ("SRO") housing in the 1970s.[7] SROs had, in part, served to

---

2. National Low Income Housing Coalition, "A Brief Historical Overview of Affordable Rental Housing." (2015). https://nlihc.org/sites/default/files/Sec1.03_Historical-Overview_2015.pdf.

3. Reagan.com, "Ronald Reagan and Small Government: Reducing the Size." Accessed September 27, 2021. https://www.reagan.com/ronald-reagan-small-government-reducing-the-size.

4. General Accounting Office, "Homelessness: A Complex Problem and the Federal Response." (1985).

5. National Low Income Housing Coalition, "Changing Priorities" (2001), Table 6. In 1974, the total was higher still: 416,788 new units.

6. National Low Income Housing Coalition, "The Gap" at 18. (2021). https://reports.nlihc.org/sites/default/files/gap/Gap-Report_2021.pdf.

7. GAO, Homelessness: A Complex Problem and the Federal Response at 23–24 (1985) (estimating some one million SRO housing units were lost in the 1970s).

house people released from mental health institutions beginning in the 1960s, as a result of legislation President Kennedy signed that provided for residential treatment centers.[8] However, only half of these centers were created, and none were fully funded;[9] many former patients were simply left to fend for themselves and, with the loss of SRO housing and cuts to federal disability benefits, some became houseless. Currently, a significant minority—but by not a majority, contrary to common stereotype—of the houseless population also experiences mental illness.[10]

The Reagan cuts also added to decades of racist policies that excluded Black and other people of color from housing,[11] including policies adopted as part of the New Deal programs. This contributed to the disproportionate representation of people of color, and especially Black people, in the houseless population, even as compared to the poverty population. Today, some 40% of people experiencing houselessness are Black, compared to 28% of the poverty population and 12% of the total U.S. population.[12]

These assaults on low-income housing, coupled with cuts in other social programs, spurred an explosion of houselessness.[13]

II. Early Advocacy, Local and National: Emergency Responses

Much early advocacy to address houselessness was centered in New York City. In 1979, advocates filed *Callahan v. Carey* in New York state court on behalf of a class of men living on that city's Bowery. The case argued for a right

---

8. The legislation was premised on the emergence of new treatments and a belief that, given adequate support, people could be treated in their communities. SROs became a default, last resort option when promised residential treatment centers were not adequately funded.

9. Community Mental Health Act. Accessed September 27, 2021. https://en.wikipedia .org/wiki/Community_Mental_Health_Act.

10. National Alliance to End Homelessness, "What Causes Homelessness." Accessed September 27, 2021. https://endhomelessness.org/homelessness-in-america/what-causes -homelessness/health.

11. Rothstein, Richard. 2017. *The Color of Law*. New York: W.W. Norton.

12. National Alliance to End Homelessness, "Racial Inequalities in Homelessness, by the Numbers." Accessed September 27, 2021. https://endhomelessness.org/resource/racial -inequalities-homelessness-numbers/.

13. GAO, "Homelessness: A Complex Problem and the Federal Response." (1985).

to shelter under state and city law, including a provision in the state's constitution imposing a duty to provide "aid, care, and support" of "the needy."[14] Just before Christmas, the court granted plaintiffs' motion for preliminary injunction, a landmark victory.[15] However, there was no ruling on the merits; instead, after lengthy negotiations, in 1981, the parties entered into a detailed consent decree spelling out the terms under which the city would provide emergency shelter to all houseless men in the city.[16] Subsequent litigation expanded the terms of the decree to women[17] and families; the latter included a ruling on the merits establishing that the New York Constitution did, in fact, protect a right to shelter.[18]

The consent decree coincided with the release of a new report that the Community Service Society of New York released in 1981, coauthored by anthropology graduate students who documented the experience of houselessness as "participant-observers," being houseless, in shelters, and eating at soup kitchens in New York City. The report also drew media coverage and public attention to houselessness in the city, adding momentum to and spurring advocacy and government response.[19] One result was the founding, in 1981, of the Coalition for the Homeless, still a prominent New York advocacy group.

The newly formed Coalition for the Homeless, monitoring compliance, repeatedly sued to enforce the consent decree over the following decades. The organization also filed several other cases, including some seeking relief aimed at preventing houselessness. Advocates in other cities also filed litigation,

---

14. *Callahan v. Carey,* Amended Complaint, https://www.coalitionforthehomeless .org/wp-content/uploads/2014/08/CallahanAmendedComplaint-1.pdf.

15. *Callahan v. Carey,* No. 42582/79, New York Supreme Court, New York County (1979).

16. *Callahan v. Carey* Consent Decree. https://www.coalitionforthehomeless.org/wp -content/uploads/2014/08/CallahanConsentDecree.pdf. See the Coalition for the Homeless website for an overview of this and other cases. Accessed March 29, 2022. https://www .coalitionforthehomeless.org/our-programs/advocacy/legal-victories.

17. *Eldredge v. Koch,* 118 Misc. 2d 163, 459 N YS.2d 960 (Sup. Ct. N.Y. Co.), *rev'd on other grounds,* 98 A.D.2d 675, 469 N.Y.S.2d 744 (1983) (Equal Protection Clause requires equivalent facilities be made available to homeless women).

18. *McCain v. Koch,* 117 A.D.2d 198 (1st Dept. 1986) (Constitution and laws of the State of New York require New York City and State to provide emergency housing to all homeless families with children).

19. Johnston, Laurie. 1981."A Journey into The City's Netherworld," *New York Times,* March 11, 1981. https://www.nytimes.com/1981/03/11/nyregion/a-journey-into-the-city-s -netherworld.html.

resulting in emergency aid based on state and local law,[20] as well as procedural protections grounded in the U.S. Constitution.[21] At the same time local coalitions were forming across the country, many focused on shelter and other emergency relief, although some also included a call for housing. In 1982, the local groups, led by the New York coalition, came together to form the National Coalition for the Homeless.[22]

Around the same time, in Washington D.C., the Community for Creative Non-Violence (CCNV) was advocating for shelter locally, relying primarily on civil disobedience.[23] CCNV also identified and began working with a handful of sympathetic members of the Reagan Administration, pressing for vacant federal buildings to be used for shelter. As a result, the Administration agreed to allow the group to use a large, dilapidated, vacant federal building in downtown D.C. as a shelter, accommodating over 1000 people.[24] On a parallel track, CCNV organized a successful campaign for a ballot initiative to establish a right to shelter in the city, and Initiative 17 was voted into law.[25] CCNV also had engaged with Congress, spurring the first hearings on the crisis in 1982, but no legislative proposal was put forth.

---

20. See, e.g., *Maticka v. Atlantic City*, 216 N. J. Super. 634 (1987) (striking down "fault" standard in assessing applications for emergency shelter by families under state's AFDC emergency assistance program and requiring hearing on time limitation); *Hodge v. Ginsburg*, 303 S.E.2d 245 (1983) (requiring state to provide emergency shelter, medical care, and food to homeless plaintiffs under state's adult protective services statute and implementing regulations); *Graham v. Schoemehl*, No. 854-00035 (Mo. Cir. Ct. 1985) (consent decree requiring emergency shelter for homeless people in St. Louis following suit based on state law creating duty to relieve the poor); *Massachusetts Coal. for the Homeless v. Sec'y of Human Servs.*, 511 N.E.2d 603 (1987) (state has obligation to provide aid to AFDC families sufficient to pay for housing and to seek sufficient funds from legislature).

21. See, e.g., *Williams v. Barry*, 490 F. Supp. 941 (D.D.C. 1980) (D.C. shelter policy created property interest protected by procedural due process; shelter residents could not be evicted without some form of process).

22. National Coalition for the Homeless. Accessed March 29, 2022. www.national homeless.org.

23. See generally Victoria Rader, *Signal through the flames: Mitch Snyder and America's Homeless* (1986).

24. Susan Baker, wife of then Presidential advisor James Baker III, played a key role in this decision by the Administration. Later that year, Mitch Snyder and other CCNV members organized a hunger strike to force the Administration to pay for renovations to the building; on the eve of the national election, with Snyder critically ill, Reagan agreed to the group's demand. People experiencing houselessness and CCNV staff lived together at the shelter, in community, a basic tenet of the group.

25. The initiative passed with over 70% of voter support.

Homelessness was clearly a national crisis. But despite the occasional helpful actions of individual members of the Reagan Administration, the overarching position of the Administration was that homelessness was not an issue for federal action; it was a matter for charity or, at most, local government. Aiming to spur a national response, the newly formed National Coalition established an office in Washington, D.C. to organize a campaign for federal action.[26]

Legal services offices around the country had begun seeing increasing numbers of unhoused clients in their offices; lawyers from their national offices, specializing in a variety of poverty issues, had been meeting to draft a blueprint for federal legislation based on the needs the local legal services offices identified. However, because no single organization was able to focus on it, the effort languished. The new Washington office of the National Coalition joined that group, taking on the job of shaping the draft into a proposal, and beginning a campaign to champion it on Capitol Hill.

The Homeless Persons Survival Act consisted of three parts: emergency relief, preventative measures, and long-term solutions. Eventually introduced in the House by Rep. Mickey Leland and in the Senate by Al Gore, it was an ambitious, multipart bill; the plan was to advocate for pieces of it separately while rallying support for the whole. A few pieces became law in 1986. Then, later that year, CCNV became involved, working with the National Coalition; the latter engaged Covington & Burling, a Washington law firm with a lobbying practice, to help pro bono. Facing steep political odds in the Reagan era, the campaign highlighted the approaching cold weather and focused on emergency relief.[27]

Carried out over the winter of 1986–87, the campaign combined traditional lobbying, coalition building, and direct-action strategies. Activists camped out in front of the Capitol building to draw attention to the campaign, national advocates mobilized local groups across the country to put pressure on their representatives in Congress, and the pro bono law firm team provided expert

---

26. The National Coalition hired the author, then a young lawyer, to go to Washington to establish that office and organize the campaign.

27. For an overview of this campaign, see Foscarinis, Maria. 2018. "Strategies to Address Homelessness in the Trump Era: Lessons from the Reagan Administration," *J. of Affordable Housing and Comm. Dev. L.*, 27, no.1: 161–181; Foscarinis, Maria. 1993. "Beyond Homelessness: Ethics, Advocacy, and Strategy," *St. Louis Univ. Pub. L. Rev.*, 12, no. 1: 37–67; Foscarinis, Maria. 1996. "The Federal Response," in Jim Baumohl, ed., *Homelessness in America* (Oryx Press:).

advice and helpful connections. Then-Speaker of the House Jim Wright got behind the campaign, providing crucial political support.

On July 22, 1987, the Stewart B. McKinney Homeless Assistance Act became the first major federal legislation addressing houselessness. Authorizing $1 billion over two years—and appropriating $712 million—it consisted primarily of the emergency parts of the HPSA; much of the funding went to emergency shelter and transitional housing, a small amount to permanent housing. Small amounts also went to job training, larger amounts to health care. The Act also created the Interagency Council for the Homeless, now known as the U.S. Interagency Council on Homelessness, to lead and coordinate federal efforts to address what the Act explicitly named a "crisis" facing the nation.[28]

Significantly, the Act also created two legal rights: Title V created a right of first refusal to "suitable" vacant federal real property for providers of services to unhoused people, including non-profits and state and local governments.[29] Title VII created a right of homeless children to enroll in and attend public school, including a right to continue in their school of origin if that was in their best interest, and to receive transportation to get there.[30]

On a parallel track, part of the campaign for a federal response included developing a litigation strategy to press the federal agencies to act. Before enactment of the McKinney Act, there was little federal law addressing houselessness specifically; however, buried in the federal statute books was a provision requiring the defense department to implement a program to make military installations available for use as shelters, and a successful suit was filed in federal court to require the Department of Defense to implement the law.[31] After the McKinney Act was enacted, advocates filed a series of lawsuits—first to get funds out and then to implement rights created by the new law; one is ongoing to this day.[32]

Much of the early advocacy was focused on emergency relief; some advocates prioritized shelter, but for many advocates, this was simply a result of the

---

28. 42 U.S.C. § 11301 (1987). For an overview of and details on the original Act and early amendments to it, see Foscarinis, "The Federal Response," *supra.*

29. 42 U.S.C. § 11411 (1987).

30. 42 U.S.C. § 11431 (1987).

31. *Bruce v. U.S. Dep't of Defense*, No. 87-0423 (D.D.C. 1987); Foscarinis, Maria, "Federal Legislative and Litigative Strategies: An Overview," *Maryland J. of Contemp. Legal Issues* 1, no. 1: 9–26 (1990).

32. Foscarinis, "Federal Legislative and Litigative Strategies," 9–26.

political constraints of the time.[33] In comments to the press at the time, advocates made clear that the McKinney Act was just a first step, and that longer term relief—primarily housing—was imperative.[34] Advocates also made sure to get key congressional sponsors to affirm this in statements they made as part of the Congressional Record.[35]

III. Fighting for More Lasting Relief: Two Steps Forward and One Step Back

Enactment of the McKinney Act, now known as the McKinney-Vento Homeless Assistance Act, was a signal event in federal policy. President Reagan and his Administration had insisted that houselessness was a "lifestyle choice" and that the federal government had no responsibility to address it; when large bipartisan majorities passed the Act, he was forced to sign it, but he did so in the evening, without the customary signing ceremony, to indicate his lack of "enthusiasm."[36]

A. Definitions and Numbers

With the enactment of the McKinney-Vento Act came significant federal funds, distributed to states and localities and, in some cases, through competitive grant applications.[37] All funds had the goal of benefiting unhoused or homeless people, and defining "homeless" was essential for this purpose. It was also essential for other non-funding provisions of the Act—for example, those protecting the right of unhoused children to enroll in and attend school. Advocates working on the legislation developed a broad formulation that reflected the reality that people typically move in and out of homelessness,

---

33. Foscarinis, Maria "Homelessness, litigation and law reform strategies: a United States perspective," *Australian J. of Human Rights*, 10:2, 105–132, (2004).

34. Pear, Robert. 1987. "President Signs $1 Billion Bill to Aid Homeless." *New York Times*, July 24, 1987.

35. Foscarinis, "Homelessness," *supra*.

36. Pear, Robert, *supra*.

37. See Foscarinis, "The Federal Response," *supra*.

resorting to a variety of makeshift arrangements.[38] Unfortunately, it led to different interpretations by the agencies charged with implementing the new law, and continuing, still ongoing controversy.[39]

The primary point of contention is between proponents of the "narrow" definition the United States Department of Housing and Urban Development ("HUD") adopted, which largely leaves out people who have lost their housing and moved in temporarily with friends or relatives, rotating among them; this is an all-too-common arrangement. The "broader" definition the Department of Education ("DOE") adopted includes this "doubled up" population in its definition of homeless children, with which it is concerned. The argument centers on whether it is better to "target" limited resources to a smaller population or spread it more thinly to a larger one. Proponents of the broader interpretation believe that approach best positions advocates to enlarge the coalition of supporters—and thus enlarge the total pie, obviating this dilemma.

The question of definition also adds to the difficulty in assessing the size of the unhoused population, another source of ongoing controversy since the early

---

38. As originally enacted, the definition read:

> For purposes of this Act, the term "homeless" or "homeless individual" includes—
>> (1) an individual who lacks a fixed, regular, and adequate nighttime residence; and
>> (2) an individual who has a primary nighttime residence that is—
>> (A) a supervised publicly or privately operated shelter designed to provide temporary living accommodations (including welfare hotels, congregate shelters, and transitional housing for the mentally ill);
>> (B) an institution that provides a temporary residence for individuals intended to be institutionalized; or
>> (C) a public or private place not designed for, or ordinarily used as, a regular sleeping accommodation for human beings.

42 U.S.C. § 11301103(a). It explicitly excluded prisoners:

> For purposes of this Act, the term "homeless" or "homeless individual" does not include any individual imprisoned or otherwise detained pursuant to an Act of the Congress or a State law.

42 U.S.C. § 11301103(c).

This formulation was based on language developed by the author, in consultation with Kim Hopper; of course, members of Congress, working with congressional legislative counsel had the final word; for example, the exclusion of prisoner, was inserted by them.

39. HUD Exchange, HUD's Definition of Homeless: Resources and Guidance (2019); U.S. Interagency Council on Homelessness, Key Federal Terms and Definitions of Homelessness Among Youth (2018).

1980s.[40] Currently, HUD requires annual counts of the unhoused populations by continuums of care, the local entities that receive and manage HUD McKinney Vento funds;[41] DOE requires counts of unhoused children by all states, which in turn collect data from local education agencies.[42] The HUD count includes both a shelter and a "street" count; the latter typically involves volunteers literally trying to identify and count people they consider unhoused in some (not all) public places in the space of a few hours on a single night of the year.

Some advocates heavily criticize the HUD "street" count as a fundamentally flawed effort that yields a significant undercount. Moreover, because each community has the option to choose its own method, and to vary its choice each year, the count is not helpful even for comparative trend purposes. The DOE count, by contrast, is an annual count that relies, ultimately, on the identification of unhoused children by schools. Because schools, despite their obligation to do so, may not be able to identify all their unhoused students—and families may also be reluctant to come forth—these numbers also are almost certainly undercounts.[43]

In 1989, the National Law Center on Homelessness & Poverty ("NLCHP") was founded to focus specifically and solely on using the power of the law to end homelessness in the United States. The name was chosen deliberately to include "poverty," to send the message that the NLCHP viewed houselessness as part of continuum—an extreme form of poverty. This was a position not widely accepted at the time; an argument that houseless people suffer personal "pathologies" that make them different from other poor people, and from other people in general, was gaining currency. The new organization placed houselessness squarely on the continuum of poverty, with a goal of taking aim at its underlying causes.[44] In 2020, after concluding that the point had been made and largely accepted, the NLCHP simplified and shortened its name,

40. See, e.g., Subcommittee, Committee on Housing and Community Development, of the Committee on Banking, Finance and Urban Affairs, and the Sub-committee on Manpower and Housing of the Committee on Government Operations, U.S. House of Representatives, Joint Hearing, HUD Report on Homelessness (1984).

41. HUD Exchange Point-in-Time Count and Housing Inventory Count. Accessed Sept 30, 2021. https://www.hudexchange.info/programs/hdx/pit-hic/.

42. National Center for Homeless Education. Accessed March 29, 2022. https://nche.ed.gov/data-and-stats/.

43. Foscarinis, Maria. 2017. "Undercounting People Experiencing Homelessness." *Huffington Post*, Feb. 6, 2017.

44. Other organizations followed suit, including the ABA Commission on Homelessness & Poverty.

dropping the word poverty, and becoming simply the National Homelessness Law Center ("Law Center").[45]

Treating houselessness as part of a larger continuum also means fully accounting for the people it affects. In 1992, a large coalition of plaintiffs—including two cities, the U.S. Conference of Mayors, service providers, unhoused people, and the Law Center—filed a lawsuit to challenge a flawed Census Bureau effort to count the unhoused population in the 1990 decennial census, in contravention of the Constitution's requirement of a full count of the entire population. The court dismissed the suit on standing grounds, but the Bureau issued a disclaimer making clear that its count was not an actual estimate of the unhoused population.[46]

B. Enforcing and Extending the McKinney-Vento Act

Much subsequent legal advocacy in the 1990s and beyond focused on enforcing the McKinney-Vento Act, protecting and expanding on its provisions and its funding. Early litigation to enforce Title V yielded a nationwide injunction, multiple enforcement orders, and a slow trickle of properties that now number over 500 and serve an estimated 2 million people each year.[47] Federal court litigation the Law Center filed in 1992 resulted in a 1995 federal appeals court ruling holding that Title VII, which protected the rights of unhoused children to a public education, is in fact enforceable;[48] this ruling has been reaffirmed on multiple occasions over the years.[49]

At the same time, policy advocacy to build on the original commitment to move beyond emergency relief also moved forward. An early advocacy effort brought together a coalition of national anti-poverty advocacy groups

---

45. National Homelessness Law Center, "Message from the Executive Director," *In Just Times*, August 2020.

46. *National Law Center on Homelessness and Poverty v. Kantor*, 91 F.3d 178 (D.C. Cir. 1996).

47. National Law Center on Homelessness & Poverty. 2017. "Public Property, Public Need." https://homelesslaw.org/wp-content/uploads/2018/10/Public-Property-Public-Need-1.pdf.

48. *Lampkin v. District of Columbia*, 27 F.3d 605 (D.C. Cir. 1994).

49. E.g., *Salazar v. Edwards*, No. 92 CH 5703, Settlement Agreement and Stipulation to Dismiss (Ill. Nov. 21, 1996); https://chicagohomeless.issuelab.org/resource/enforcing-the-educational-rights-of-homeless-children-and-youth-focus-on-chicago.html; *National Law Center on Homelessness and Poverty v. State of New York,* 224 F.R.D. 314 (E.D.N.Y. 2004).

to develop and push for "Beyond McKinney: Policies to End Homelessness," an ambitious agenda that aimed to build on and push forward the unfinished work of the original Homeless Persons Survival Act. The Coalition set a consensus agenda for housing, income, services, and civil rights that helped steer advocacy focused on prevention and long-term solutions.

Some portions of this agenda were adopted following legislative and regulatory advocacy. Among these were a requirement that earned income credits be made available to unhoused families, including a requirement that the IRS conduct outreach to unhoused workers. A law was enacted authorizing funding for a new "demonstration program" to increase access to federal disability benefits for unhoused people who were physically or mentally disabled.[50] A requirement to address the needs of unhoused people in the conversion of military bases followed.[51]

But in 1996, President Clinton's welfare reform legislation, which repealed welfare for families with children, replacing it with a new block grant program, removed a key, albeit grossly inadequate, entitlement for poor families, many of whom were either houseless or on its brink. Newt Gingrich became Speaker of the House, and his "Contract with America" proposed draconian cuts to many social programs.[52] Both developments ushered in a period of defensive

---

50. Pub. L. No. 100-203, 101 Stat. 1330, 42 U.S.C. § 1383 *note*, Sec. 917 (1987). This law led to the development of a successful program to help homeless people sign up for disability benefits known as SSI/SSDI Outreach, Access and Recovery ("SOAR"), which is now administered through the Substance Abuse and Mental Health Services Administration ("SAMHSA"). Accessed March 29, 2022. https://www.samhsa.gov/soar.

51. Base Closure Community Redevelopment and Homeless Assistance Act of 1994, 10 U.S.C. § 2687 (1994). National Law Center on Homelessness & Poverty. 2007. "Utilizing the Base Closure Community Redevelopment and Homeless Assistance Act: A Toolkit for Non-Profits." https://homelesslaw.org/wp-content/uploads/2018/10/BRACtoolkit.pdf.

52. The Contract with America included a proposal to cut cash welfare programs by, among other things, prohibiting welfare to mothers under 18 years of age, denying increased aid (under what was then the main federal cash assistance program for poor families, Aid to Families with Dependent Children or AFDC) for additional children born while the mother was on welfare, and enacting a two-years-and-out provision with work requirements to promote individual responsibility and complete termination of AFDC payments after five years. This proposal was passed by the House and Senate but vetoed twice by President Clinton; a slightly less harsh alternative, the Personal Responsibility and Work Opportunity Reconciliation Act, which offered many of the same policies, was enacted August 22, 1996. Many other proposals included in the original Contract with America passed the House but not the Senate and did not become law.

advocacy, including fighting—not always successfully—concerted efforts to cut funding for the McKinney-Vento Act as well as other critical programs.[53]

Nevertheless, despite periods of significant setbacks, in the coming years, overall funding for McKinney-Vento programs increased. The Clinton Administration and Andrew Cuomo, then HUD Assistant Secretary for Community Planning and Development, developed a continuum of care model for the allocation of HUD-administered homelessness funds.[54] In this model, a coalition of service providers, including and sometimes consisting of local government, comes together to constitute a "continuum-of-care."[55] The continuum develops a plan and applies collectively to HUD for McKinney Act funds to address houselessness in their communities.

The infusion of federal funds and this model also meant that service providers were increasingly beholden to local governments, which often dominated the local continuums of care that applied for, received, and distributed federal funds. Whereas in the early days, providers were often the fiercest advocates, they were becoming increasingly constrained by their dependence on government funding. This is sometimes referred to as the "institutionalization" of houselessness.[56]

The emergence of "ten-year plans" to end homelessness dovetailed with this trend. The first such plan was developed and released by the National Alliance to End Homelessness (NAEH) in 2000.[57] Subtitled "a plan, not a dream,"

---

53. Foscarinis, Maria, "The Federal Response," 1996, in *Homelessness in America*, edited by Jim Baumohl, 160–171, 170. Phoenix: Oryx Press; National Law Center on Homelessness & Poverty, 1996, "Federal Funding for FY96 Finalized," *In Just Times* 7, no. 4, April 1996.

54. U.S. Department of Housing and Urban Affairs Archives, "Andrew M. Cuomo, Highlights of HUD Accomplishments 1997–2000." https://archives.hud.gov/secretaries /cuomobio.cfm.

55. HUD Exchange, "The Continuum of Care Program;" https://www.hudexchange .info/programs/coc/ (visited March 29, 2022).

56. See, e.g., Foscarinis, Maria, 1993, "Beyond Homelessness: Ethics, Advocacy, and Strategy," *St. Louis Univ. Public L. Rev.*, 12, no. 1: 37–67; Beck, Elizabeth and Twiss, Pamela, 2018, The Homelessness Industry: A critique of U.S. social policy, Boulder and London: Lynne Rienner Publishers, Inc.

57. Formed in 1983 as the Committee on Food and Shelter, and co-founded by Susan Baker, wife of James Baker III, former chief of staff and Treasury Secretary to Ronald Reagan and Secretary of State to George H.W. Bush, it later rebranded as the National Alliance to End Homelessness. Accessed March 29, 2022. https://endhomelessness.org/who-we-are /our-mission-and-history/?gclid=CjwKCAiAksyNBhAPEiwAlDBeLLGnwpbRB4EFerVB JMUy0jvmJrCmQmI9fBtY87rthNHO3DuUOLemjRoCzQIQAvD_BwE.

it was embraced the following year by the George W. Bush Administration, which then challenged cities across the country to develop their own plans.[58] While the initiative effectively passed the responsibility back to the local level, it also galvanized many local governments and groups, and hundreds developed plans.

Some of the plans collected significant data and developed policy ideas. But the lack of federal funds accompanying the initiative limited its impact; not surprisingly, it did not end homelessness locally or nationally. In 2009, Congress directed the U.S. Interagency Council on Homelessness to create a federal plan to end homelessness, reasserting federal responsibility.[59] Since that time, each Administration has developed a plan. Advocacy has included efforts to shape the plans; however, despite the urging of advocates, the plans have not included budgets or funding requests.

Other advocacy efforts focused on including the needs of houseless people in larger, "mainstream" anti-poverty programs. As a result, in 2004, unhoused children with special needs were included in the Individuals with Disabilities Act; also in 2004, all unhoused schoolchildren were made automatically eligible for assistance under Title I, the major federal program for low-income schoolchildren.[60] In 2007, unhoused preschoolers were included in Head Start and other early childhood programs.[61] In 2005, housing protections were added to the Violence Against Women Act, VAWA, an effort to prevent domestic violence survivors—primarily women and their children—from losing housing.[62]

---

58. See S. Berg, Ten Year Plans, 2015 Advocates Guide, National Low Income Housing Coalition (2015).

59. This was included in the HEARTH Act, which reauthorized and amended the HUD McKinney-Vento programs, and followed advocacy by the Law Center and others. That Act also included a directive to the USICH to work to develop alternatives to the criminalization of homelessness. Accessed March 29, 2022. https://www.hud.gov/sites /documents/HAAA_HEARTH.PDF.

60. National Center for Homeless Education. 2014. "Serving Students Experiencing Homelessness Under Title I, Part A." https://files.eric.ed.gov/fulltext/ED574592.pdf.

61. Improving Head Start for School Readiness Act of 2007, Pub. Law 110-134 121 Stat. 1363 (2007). The applicability of the McKinney-Vento Act provisions to public preschool was clarified in amendments enacted in 1994. Foscarinis, "The Federal Response," *supra*, 169.

62. National Law Center on Homelessness & Poverty, "Insult to Injury: Violations of the Violence Against Women Act," 1–2 (2009). A comprehensive 2005 study found that one in four homeless women became homeless after experiencing violence. Jasinski, Jana L. et al. 2005. "The Experience of Violence in the Lives of Homeless Women: A Research Report 2, 65," *American J. of Pub. Health* 6 (January): 1–101, 2, 65. In a 2007 study, domestic violence

Enacted in response to advocacy by a coalition of houselessness, housing and domestic violence organizations, these protections amended the federal public housing and Section 8 housing assistance statutes to ensure that survivors and their families are not evicted from or denied housing based on their survivor status.[63] In 2013, important new amendments significantly expanded these protections, expanding their coverage to nine additional federally subsidized housing programs, including otherwise private developments benefiting from federal Low Income Housing Tax Credits. They also made clear that survivors of sexual assault are covered and mandated that housing agencies create and implement emergency housing transfer options.[64] Several jurisdictions also enacted state counterparts. Amendments to further strengthen these protections are pending but have not been enacted.

In late 2007, the "great recession" and foreclosure crisis precipitated large increases in houselessness, rivaling the initial explosion in the 1980s.[65] Under state and local landlord tenant law, foreclosures could occur with virtually no notice to tenants renting the subject property—putting them at risk of eviction and houselessness.[66] Reports by houselessness and housing organizations

---

was the most common reason women gave for their homelessness. Tischler, V., Rademeyer, A. and Vostanis, P. (2007), "Mothers experiencing homelessness: mental health, support and social care needs." *Health & Social Care in the Community*, 15: 246–253, https://doi .org/10.1111/j.1365-2524.2006.00678.x.

63. See National Law Center on Homelessness & Poverty and National Coalition to End Domestic Violence, "Lost Housing, Lost Safety: Survivors of Domestic Violence Experience Housing Denials and Evictions Across the Country," 2, 5–6 (2007).

64. National Law Center on Homelessness & Policy. "Fact Sheet: The impact of the Violence Against Women Reauthorization Act of 2013 on the housing rights of survivors of domestic violence." https://homelesslaw.org//wp-content/uploads/2018/10/VAWA_Fact _Sheet.pdf.

65. Sard, Barbara. 2009. Recovery Package Should Include New Housing Vouchers and Other Measures to Prevent Homelessness. Washington, DC: Center on Budget and Policy Priorities, https://www.cbpp.org/research/number-of-homeless-families-climbing -due-to-recession; National Coalition for the Homeless et al., Foreclosure to Homelessness (2009). Accessed March 29, 2022. https://www.nationalhomeless.org/factsheets /foreclosure.html.

66. National Law Center on Homelessness & Poverty and National Low Income Housing Coalition, *Without Just Cause: A 50 State Review of the (Lack of) Rights of Tenants in Foreclosure* (2009). The report detailed the shocking lack of protections afforded to renters in foreclosed properties: renters who had been paying rent regularly, in full compliance with their lease, could be summarily evicted without notice, based on their landlord's default on their mortgage—even if they had no knowledge of the landlord's non-payment.

detailed the impact of the foreclosure crisis,[67] and a national survey report detailed the lack of legal protections for tenants in many states.[68] As part of an advocacy strategy, the survey report was widely publicized and shared with lawmakers and, in 2009, Congress passed and President Obama signed the Protecting Tenants at Foreclosure Act, which required (among other provisions) at least 90 days' notice before a bona fide tenant could be evicted; if the tenant had a lease for a longer period, it had to be honored.[69]

IV. Criminalization of Houselessness: Advocacy for "Housing Not Handcuffs" Emerges

When it first came to public attention, houselessness had been shocking. Beginning in the 1990s, news reports of "compassion fatigue" became more prevalent.[70] While public opinion polls during this time did not reflect diminution of compassion, according to a comprehensive study,[71] the public narrative began to shift, with houselessness increasingly portrayed as part of a landscape to which many had become accustomed. Even worse, this portrayal set the stage for an assumption that the problem had been solved—but

---

67. National Coalition for the Homeless, the National Health Care for the Homeless Council, the National Alliance to End Homelessness, the National Association for the Education of Homeless Children and Youth, the National Law Center on Homelessness & Poverty, the National Low Income Housing Coalition and the National Policy and Advocacy Council on Homelessness, *Foreclosure to Homelessness 2009: The Forgotten Victims of the Subprime Crisis.* https://nationalhomeless.org/wp-content/uploads/2013/01/Foreclosureto Homelessness0609.pdf.

68. National Law Center on Homelessness & Poverty and National Low Income Housing Coalition, *supra.*

69. The law was first enacted in 2009 with a sunset clause until 2012; it was extended in 2010 by the Dodd-Frank Act until 2014; Congress then allowed it to lapse, based on the assumption that the foreclosure crisis was over. Following persistent advocacy, it was reinstated and made permanent in 2018. Johnson, Kimberly, "Protecting Tenants at Foreclosure." National Low Income Housing Coalition, 2021. https://nlihc.org/sites/default/files/AG-2021/06-06_PTFA.pdf.

70. Buck, P.O., Toro, P.A. and Ramos, M.A. (2004), Media and Professional Interest in Homelessness over 30 Years (1974–2003), Analyses of Social Issues and Public Policy, 4: 151–171, 154. https://doi.org/10.1111/j.1530-2415.2004.00039.x.

71. Ibid. In *Reversals of Fortune: America's Homeless Poor and their Advocates in the 1990s*, New Formations, 1992 (17), Mary Ellen Hombs argues that the shift in public reaction reflected not callousness but powerlessness.

that people were simply not availing themselves of solutions.[72] A return to the Reagan-era narrative—that people "choose" to be houseless—was on the horizon, along with the emergence of a destructive new trend: the criminalization of houselessness.[73]

Unfolding primarily at the city level, the criminalization of houselessness paralleled the growth of punitive responses to poverty at all levels of government during the 1990s. At the national level, these included the "Contract with America," promoted by Newt Gingrich as his legislative agenda as Speaker of the U.S. House of Representatives and Bill Clinton's pledge to "end welfare as we know it." At the state level, the repeal of or limitations on state "general assistance" programs that aid poor individuals has severely eroded that extremely limited and inadequate source of aid.[74] At the city level, in addition to increased criminalization, time limits and other restrictions on shelter—including repeal of a city's right to shelter in Washington, D.C.—removed even that emergency support.[75]

Laws criminalizing poverty, and houselessness specifically, are not new. Laws controlling the use of public space in the U.S. have roots in Elizabethan poor laws and, later, in efforts to control newly freed enslaved persons.[76] The U.S. Supreme Court limited some of their broadest, most egregious formulations in a 1972 decision striking down an ordinance that criminalized "wandering... without any lawful purpose," being a "vagabond," being a "habitual loafer[]," being a person "neglecting all lawful business," and similar offenses.[77] The decision did not invalidate vagrancy and loitering laws

---

72. Goodman, Ellen. 1990. "Compassion Fatigue," *Washington Post*, February 3, 1990. https://www.washingtonpost.com/archive/opinions/1990/02/03/compassion-fatigue /c9a84236-da58-4f2e-b7d8-c08b283cae10/.

73. See National Law Center on Homelessness & Poverty, Go Directly to Jail: A Report Analyzing Anti-Homeless Ordinances (1991). This was the first of what became a series of national survey reports documenting this trend and advocating for its reversal in favor of constructive solutions.

74. See Schott, Liz, "State General Assistance Programs Very Limited in Half the States and Nonexistent in Others, Despite Need," Center on Budget and Policy Priorities (July 2, 2020). https://www.cbpp.org/research/family-income-support/state-general-assistance -programs-very-limited-in-half-the-states.

75. See Hombs, *Reversals of Fortune, supra.*

76. See, e.g., Hopper, Kim, and Milburn, Norweeta, 1996, "Homelessness Among African-Americans: A historical and Contemporary Perspective," in *Homelessness in America*, 123–131; Edelman, Peter, 2017. *Not a Crime to Be Poor*, New York: New Press.

77. *Papachristou v. Jacksonville*, 405 U.S. 156 (1972).

generally, however; following this ruling, many cities simply amended their ordinances to make them more specific.[78]

Over time, laws regulating the use of public space have evolved to target houseless people, in the often-highly specific form they take today. Examples of current laws include bans on camping, sleeping, vehicle habitation, panhandling, aggressive panhandling, "sit-lie" bans, public urination and defecation, and property storage—among others.[79] They also include laws regulating the conduct of would-be helpers; for example, restrictions on offering food to people in public places.[80] By the early 1990s, these became increasingly prevalent, becoming a primary form of local government response to houselessness in many cities across the country.[81]

In 1991, the NLCHP began documenting the trend of criminalization in national survey reports; beginning in 2006, these surveys focused on the same 187 cities, allowing comparison over time, and revealing the growth of this trend.[82] The reports, which also included arguments against criminalization and data demonstrating its cost-ineffectiveness, served as well to publicize the trend and the arguments against it. Resistance to these laws became, and continues to be, a primary focus of advocacy for many local groups, and a focus of national advocacy as well.

Litigation challenging such laws as violative of the U.S. Constitution has been a leading form of that advocacy. A federal court case first filed in 1988, *Pottinger v. Miami*, led to an important court ruling that criminally punishing a person for sleeping in public in the absence of an alternative place to sleep is cruel and unusual punishment, in violation of the Eighth Amendment to the U.S. Constitution.[83] Most recently, in *Martin v. Boise*, an en banc panel of

---

78. Poulos, Peter. 1995. "Chicago's Ban on Gang Loitering: Making Sense of Vagueness and Overbreadth in Loitering Laws." Cal. L. Rev. 83 (January 1995): 379–417 (discussing "loitering plus" laws).

79. See National Law Center on Homelessness & Poverty, Housing Not Handcuffs: A Litigation Manual (2019). https://homelesslaw.org//wp-content/uploads/2018/10/Housing -Not-Handcuffs-Litigation-Manual.pdf. For more discussion of these laws criminalizing the state of being unhoused see Chapter 4.

80. See Guarneri, Grace. 2018. "Why it's Illegal to Feed the Homeless in Cities Across America." *Newsweek*, January 16, 2018.

81. See Foscarinis, Maria, "Downward Spiral: Homelessness and its Criminalization," *Yale L. and Pol'y Rev.* 14, no. 1: 1–63, https://digitalcommons.law.yale.edu/ylpr/vol14/iss1/2/.

82. National Coalition for the Homeless and National Law Center on Homelessness & Poverty, A Dream Denied: The Criminalization of Homelessness in U.S. Cities (2006).

83. *Pottinger v. Miami*, 810 F. Supp. 1551 (S.D. Fla. 1992).

the Ninth Circuit affirmed this reasoning in even stronger terms, and the U.S. Supreme Court denied the city's petition for certiorari.[84]

Advocates have also used policy advocacy to challenge laws criminalizing houselessness. At the city council level, local as well as national advocates have occasionally successfully argued against enactment of such laws, or mitigated their impact, relying on persuasion as well as the threat of litigation. In several cases, advocates successfully argued for "constructive alternatives" to such laws. At the state level advocates have pushed for, and in some state legislatures have enacted, Homeless Bills of Rights which protect the rights of people experiencing houselessness to use public space.[85]

However, this advocacy often operated like a game of "whack-a-mole": no sooner was one objectionable law struck down than another was enacted. Following up from earlier efforts in the 90s, advocates again focused on pushing the federal government to act. Starting from a goal of getting federal funding agencies to use the power of their purse to bar local governments from adopting laws criminalizing houselessness, advocates eventually won, in 2009, a congressional directive to the USICH (the HEARTH Act) to develop constructive alternatives to criminalization. The following year, USICH, together with the Justice Department, held a summit on the topic and published a report.[86] While not the broad prohibition advocates had wanted, the congressional action and the Council's follow up provided an opening for more advocacy.[87]

---

84. *Martin v. Boise*, 902 F.3d 1031 (9th Cir. 2018), *opinion amended and superseded on denial of rehearing en banc*, 920 F.3d 584 (9th Cir. 2019), *cert. denied*, 140 S. Ct. 674 (2019).

85. Rhode Island was the first state to enact such a law in 2012, followed by Illinois and Connecticut in 2013; Puerto Rico preceded them in 1998. See National Law Center on Homelessness & Poverty, *From Wrongs to Rights: The Case for Homeless Bills of Rights Legislation* (2014).

86. U.S. Interagency Council on Homelessness, 2010, *Searching out Solutions: Constructive Alternatives to the Criminalization of Homelessness,* https://www.usich.gov/tools-for-action/searching-out-solutions/; https://www.usich.gov/resources/uploads/asset_library/RPT_SoS_March2012.pdf.

87. Federal action on criminalization had been a key goal of the earlier Beyond McKinney campaign and had then led to favorable actions by the U.S. Department of Justice, including submitting amicus briefs on the side of homeless litigants in two cases. Brief for the United States as Amicus Curiae, *Joyce v. City and County of San Francisco*, No. 95-16940 (9th Cir. Mar. 29, 1996); Brief for the United States as Amicus Curiae, *Tobe v. City of Santa Ana*, No. S03850 (Cal. June 9, 1994). In 2015, the U.S. Department of Justice also filed an amicus brief on the side of the homeless plaintiffs in *Martin v. Boise* (then styled *Bell v. Boise*). Statement of Interest of the United States, *Bell v. Boise*, Civil Action No. 1:09-cv-540-REB (filed August 6, 1915), https://www.justice.gov/opa/file/643766/download.

Human rights mechanisms also were and continue to be an important strategy in pressing the federal government to address criminalization. Along with others, NHLC began using these mechanisms to submit "shadow reports" to U.N. committees reviewing U.S. compliance with treaties that it had signed and ratified, as part of a regular review process. In addition, advocates drafted questions for the committees to pose to the U.S. government representatives appearing before them. This yielded strong condemnations from human rights committees that advocates could in turn rely on to advocate for federal policies to counter criminalization. One result was a HUD policy that prioritized funding to communities that do not criminalize houselessness.[88]

In 2016, advocates launched the Housing Not Handcuffs Campaign to bring together groups around the country advocating against criminalization—as well as to link explicitly the call against criminalization to the call for housing.[89] This latter point was intended to guard against the danger that fighting criminalization would be viewed as fighting for a right to live on the street—feeding into a narrative that people choose to be unhoused—instead of fighting for a right to housing. But while it is the ultimate goal of this work, making the case for the right to housing in the U.S. was and remains a much harder proposition.

V. U.S. Legal System: "Negative" vs. "Positive" Rights?

Unlike other countries, the U.S. does not explicitly include a right to housing in its constitution.[90] A 1972 U.S. Supreme Court case, *Lindsey vs. Normet*,[91] is commonly cited for the proposition that no implicit right to housing exists;

88. National Law Center on Homelessness & Poverty, Scoring Points: How Ending the Criminalization of Homelessness Can Increase HUD Funding to Your Community (2018). https://homelesslaw.org//wp-content/uploads/2018/10/NOFAtoolkit2018.pdf.

89. See Housing Not Handcuffs, https://homelesslaw.org/housing-not-handcuffs/.

90. National Law Center on Homelessness & Poverty, Homelessness in the United States and the Human Right to Housing (2004) noting that France, Scotland, South Africa and other countries have a constitutional right to housing for their citizens; see also Foscarinis, Maria et al. 2004. *The Human Right to Housing: Making the Case in US Advocacy*; Tars, Eric, et al. 2012, "The Champagne of Housing Rights: France's Enforceable Right to Housing and Lessons for U.S. Advocates," *Northeastern Univ. L. J.* 4, no. 2. (October): 429–482.

91. *Lindsey v. Normet*, 405 U.S. 56 (1972).

in fact, the holding is more limited. The constitutional issue in the case is whether an Oregon statute defining the process for eviction on its face violated the Equal Protection Clause and the Due Process Clause. Writing for the Court, Justice White stated that there was no "constitutional guarantee of access to dwellings of a particular quality," nor was there any "right of a tenant to occupy the real property of his landlord beyond the term of his lease without the payment of rent or otherwise contrary to the terms of the relevant agreement." Thus, no strict scrutiny was required, and the Court used a rational basis analysis, upholding all but one of the statute's provisions.[92]

Interestingly, the Court noted that historically, landlord tenant law was one of few areas of common law to recognize a right of self-help on the part of the property owner. Statutes like the one at issue in the case were enacted to provide a process and reduce the violence and bloodshed that self-help often entailed, thus representing a step forward in greater protection for tenants.[93] Nonetheless, the Court rejected all but one of plaintiffs' constitutional challenges. But the ruling falls short of a clear holding that no federal constitutional right exists to any form of shelter at all.

The first federal housing programs were created following the devastation of the Great Depression, another time of mass houselessness in this country; housing was a key part of the New Deal President Franklin D. Roosevelt (FDR) championed. FDR also explicitly included economic rights generally in articulating his vision for the world and the country. In 1941, as the country was heading into World War II, Roosevelt set out his vision of the "four freedoms" essential for world peace: freedom of speech, freedom of religion, freedom from want, and freedom from fear. In his 1944 State of the Union address, Roosevelt called for a "second bill of rights," including among others, "the right of every family to a decent home." Indeed, he argued that these rights had already been accepted as "self-evident."[94]

In 1949, the Housing Act stated a "goal" of a "decent home and a suitable living environment for every American family."[95] But it did not guarantee it as a right. Funding was and remains discretionary—and thus easily subject to cuts.

---

92. However, it struck down one provision as violative of the Due Process Clause, under a rational basis analysis.

93. It also noted that the Constitution does explicitly protect private property.

94. See National Law Center on Homelessness & Poverty, *"Simply Unacceptable:" Homelessness and the Human Right to Housing in the United States* (2011).

95. Housing Act of 1949, Pub. L. No. 81-171 (1949). The Act was part of President Harry S. Truman's "Fair Deal." https://en.wikipedia.org/wiki/Housing_Act_of_1949. See

In fact, funding has varied significantly over time. In 1978, over 300,000 new housing units were funded; by 1982, that number had been slashed to under 2,000. As of 2021, only one in four of those poor enough to be eligible for housing assistance actually received it, due to insufficient funding.[96]

FDR's clearly articulated view of the interdependent nature of political and economic rights was incorporated as a key part of the Universal Declaration of Human Rights Eleanor Roosevelt spearheaded. But ultimately, political, and economic rights were separated in the two main treaties implementing the declaration—and the U.S. ratified only the one on civil and political rights. President Jimmy Carter signed the other foundational human rights treaty that enshrines other economic, social, and cultural rights, but it has not been ratified by the Senate—yet.

The U.S. legal system is often described as one of negative, as opposed to positive, rights.[97] FDR's formulation, "freedom from want," illustrates some of the difficulty and arguably artificial nature of this distinction, as does his observation that "necessitous men are not free men." Regardless, the U.S. legal system does protect economic rights; for example, as the court in *Lindsey v. Normet* noted, the Constitution explicitly protects private property.[98] A few scholars have argued that the Constitution should or may be interpreted to provide a right to minimum subsistence for all, including housing, food, livelihood, and health care.[99] These include arguments based on the Declaration of

---

Foscarinis, Maria, "Advocating for the Human Right to Housing: Notes from the United States," *N.Y.U. Rev. of L. & Soc. Change* 30, no. 3: 447–481. (2006).

96. Center on Budget and Policy Priorities, 2021, https://www.cbpp.org/research/housing/three-out-of-four-low-income-at-risk-renters-do-not-receive-federal-rental-assistance.

97. See, e.g., *Bowers v. Devito*, 686 F.2d 616 (7th Cir. 1982) (Posner, J., writing for the majority); see also Cass Sunstein, "Why Does the American Constitution Lack Social and Economic Guarantees?", 56 *Syracuse L. Rev.* 1, 3 (2006).

98. *Lindsey v. Normet*, 405 U.S. 56 (1972).

99. Charles L. Black, Jr. 1986, "Further Reflections on the Constitutional Justice of Livelihood," *Columbia L. Rev.* 86, no. 6 (October): 1103–1117. Black argues that the Declaration of Independence, the preamble, the Ninth Amendment, and other parts of the Constitution support "a constitutional right to a decent material basis for life" noting that poverty "is overwhelmingly, in the whole world, the commonest, the grimmest, the stubbornest obstacle we know to the pursuit of happiness." Amar, Akhil R. 1990, "Forty Acres and a Mule: A Republican Theory of Minimal Entitlements," 13 *Harvard J.L. & Pub. Pol'y* 13: 37–43 (argues that the 13th Amendment creates a federal duty "to provide all individuals with a minimum level of sustenance and shelter" so that no one is forced into slavery); Michelman, Frank I. 1979, "Welfare Rights in a Constitutional Democracy," *Wash. U. L.Q.*, 1979, no. 3.

Independence and the preamble to the Constitution's "general welfare" clause, the Thirteenth Amendment, and the Fourteenth Amendment. However, as currently interpreted by most scholars and courts, the Constitution protects economic rights only for some, not all; most obviously, it protects property rights for those who already possess them. Those who lack property rights will have a hard time finding a basis to argue for them.[100]

Similarly, and more broadly, the legal system as a whole protects the interests of those who are already in privileged positions, including those who hold property. Indeed, in at least some ways, it has not only protected those with privilege but actively harmed those without it. For example, Richard Rothstein and a growing number of other scholars have documented how U.S. law at all levels has served explicitly exclusionary purposes, sometimes quite intentionally, and especially for Black and other people of color; indeed, FDR's housing programs explicitly excluded Black would-be homeowners.[101] Local zoning laws that require single family homes on lots of specified size exclude those who cannot afford them—disproportionately and sometimes explicitly affecting people of color. Discrimination pervades not just housing programs and laws but employment, health care, public benefits as well as civic participation—indeed, all aspects of life.[102]

VI. Toward a Right to Housing

In the mid-1990s, a small group of U.S. advocates working on houselessness began engaging with preparations for Habitat II, a U.N. conference focused on

---

(Summer): 659–693 (enjoyment of political rights requires a certain level of subsistence); Ely, John H. 1980, *Democracy and Distrust: A Theory of Judicial Review*. Cambridge: Harvard University Press.

100. For an interesting discussion of homelessness as a property (or no property) problem, see Baron, Jane B., "Homelessness as a Property Problem," 2004, *Urban Lawyer*, 36: 273–88 (Spring), https://ssrn.com/abstract=569843. For a discussion of the far-reaching implications of such extreme poverty, see Ned Resnikoff, "It's Hard to Have Faith in a State That Can't Even House its People," *N.Y. Times*, July 26, 2021.

101. Richard Rothstein, *The Color of Law: A Forgotten History of How Our Government Segregated America,* New York: W.W. Norton (2017).

102. As discussed above, the impact on access to housing is among the most severe, as evidenced by the disproportionate percentage of Black Americans who are houseless: Black Americans make up 13% of the U.S. population, but 28% of the poverty population, and 40% of the houseless population.

the right to housing to be held in Istanbul in 1996. At the extended lead up, or "Prep Com," the official U.S. position, led by the State Department, was that there is no right to housing, and the U.S. worked to remove mention of it at the upcoming conference. Enraged by the government's stance, U.S. advocates together with other countries lobbied against this—eventually succeeding in getting the right to housing back into the conference on the right to housing.

The conference itself offered an education on the human right to housing, a concept that is increasingly well developed in international law, policy, and practice, and adopted by several countries, including developed countries like the U.S. That first introduction to the human right to housing, and human rights more broadly, spurred interest in developing new advocacy strategies in the U.S. Coming out of Habitat II, a small group of U.S. organizations that had taken part developed a project to apply some of its lessons here in the U.S. With some funding from HUD, Meeting America's Housing Needs developed a series of convenings around the country, bringing together stakeholders to learn about different aspects of the right to housing and how it might apply to issues they were facing.[103]

Follow up research on potential legal applications began with developing an understanding among advocates on houselessness of how human rights law could be used in U.S. courts to supplement arguments based solely on domestic law.[104] Unlike U.S law, human rights law recognizes economic rights for all; it also takes as a fundamental principle the interdependence of all rights; thus, violations of economic rights also can be taken to violate civil rights. The U.S. had ratified the International Covenant on Civil and Political Rights in 1992; in 1995, the U.N. Human Rights Committee, which oversees international compliance with the treaty, conducted its first review of U.S. compliance and noted this interdependence. Citing the disproportionate impact of poverty on Native Americans, African Americans, Hispanics, and single parent families headed

---

103. Dolbeare, Cushing, January 1997-June 1999, Final Project Report: Meeting America's Housing Needs: A Domestic Follow-Up to the UN Habitat Conference. (On file with author.)

104. Foscarinis, Maria, Brad Paul, Bruce Porter & Andrew Scherer. "The Human Right to Housing: Making the Case in U.S. Advocacy," *Clearinghouse Review*, 38, no. 3–4: 97–114. This work built on that of other advocates who had looked to U.S. law to make the case for a right to housing. Florence. Roisman, "Establishing a Right to Housing: A General Guide," *Clearinghouse Review* 25, no. 3 (1991): 201–227; Chester Hartman "The Case for a Right to Housing," *Housing Policy Debate*, 9, no. 2 (1998): 223.

by women in the U.S., the Committee expressed concern for their ability "to enjoy rights under the Covenant on the basis of equality."[105]

In 2003, the first of what would become an annual National Forum on the Human Right to Housing brought together advocates from around the country to learn about human rights law and to develop strategies to use it to advance work to address houselessness in the U.S.[106] Following the success of the national forums, the convening organizations began hosting regional and local forums and other trainings, in partnership with state and local groups, tying human rights training to specific advocacy strategies to advance the priorities of local partners. These events brought local attention to the human right to housing and, over time, helped support the adoption of resolutions and policies promoting it in several local jurisdictions.[107]

On a parallel track, advocates engaged human rights mechanisms submitted "shadow reports" to U.N. committees reviewing U.S. compliance with treaties that it had signed and ratified, as part of a regular review process.[108] At the same time, advocates recommended questions for the committees to pose to the U.S. government representatives appearing before them. Because the U.S. had not signed on to the economic and social rights treaty, advocates focused primarily on the civil and political rights treaties that it *had* adopted,

---

105. Concluding Observations of the Human Rights Committee: United States of America, 03/10/95 Para. 291 (1995). See generally Foscarinis, Maria, et al., The Human Right to Housing: Making the Case in U.S. Advocacy.

106. Organized by the National Homelessness Law Center and the Centre on Housing Rights and Evictions ("COHRE"). COHRE was then a leading international housing rights organization; it ceased operations in December 2014. Accessed December 7, 2021. https://www.cohre.org/.

107. For example, as a result, Cook County, IL, where Chicago is located, adopted a right to housing resolution; advocates then followed up to use it to advocate successfully for increased funding for housing. Cook County, IL, Resolution to Support House Bill 4100 (March 23, 2004). Los Angeles included the right to housing in "Bring LA Home," its ten-year plan to end homelessness. Foscarinis, Maria, and Tars, Eric, 2008, Housing Rights and Wrongs. Madison, WI, and Dane County, where it is located, also passed right to housing resolutions. Schneider, Pat, 2011, "Grassroots: Madison Recognizes Housing as a Human Right," *The Capital Times*, December 2, 2011, https://madison.com/ct/news/local/grassroots/grass-roots-madison-recognizes-housing-as-a-human-right/article_30d9d280-1c7b-11e1-858a001871e3ce6c.html#:~:text=A%20resolution%20passed%20on%20Nov,met%20both%20temporarily%20and%20permanently.%22.

108. For an overview of the process and how it can be used in advocacy, see, e.g., Tars, Eric, 2009, "Human Rights Shadow Reporting: A Strategic Tool for Domestic Justice," *Clearinghouse Review* 49, nos. 9–110: 475–485.

with a goal to advance their policy priorities with the U.S. government; thus, they focused on those issues, soliciting a wide coalition of organizations to sign on to their reports.

In a 2006 report to the U.N. Human Rights Committee, which monitors compliance with the International Covenant on Civil and Political Rights, advocates noted myriad violations of the treaty related to their advocacy priorities, including the disproportionate racial impact of houselessness.[109] In its official statement following its review of the U.S., titled "concluding observations," the Committee focused specifically on that impact and for the first time addressed the discriminatory impact of houselessness in the U.S., urging the U.S. to "take measures, including adequate and adequately implemented policies, to bring an end to such de facto and historically generated racial discrimination."[110]

The U.S. has also ratified, in 1994, the Covenant on the Elimination of Racial Discrimination (CERD), and advocates submitted shadow reports in 2006 and 2014 to the monitoring committee reviewing U.S. compliance with that treaty. The first report yielded general findings from the Committee on a variety of concerns it raised;[111] thus, the 2014 submission was targeted to focus more narrowly and specifically on the disproportionate racial impact of inadequate funding for low-income housing, the foreclosure crisis, and criminalization—with a goal of securing more specific recommendations that could better support follow-up advocacy with the U.S. government.[112] This strategy succeeded in part, resulting in a paragraph expressing concern about houselessness, its criminalization, and its disproportionate impact on racial and ethnic minorities. The Committee recommended two specific actions focused on criminalization, including using federal funding incentives to discourage criminalization, a policy advocates had been pushing.[113]

---

109. National Law Center on Homelessness & Poverty, Homelessness and United States Compliance with the International Covenant on Civil and Political Rights, Submitted to the Human Rights Committee, May 31, 2006.

110. UN Human Rights Committee, Concluding Observations, July 28, 2006, para. 22.

111. UN Committee on the Elimination of Racial Discrimination, Concluding Observations, March 5, 2008.

112. National Law Center on Homelessness & Poverty and Los Angeles Community Action Network, Racial Discrimination in Homelessness and Housing in the United States, Report to the UN Committee on the Elimination of Racial Discrimination, July 3, 2014, https://tbinternet.ohchr.org/Treaties/CERD/Shared%20Documents/USA/INT_CERD _NGO_USA_17800_E.pdf.

113. UN Committee on the Elimination of Racial Discrimination, Concluding Observations, Aug. 26, 2014, para. 12. In addition to recommending the abolishing of laws making

Advocates followed up by pushing for further federal action on criminalization, securing new HUD funding incentives to local governments that discouraged criminalization and encouraged constructive alternatives to it. This was a significant step forward that also pushed the federal government to increasingly strong public positions and action arguing against criminalization, including filing an amicus brief in an important court challenge that led to a landmark victory.[114] Federal agencies began increasingly to reflect the case advocates made—that criminalizing houselessness is not only extremely harmful to the people it targets, it is a waste of resources that does nothing to solve houselessness, and makes it much harder for people to exit homelessness, impeding efforts to end it. The 2014 CERD shadow report and the Committee's response also contributed to the growing public awareness of, and activism aimed at the disproportionate racial impact of houselessness.

Still, the goal of advocates was to make the case for the right to housing in the U.S., a much harder proposition, especially given the failure of the U.S. to ratify the treaty that directly protects economic and social rights. And while U.S. law protects civil rights, de jure if not always in practice, it does not currently recognize their interdependence with economic and social rights. The Universal Periodic Review, a U.N. process conducted by the Human Rights Council, reviewing the human rights records of all member countries, not tied to ratification of particular treaties,[115] offered an opportunity for broader review, and an opening to press the U.S. on the status of the human right to housing in the country. A broad coalition of organizations submitted reports to the U.N. Human Rights Council on the status of housing rights in the U.S. in 2010, 2014, and 2019.[116]

---

homelessness a crime, the Committee recommended that the US: "Offer incentives to decriminalize homelessness, including by providing financial support to local authorities that implement alternatives to criminalization, and withdrawing funding from local authorities that criminalize homelessness." Ibid. It also included a general recommendation calling for "all relevant stakeholders … to intensify efforts to find solutions for the homeless, in accordance with human rights standards." Ibid.

114. *Martin v. Boise* (then styled *Bell v. Boise*), Statement of Interest of the United States, *Bell v. Boise*, Civil Action No. 1:09-cv-540-REB (filed August 6, 1915), https://www.justice.gov/opa/file/643766/download.

115. See generally UN Human Rights Council, Universal Periodic Review.

116. Beyond Shelter, et al., "A Report to the UN Human Rights Council on the Right to Adequate Housing in the United States of America," April 19, 2010; National Law Center on Homelessness & Poverty, Chair, US Human Rights Network UPR Housing Working Group, "Housing and Homelessness in the United States of America," September 14, 2014; National

Around this time, organizations working on a variety of issues were beginning to work to "bring human rights home"—to apply human rights to the U.S.[117] Housing and houselessness advocates were part of this larger broader effort, specifically on the right to adequate housing.[118] A key moment previewing the beginning of change was the shift in public discourse on health care; mainstream politicians and commentators began calling healthcare a right, not a privilege. The Housing Not Handcuffs campaign sought to harness the energy driving criminalization, and the opposition to it, to a drive for the right to housing. Growing attention to the crisis in affordable housing—driven by the deepening crisis itself—spurred federal legislative proposals to address it from key members of Congress, in both the House and the Senate; several began speaking about housing as a right, not a privilege.[119]

In 2020, during the Democratic presidential primary, four candidates specifically called for recognition of housing as a right.[120] President-elect Biden did as well, and his Administration included it in its policy platform. Key aspects of his agenda on housing, such as the proposal to make housing vouchers an entitlement, are credible as aspects of that agenda, and although currently framed as a goal over time, are backed up by proposed major increases in funding, though whether they will be enacted by Congress is unclear.[121] Additionally,

---

Law Center on Homelessness & Poverty, "Housing and Homelessness in the United States of America," October 3, 2019.

117. "Portraits of the Movement," in *Bringing Human Rights Home*, Vol. 3, edited by Cynthia A. Soohoo, Catherine Albisa, and Martha F. Davis, Praeger (2008).

118. Maria Foscarinis and Eric Tars, "Human Rights and Wrongs: The U.S. and the Right to Housing," 149- 172, in *Bringing Human Rights Home*, Vol. 3, Portraits of the Movement, edited by Cynthia A. Soohoo, Catherine Albisa, and Martha F. Davis, Praeger (2008).

119. Robillard, Kevin and Delaney, Arthur. 2019. "2020 Democrats Think the Rent is Too Damn High." *Huffington Post,* March 21, 2019, https://www.huffpost.com /entry/2020-democrats-housing_n_5c92788be4b01b140d34a891; Badger, Emily, 2019, "Renters are Mad. Presidential Candidates Have Noticed," *New York Times*, April 23, 2019; Rosen, Eva, 2021, "If Housing is a Right, How Do We Make It Happen?" *New York. Times*, February 17, 2021.

120. See, e.g., M. Fudge, "How the Biden Administration is Pushing the Country to Fairer Housing," Washington Post, June 10, 2021; https://www.federalregister .gov/documents/2021/06/10/2021-12114/restoring-affirmatively-furthering-fair-housing -definitions-and-certifications.

121. W. Fischer and Eric Gartland, Housing Vouchers in Economic Recovery Bill Would Sharply Cut Homelessness, Housing Instability, Center on Budget and Policy Priorities, Sept. 23, 2021. https://www.cbpp.org/research/housing/housing-vouchers-in-economic -recovery-bill-would-sharply-cut-homelessness-housing.

other adopted policies further the right to housing, such as the reinstatement of the rule requiring communities to affirmatively further fair housing.

In 2020 and again in 2021, U.S. Representative Pramila Jayapal from Washington's 7th congressional district introduced the Housing is a Human Right Act, aimed at reducing houselessness. In 2020, California developed a proposal to add a right to housing to its constitution; this has since been tabled, but reports are that the legislature will return to it soon.[122] In Connecticut, the State Senate passed a "right to housing" bill, but the House has not—yet. While not a true right to housing, it is a step in that direction.[123] The right to counsel in eviction cases, an important protection that prevents houselessness and advances the right to housing, is also gaining momentum nationally and in some local jurisdictions.[124]

It is important to understand what a right to housing means. While its meaning may vary depending on circumstances, in general, it means that the government adopts policies designed to ensure that everyone has access to safe, decent, affordable housing.[125] It does not mean a free house for every person in the U.S. Specifics vary; a given country would develop its own legislative framework reflecting the right. For example, Scotland has adopted legislation based on the right designed specifically to end houselessness; it includes the ability to enforce the right in court.[126]

A. Current Developments and Implications

The COVID-19 pandemic has heightened awareness of the critical importance of housing, while also peeling back the veil on the gross inequalities now

---

122. Molly Solomon, "Will California Guarantee Housing as a Right? Here's How the Pandemic is Shaping the Debate," KQED, May 21, 2020. https://www.kqed.org/news/11819691/will-california-guarantee-housing-as-a-right-heres-how-the-pandemic-is-shaping-the-debate.

123. Connecticut Coalition to End Homelessness, "Establishing a Right to Housing." https://cceh.org/right-to-housing-ct/.

124. National Coalition for a Civil Right to Counsel. http://civilrighttocounsel.org/legislative_developments/20212022_bills.

125. Office of the United Nations High Commissioner for Human Rights, The Human Right to Adequate Housing, https://www.ohchr.org/EN/Issues/Housing/Pages/AboutHRand Housing.aspx. Accessed December 20, 2021.

126. Tars, Eric and Egleson, Caitlin. 2009, "Great Scot!: The Scottish Plan to End Homelessness and Lessons for the Housing Rights Movement in the United States," *Geo. J. on Poverty L. & Pol'y*, 16, no. 1:187–216.

prevalent in American society, and their harsh and disproportionate impact on Black Americans and other people of color. People without housing are highly susceptible to the virus because of their poor health—tied to their unhoused status—and their inability to engage in preventive measures such as social distancing, handwashing, or a healthy diet. Research studies indicate that once infected, unhoused people would be twice as likely to be hospitalized, two to four times as likely to require critical care, and two to three times as likely to die from the illness as the general population.[127] Advocates formulated policy recommendations to protect unhoused people; many of these are reflected in guidance the Centers for Disease Control and Prevention (CDC) issued.[128] The Guidance urges communities to place unhoused people in housing and, if that is not feasible, to refrain from sweeps of encampments. Instead, the CDC recommends that communities provide handwashing and portable toilets at the sites to support sanitation efforts. Congress enacted the Coronavirus Aid, Relief, and Economic Security Act ("CARES Act"),[129] providing significant additional funding to existing homeless assistance programs. Many communities put people in hotel and motel rooms, many of which were vacant due to the pandemic-induced economic crisis, and the Federal Emergency Management Agency reimbursed communities for such efforts. The CDC issued an eviction moratorium to prevent people from being evicted during the pandemic; several state and local governments did as well.

Public opinion has long favored structural solutions to houselessness;[130] such support rose dramatically in the wake of the pandemic and its attendant economic crisis. A 2021 national Gallup poll found that the combined issues of hunger and homelessness topped the list of Americans' worries, with 58% say-

---

127. Dennis Culhane, Dan Treglia, Ken Steif, Randall Kuhn and Thomas Byrne, "Estimated Observational and Emergency/Quarantine Capacity Need for the U.S. Homeless Population Related to COVID-19 Exposure by County; Projected Hospitalizations, Intensive Care Units, and Mortality." (2020). https://works.bepress.com/dennis_culhane/237/.

128. CDC, "Interim Guidance for People Experiencing Unsheltered Homelessness." https://www.cdc.gov/coronavirus/2019-ncov/community/homeless-shelters/unsheltered -homelessness.html; "Interim Guidance for Homeless Service Providers to Plan and Respond to Coronavirus Disease 2019 (COVID-19)." https://www.cdc.gov/coronavirus/2019-ncov /community/homeless-shelters/plan-prepare-respond.html.

129. Pub. L. No. 116–136, 134 Stat. 281 (2020).

130. Paul Toro and D.M. McDonnell, "Beliefs, Attitudes, and Knowledge About Homelessness," *Am. J. of Comm. Psy.* 20(1):53–80 (1992); Jack Tsai, Crystal Y.S. Lee, Jianxun Shen, Steven M. Southwick, Richard H. Pietrzak, "Public exposure and attitudes about homelessness," *J. Comm. Psy.* 2019; 47:76–92. https://doi.org/10.1002/jcop.22100.

ing they worry about them "a great deal," the highest percentage in two decades of measurement, and the first time they rose to the top.[131] At least some of the worry is personal: A 2021 CBS News poll found that 28% of Americans fear not having a place to live, and 41% reported knowing someone or themselves being evicted or losing their home.[132] Polls also show that significant majorities believe that housing is a basic human right.[133]

The role of race in houselessness is not only highly significant in its own right but also plays a role in advocacy to recognize housing as a human right in the U.S. Houselessness disproportionately affects people of color, more so even than poverty generally does: African Americans comprise 28% of the poverty population, compared to 40% of the houseless population. This is no coincidence: housing policies—including federal policies in the New Deal—have explicitly discriminated against African Americans.[134] Perhaps less overtly, zoning and other policies that favor development of housing that is unaffordable to poor people, who are more likely to be people of color, keep people out. Advocates have argued that human rights instruments, including the Covenant to End Racial Discrimination, which the U.S. has signed and ratified, not only preclude such discrimination, but also require eliminating the lack of affordable and adequate housing that underlies it.[135]

Racism in the criminal legal system and the advocacy to fight it are also helping to highlight the criminalization of houselessness, placing it in the larger context of overcriminalization and the misuse of police to address social issues such as houselessness and illuminating the interdependence of civil and

131. Megan Brenan, "Record High Worry in US About Hunger, Race Relations," Gallup (March 26, 2021). https://news.gallup.com/poll/341954/record-high-worry-hunger-race-relations.aspx?utm_source=alert&utm_medium=email&utm_content=morelink&utm_campaign=syndication.

132. Fred Backus, "Over a Quarter of Americans Have Worried About Homelessness—CBS News Poll." *CBS News* (May 20, 2021).

133. Opportunity Agenda, Human Rights in the U.S.: Opinion Research with Advocates, Journalists, and the General Public, 19, 22 (2007); Alan Jenkins and Kevin Hsu, "American Ideals & Human Rights: Findings From New Public Opinion Research by the Opportunity Agenda," *Fordham L. Rev.* 77: 439 (2008); Carr Center, "2021 Poll on Reimagining Rights and Responsibilities in the U.S.," Harvard Kennedy School, 2021. https://carrcenter.hks.harvard.edu/reimagining-rights-responsibilities-2021-poll.

134. Rothstein, Richard. 2017. *The Color of Law*. New York: W.W. Norton.

135. National Law Center on Homelessness & Poverty and Los Angeles Community Action Network, Racial Discrimination in Housing and Homelessness in the United States: A Report to the UN Committee on the Elimination of Racial Discrimination (2014).

economic rights.[136] The call to take resources away from police response and to invest them instead in community needs such as housing dovetails with goals of the Housing Not Handcuffs Campaign, which works to link fighting against the criminalization of houselessness with fighting for the human right to housing.

Linking race, criminal legal reform, and housing rights can begin to bridge the gap between civil and economic rights and lay a foundation for recognition of the right to housing—and other economic, social, and cultural rights—in American law and policy. Forging these links can help expand and mobilize the constituency of support for recognizing such rights, including women, LGBTQ people, Native Americans, Latinx people, immigrants, currently and formerly incarcerated people, and African Americans.[137] Coming together in common cause on a united progressive agenda can push the shift in resource allocation that is needed to make real change.

Recent years have seen a growth in activism by people with lived experience of houselessness—including the emergence of policymakers with such experience. Early on, an initiative to organize a movement of houseless people themselves gained some traction but proved difficult to sustain. More recently, grassroots groups composed of and led by houseless people have emerged more consistently, often connected to fights over encampments, and they become more permanent in the absence of housing.[138] Such groups are powerful advocates on their own or as partners with other advocates. Policymakers with lived

---

136. Measure J was adopted by ballot initiative in LA County in 2020, and provides that 10% of the existing local budget (42 % of which allocated to law enforcement) must be spent on community needs including mental health care, job creation, and affordable housing. ReImagine LA, Measure J, https://reimagine.la/measure-j/. In June 2021, the measure was struck down by a judge based on its passage by ballot initiative; the ruling—which is not yet permanent—would not prevent its adoption as a county ordinance. https://laist .com/news/criminal-justice/judge-strikes-down-measure-j-which-comes-as-a-blow-to -the-criminal-justice-reform-movemen.

137. Research shows that houseless youth are disproportionately LGBTQ, Black, Latinx, and low-income. Morton, M.H., Dworsky, A., & Samuels, G.M. Missed opportunities: Youth homelessness in America. National estimates. Chicago, IL: Chapin Hall at the University of Chicago (2017).

138. Such groups include Moms 4 Housing in Oakland, CA, https://moms4housing .org/, and Denver Homeless Out Loud in Colorado, https://denverhomelessoutloud.org/, to name just a few.

experience, such as U.S. Representative Cori Bush, are serving as powerful and effective advocates within government.[139]

These developments also illustrate the potential for a convergence of advocacy strategies. While this chapter has focused on legal strategies—writ large to include policy more broadly—this advocacy has been most powerful when paired with other strategies such as grassroots and direct action. Cori Bush's action in staging a sit-in outside the Capitol and speaking openly about her own experience as a mother who had been evicted and become houseless was a powerful testament that galvanized public attention; her ability to focus that attention on a specific policy demand made it effective, bringing real change.

Realizing the right and making it real will require much work. But housing and other economic and social rights have a history in the U.S. as well as around the world. Perhaps it is realistic to hope that with continued, persistent advocacy the goal of decent housing for all will become a fundamental right—and a reality.

---

139. Noor, Poppy, "'It was Just Unconscionable,' Cori Bush on her Fight to Extend the Eviction Moratorium," *The Guardian*, August 8, 2021. https://bush.house.gov/media /press-releases/congresswoman-cori-bush-introduces-unhoused-bill-rights-first-ever -federal.

TWO

Foundational Principles of Homeless Advocacy

Building an effective homeless services delivery system or advocacy practice to address homelessness requires implementing a core set of foundational principles, also known as "Philosophies of Care," that emerged to place primacy on client empowerment and getting the person housed as quickly as possible; these include Trauma-Informed Care, Housing First, and Harm Reduction. Legal advocates should also be open to adopting other client-centered advocacy practices and procedures when working with unhoused people and with people who are facing imminent risk of homelessness.[140]

I. Trauma-Informed Care (TIC)

Ensuring that providers and advocates respect the individuals they are serving and address their unique circumstances and challenges lies at the core of trauma-informed care ("TIC"). A trauma-informed approach to an organization, program, or system realizes the widespread impact of trauma; understands potential paths for recovery; recognizes the signs and symptoms of trauma in clients, families, staff, and others involved with the system;

---

140. "Imminent risk of homelessness" is a term of art in homeless services, typically defined to include a low-income requirement and involving a notice to vacate within a narrow time, usually 14–30 days.

responds by fully integrating knowledge about trauma into policies, procedures, and practice; and seeks to actively resist re-traumatization.

Recent literature is almost solely focused on TIC—interchangeably referred
to as "trauma-informed approach"[141]—but this philosophy and framework
has also been called other names such as "trauma and resiliency-informed
care,"[142] "person-centered trauma-informed care,"[143] or, in the legal setting,
"trauma-informed lawyering." The goal of this section is to provide a foundational understanding of why TIC became a mandated model for working
with unhoused people and to demonstrate how legal advocates should develop
practices that implement TIC.

A. Brief History

Organizations serving youth and children populations pioneered research
regarding trauma and its impact in the 1970s.[144] The other context that initially
developed the impact of trauma was with combat veterans and research surrounding post-traumatic stress. However, it was through the advancements
in understanding how to treat trauma in children from the late 1990s into the
early 2000s that organizations realized that both the service environment and
treatment itself had to be trauma informed.[145] As trauma research began to be
supplemented by advances in neuroscience, a wealth of research documenting the relationships between trauma exposure, behavioral health risks, and

---

141. Substance Abuse and Mental Health Services Administration, *SAMHSA's Concept
of Trauma and Guidance for a Trauma-Informed Approach* (2014), 9. https://store.samhsa
.gov/sites/default/files/d7/priv/sma14-4884.pdf.

142. See, for example, Downtown Women's Center, *Trauma & Resiliency Informed Care
Toolkit: A Resource for Service Providers* (2020). https://fz5.d4b.myftpupload.com/wp-con-
tent/uploads/2020/07/Trauma-and-Resiliency-Informed-Care-Toolkit-updated-12.10.18
.pdf.

143. Person-centered planning appears to be used frequently in connection with
homeless services pre-2017, but despite the absence of the "person-centered" label, its fundamental principles are adopted in the TIC model set forth by the Substance Abuse and
Mental Health Services Administration (SAMHSA). See the section on Defining Trauma
and Trauma-Informed Care later in the chapter.

144. Karen Heller Key, *Foundations of Trauma-Informed Care: An Introductory Primer*, Jill Schumann ed. (2018), 6. https://www.leadingage.org/sites/default/files/RFA%20
Primer%20_%20RGB.pdf.

145. Substance Abuse and Mental Health Services Administration, *Treatment Improvement Protocol: Trauma-Informed Care in Behavioral Health Services* (Rockville, MD:
Substance Abuse and Mental Health Services Administration, 2014), Appendix C, 268–69.

weakened neurological development and immune system responses emerged to create the evidence-based TIC model.[146]

Now, TIC is a common principle applied within various service contexts across all demographics, and it is widely adopted by advocates and practitioners assisting unhoused people. Specifically, TIC reframes the question for those seeking services from "What is wrong with you?" (patient/victim) to "What has happened to you?" (survivor). Another key component of TIC is avoiding re-traumatizing survivors. Thus, under the TIC model, survivors are empowered to take control of their progress, and organizations are encouraged to move away from traditional "top down" hierarchical clinical models to create a psychosocial empowerment partnership. In fact, undergirding TIC is the importance of addressing clients individually, rather than applying general treatment approaches. Reflecting a compassionate perspective, TIC can provide a greater sense of safety for clients and can improve organizational processes, treatment planning, and placements because of the decreased risk of re-traumatization.[147]

B. Defining Trauma and Trauma-Informed Care

Today, and for the last twenty years, the U.S. Substance Abuse and Mental Health Services Administration (SAMHSA) shapes how institutions and service providers recognize and address trauma. SAMHSA describes trauma as "an event, series of events, or set of circumstances that is experienced by an individual as physically or emotionally harmful or threatening and that has lasting adverse effects on the individual's functioning and physical, social, emotional, or spiritual well-being."[148] A traumatic experience can affect individuals, groups, communities, and generations and generally overwhelms one's ability to cope, ignites the "fight, flight, or freeze" reaction at the time of the event, and frequently results in feelings of fear, vulnerability, and helplessness.[149]

---

146. Los Angeles Homeless Services Authority, *Trauma Informed Care: A Core System Approach to the Los Angeles Homeless Services Delivery* (2020), 1–2. https://www.lahsa.org/documents?id=4912-trauma-informed-care.pdf.

147. Ibid., 8–9; SAMHSA, *Studies Back Trauma-Informed Approaches in Homeless Services.* https://www.samhsa.gov/homelessness-programs-resources/hpr-resources/studies-back-trauma-informed-approaches.

148. Substance Abuse and Mental Health Services Administration, *Treatment Improvement Protocol*, 7.

149. Ibid.

Simply put, TIC is essential for practitioners and advocates of any population because trauma exposure is pervasive.[150] Potential trauma can arise from experiencing or witnessing, for example: sexual violence, natural disasters, war, displacement, violent crime, discrimination, hate crimes, and houselessness. It is important to note, however, that such events are *potentially* traumatic—that is, not every individual will register these events as being traumatic but a person *can* be traumatized by such events. Thus, being trauma-informed is being aware of an individual's different life experiences and the possible lingering trauma that may be preventing him or her from being successful.

Notably, housing instability and loss has been recognized as a potentially traumatic event, and rates of trauma symptoms are high amongst unhoused people.[151] Further, these individuals report high levels of trauma even preceding their unhoused status.[152] Because of the likelihood of trauma exposure, TIC is a mandated practice model for working with unhoused people and is a competency that advocates and practitioners should develop to avoid re-traumatization and better encourage positive program or goal outcomes.[153]

SAMSHA defines TIC as "an intervention and organization approach that focuses on how trauma may affect an individual's life and his or her response to behavioral health services from prevention through treatment."[154] Although there are some nuanced differences between different programs and organizations, SAMHSA sets forth six guiding principles for TIC, which programs and organizations on the federal, state, and local levels have adopted.[155]

---

150. Trauma has been suggested to be a public health issue due to its pervasiveness and significant associated costs to society. See, for example, Kathryn M. Magruder, Katie A. McLaughlin, and Diane L. Elmore Borbon, "Trauma is a public health issue," *European J. of Psychotraumatology* 8, no. 1 (2017), DOI: 10.1080/20008198.2017.1375338.

151. One SAMHSA study that found 76 to 100 percent of women and 67 percent of men experiencing homelessness exhibit trauma symptoms. *Treatment Improvement Protocol*, 57.

152. Ibid.

153. In fact, re-traumatization is one of the reasons why people living unsheltered on the streets refuse to live in a shelter. See, for example, Joe Colletti, *The Increasing Need for Trauma-informed Care Shelters* (2020). https://homelessstrategy.com/the-increasing-need-for-trauma-informed-care-shelters/.

154. Substance Abuse and Mental Health Services Administration, *Treatment Improvement Protocol*, 11.

155. United States Interagency Council on Homelessness, *Expanding the Toolbox: The Whole-of-Government Response to Homelessness* (2020), 14.

These principles are:

1. **Safety**: Throughout an organization, staff members and the people they serve feel physically and psychologically safe; the physical setting is safe and interpersonal interactions promote a sense of safety. Understanding safety as defined by those served is a high priority.

2. **Trustworthiness and Transparency**: Organizational operations and decisions are conducted with transparency with the goal of building and maintaining trust with clients and family members, among staff, and others involved in the organization.

3. **Peer Support**: Peer support and mutual self-help are key vehicles for establishing safety and hope, building trust, enhancing collaboration, and utilizing their stories and lived experience to promote recovery and healing. The term "Peers" refers to individuals with lived experiences of trauma, or in the case of children this may be family members of children who have experienced traumatic events and are key caregivers in their recovery.

4. **Collaboration and Mutuality**: Importance is placed on partnering and the leveling of power differences between staff and clients and among organizational staff from clerical and housekeeping personnel to professional staff to administrators, demonstrating that healing happens in relationships and in the meaningful sharing of power and decision-making. The organization recognizes that everyone has a role to play in a trauma-informed approach. As one expert stated, "one does not have to be a therapist to be therapeutic."

5. **Empowerment, Voice, and Choice**: Throughout the organization and among the clients served, individuals' strengths and experiences are recognized and built upon. The organization fosters a belief in the primacy of the people served, in resilience, and in the ability of individuals, organizations, and communities to heal and promote recovery from trauma. Operations, workforce development and services are organized to foster empowerment for staff and clients. Clients are supported in shared decision-making, choice, and goal setting to determine the plan of action they need to heal and move forward. They are supported in cultivating self-advocacy skills. Staff are facilitators of recovery rather than controllers of recovery.

6. **Cultural, Historical, and Gender Issues:** The organization active-ly moves past cultural stereotypes and biases (e.g., based on race, ethnicity, sexual orientation, age, religion, gender-identity, geog-raphy, etc.); offers access to gender responsive services; leverages the healing value of traditional cultural connections; incorporates policies, protocols, and processes that are responsive to the racial, ethnic and cultural needs of individuals served; and recognizes and addresses historical trauma.[156]

SAMHSA also developed the four "R's" as being key assumptions of TIC, which provide further insight into these core principles.

1. *Realizes* the widespread impact of trauma and understands poten-tial paths for recovery.

2. *Recognizes* the signs and symptoms of trauma in clients, families, staff, and others involved with the system.

3. *Responds* by fully integrating knowledge about trauma into poli-cies, procedures, and practices.

4. Seeks to actively *resist re-traumatization*.[157]

Legal and policy advocates should pay particular attention to these assump-tions and adopt them into the provision of supportive and representative services. First, by seeing a broad view of what the client needs for a transi-tion into being housed; second, being aware of the indicators of the trauma of being unhoused; third, working at the direct services and policy levels to support individual and systems efforts to prevent homelessness; and fourth, being mindful of interview and service methods that prevent re-traumatiza-tion. For example, intake procedures should ensure that information about the traumatic events a client has experienced is gathered in a sensitive manner and is memorialized appropriately to avoid the need to ask the client about the traumatizing event again. Indeed, successful adoption and implementation of TIC practices can help individuals seeking assistance feel more comfortable and lead to more successful outcomes.

Although agencies are adopting TIC or other trauma-informed models, many service providers are not aware of this principle and unwittingly contrib-

---

156. Substance Abuse and Mental Health Services Administration, *Concept of Trauma,* 10.

157. Ibid., 9.

ute to the re-traumatization of individuals. As Elizabeth Hopper, Ellen Bassuk, and Jeffrey Olivet aptly described: "Homeless services have a long history of serving trauma survivors, without being aware of or addressing the impact of traumatic stress. Overwhelmed by the daily needs of their clients, providers in these settings often have few resources to address issues of long-term recovery."[158] Further, as mentioned above, traumatic stress leads to negative outcomes because it causes increased physical symptoms, behavior management problems, relapse, and recidivism.[159]

Fortunately, through education, legal practitioners and other advocates can learn more about how to implement TIC practices to provide more compassionate care to this vulnerable group and to help prevent and reduce the number of unsheltered or transient individuals in our community. For more in-depth information regarding TIC and its evidence-based practices, see SAMHSA's Concept of Trauma and Guidance for a Trauma-Informed Approach[160] or Treatment Improvement Protocol (TIP) Series 57 on Trauma-Informed Care in Behavioral Health Services.[161]

C. Critiques

Although health, social work, and other human service professionals widely embrace TIC as a model, the approach has several critiques. The most prominent one was that TIC was an "amorphous concept" with a lack of uniform terminology and practices.[162] This is unsurprising, as organizations incorporate TIC practices in varying ways, depending on the community on which they primarily serve or on the, often limited, training or resources available to them. Varied application could make TIC a confusing (set of) principle(s) to implement; after all, is there a correct way? Thus, the greatest success of

---

158. Elizabeth K. Hopper, Ellen L. Bassuk, and Jeffrey Olivet, "Shelter from the Storm: Trauma-Informed Care in Homelessness Services," *The Open Health Services and Policy Journal* 2010, 3: 80–100.

159. Institute for Health and Recovery, *Person-Centered Trauma-Informed Approach* (2016). https://event.capconcorp.com/wp/hpog-2016/wp-content/uploads/sites/7/2016/09/Schilling_IPerson-centered-TI-approach-508.pdf.

160. HHS Publication No. (SMA) 14-4884 (Rockville, MD: Substance Abuse and Mental Health Services Administration, 2014).

161. Ibid.

162. Shira Birnbaum, "Confronting the Social Determinants of Health: Has the Language of Trauma Informed Care Become a Defense Mechanism?," *Issues in Mental Health Nursing* 40, no. 6 (2019), 476–81, DOI: https://doi.org/10.1080/01612840.2018.1563256.

SAMHSA may be providing concrete guidance and definitions, which appears to create some unity among organizations. Legal and policy advocates still have the challenge of adapting these definitions and applying the working assumptions to legal services and legislative processes based on their clients and communities.

More concerning are the political criticisms of SAMHSA itself.[163] Shira Birnbaum discusses one particular book in which D.J. Jaffe, a patient advocate and policy analyst, observed that the language of TIC dominated SAMHSA at a time when federal and state resources were being shifted away from programs and services serving the most severely mentally ill and that TIC renders the acute needs of this particular population invisible by "submerging them under vague definitions of trauma that can include virtually any self-reported subjective sense of injury, victimization, or loss."[164] SAMHSA's approach was similarly criticized to be "so vague and all-inclusive as to trivialize severe mental illness, diverting attention from the clinical needs of some of the most vulnerable and highly traumatized Americans."[165]

Others also warned that framing trauma in terms of interventions and interpersonal facts, as SAMHSA does, can shift the focus from trying to dismantle the systems of oppression that create trauma to the trauma survivors and their symptoms.[166] It is important to note that this danger of homogenization is the opposite of the individualized, personalized care, or representation that TIC intends to achieve. Nonetheless, this criticism of TIC is important as it points out a potential flaw—that by becoming a widely applied approach, TIC may inadvertently erase the unique experiences of individuals exposed to trauma and may trivialize or even normalize truly horrific experiences or severe mental illnesses. Yet, it's possible that TIC became so widely applicable and embraced in part because of its flexibility (or vagueness, a critic may say) and facilitates increased awareness by practitioners and organizations across populations, including subgroups of unhoused people.

How human services now defines and understands trauma may be shifting the focus from a macro perspective to a micro perspective, possibly reflecting a human desire to make tangible change. Although it is true that losing sight

---

163. Ibid. Although not discussed here, Birnbaum (2019) reiterates a criticism that shifts in language are deliberate, which appears to make this shift in how human services defines trauma more deserving of scrutiny.

164. Ibid., 477–78.

165. Ibid., 478.

166. Ibid., 477–78.

of the causes of these trauma (whether they be from a who or what or where or why perspective) may make it more difficult to prevent future traumas and distract advocates from dismantling the institutional inequity that can create or prolong traumatic instances, it does not make treatment any less important. Rather than a zero-sum game, advocates can consider TIC as a positive practice at the individual or service-provider level while also being aware of larger social and worldly events that create the need for TIC.

D. Current Models & Best Practices

Best practices for implementing TIC strategies differ depending on the community being served. No two traumas are the same, and approaches will differ depending on an individual's or community's experiences. Virtually all organizations, however, reference or rely on SAMHSA's general guidelines. Some advice from providers serving various communities is briefly discussed below to provide a glimpse of the broad applicability of TIC. This list is by no means exhaustive, and is not ordered by importance nor suggesting any opinion of whether these applications of TIC are correct per se. More importantly, it is important for future practitioners and advocates to realize how these different group identities might intersect,[167] which further emphasizes how individual experiences are unique and may affect the ability to obtain and maintain permanent housing.

1. Youth

A webinar sponsored by the Interagency Working Group on Youth Programs (IWGYP), in collaboration with eighteen federal departments and agencies,[168] explored the effects of trauma exposure on youth and outlined specific elements for implementing TIC within youth programs and services were outlined. But because TIC is not just about raising awareness but also changing

---

167. For example, in Skid Row, located in downtown Los Angeles, 317 surveys collected in 2016 to conclude a longitudinal analysis from 2001 to 2016 by the Downtown Women's Action Coalition (DWAC) in their 2016 Downtown Women's Needs Assessment concluded that "women in Skid Row are far more likely to be older and African-American than women in LA county, suggesting that these groups experience homelessness and extreme poverty at disproportionately high levels." https://downtownwomenscenter.org/wp-content/uploads/2017/08/2016DowntownWomensNeedsAssessment-web.pdf.

168. *Implementing a Trauma-Informed Approach for Youth across Service Sectors* (2012). https://youth.gov/docs/Trauma_Informed_Approach_508.pdf.

concrete behaviors, actions, and responses, the IWGYP calls upon child protection systems, lawyers, juvenile judges, law enforcement, schools, mental health providers, and caretakers to play central roles in creating a trauma-informed system. That is, providers and systems can either help or re-traumatize, and it is the myriad caregivers who help promote a youth's natural resiliency and provide tools for managing stress. The IWGYP suggests the following central elements for implementing TIC in youth programs and services: (1) maximizing physical and psychological safety of youth and families; (2) identifying trauma-related needs of youth; (3) enhancing the well-being and resilience of youth, families, and practitioners, service providers or advocates; and (4) partnering with youth, families, and the agencies that interact with those groups.

2. Women

The Downtown Women's Center in Los Angeles (DWC)[169] created a toolkit for service providers, which delves into the value of implementing TIC principles for services provided to women and provides checklists and concrete advice for an organization to become trauma informed.[170] Relying on the 2016 Downtown Women's Needs Assessment,[171] which surveyed 317 women in Skid Row (located in Los Angeles, California), DWC noted that more than half of these survey respondents (54.3%) reported "not receiving services to deal with the after-effects of trauma."[172] This high rate of trauma exposure and lack of support following such traumatic events speak to the need for implementing TIC, especially because "the staggeringly high prevalence of violence is the most distinguishing difference between women and men experiencing homelessness."[173] Adopting SAMHSA's six core principles, listed above, DWC is one example of a services agency that has outlined concrete steps towards becoming trauma informed, which includes cultural and gender competency trainings and ensuring women are connected with recovery services.

---

169. Downtown Women's Center. https://downtownwomenscenter.org/trauma-informed-care/.

170. Downtown Women's Center, *Trauma & Resiliency Informed Care Toolkit: A Resource for Service Providers*. https://fz5.d4b.myftpupload.com/wp-content/uploads/2020/07/Trauma-and-Resiliency-Informed-Care-Toolkit-updated-12.10.18.pdf.

171. Downtown Women's Center. https://downtownwomenscenter.org/wp-content/uploads/2017/08/2016DowntownWomensNeedsAssessment-web.pdf.

172. Ibid., 7.

173. Ibid.

3. Older Adult Populations

TIC is widely implemented for older adult populations, who may have more complex trauma histories as they age. In fact, it is estimated that approximately 55–90% of adults in the United States have experienced at least one traumatic event.[174] Older adults are also more at risk of experiencing trauma resurgence due to social, financial, and physical change—for example, after losing one's independence or due to the emergence of health problems—and previously used coping mechanisms may become less helpful.[175] For these reasons, service providers interacting with older adults have been encouraged to implement TIC in their practices.

4. Survivors of Intimate Partner Violence (IPV)

Relying on SAMHSA and other TIC developments, in 2015, Joshua Wilson, Jenny Fausi, and Lisa Goodman attempted to synthesize observed TIC practices to better understand its application for domestic violence programs. They identified six principles for implementing a trauma-informed approach in IPV intervention, which include: (1) promoting emotional safety, (2) restoring client choice and control, (3) facilitating connection, (4) supporting coping, (5) responding to identity and context, and (6) building strengths.[176]

---

174. Karen Heller Key, *Foundations of Trauma-Informed Care: An Introductory Primer,* 8 (2018). https://www.leadingage.org/sites/default/files/RFA%20Primer%20_%20RGB.pdf.

One study found that traumatic event exposure in a national sample of 2,953 U.S. adults was 89.7% using the American Psychiatric Association's *Diagnostic and Statistical Manual* 5th ed. (*DSM-5*; 2013). Kilpatrick, D.G., Resnick, H.S., Milanak, M.E., Miller, M.W., Keyes, K.M., & Friedman, M.J. (2013). "National estimates of exposure to traumatic events and PTSD prevalence using DSM-IV and DSM-5 criteria." *J. of Traumatic Stress,* 26(5), 537–547. https://doi.org/10.1002/jts.21848.

175. The Jewish Federations of North America & Center on Aging and Trauma, *Aging and trauma,* 1 https://cdn.fedweb.org/fed-42/2/AgingAndTrauma_FactSheet_CenterOnAgingAndTrauma%25281%2529.pdf; "From Late-Onset Stress Symptomatology to Later-Adulthood Trauma Reengagement in Aging Combat Veterans: Taking a Broader View." *The Gerontologist,* 56(1), 14–21. https://doi.org/10.1093/geront/gnv097; Ladson, D., & Bienenfeld, D. (2007). "Delayed reaction to trauma in an aging woman." *Psychiatry* (Edgmont), 4(6), 46–50, https://www.ncbi.nlm.nih.gov/pmc/articles/PMC2921251/; Paratz, E.D., & Katz, B. (2011). "Ageing Holocaust survivors in Australia." *The Medical J. of Australia,* 194(4), 194–197. https://doi.org/10.5694/j.1326-5377.2011.tb03771.x).

176. Joshua M. Wilson, Jenny E. Fauci, and Lisa A. Goodman, "Bringing Trauma-Informed Practice to Domestic Violence Programs: A Qualitative Analysis of Current Approach," *Am. J. of Orthopsychiatry* (2015): 594–95.

TIC is about empowering trauma survivors to better cope and reassimilate into every-day society. Thus, when working with IPV survivors, it is important to consider person-specific facts such as the location of the client housing in relation to where their abuser lives or considering characteristics of a neighborhood and whether it will provide emotional and physical safety.[177] In one 2017 study of a single domestic violence program in the Southwest U.S., participants identified how housing can "trigger" survivors of IPV or lead to flashbacks of their trauma.[178] This is a clear example of the risk of re-traumatization when there is a lack of awareness and application of TIC. With this knowledge, it is strongly encouraged that practitioners prepare and assist clients by strengthening and developing coping strategies such as: (1) helping survivors recognize their trauma through a "user-sensitive checklist," (2) teaching "containment skills" for flashbacks and dissociation, and (3) encouraging efforts to reach out for help from the survivor's personal support net of friends and family.[179]

II. Housing First

A. What Is Housing First?

Housing First ("HF") is an empirically proven[180] and nationally recognized guiding philosophy that prioritizes immediate, low-barrier, non-abstinence-based, unconditional, and permanent housing[181] for unhoused people.[182] The goal of HF is to connect unhoused individuals and families quickly and successfully to permanent housing. It represents a dramatic shift away from

---

177. Ibid.

178. Ward-Lasher et al., *Implementation of Trauma-Informed Care in a Housing First Program for Survivors of Intimate Partner Violence: A Case Study* (2017). at 207. This study focused on the intersection of trauma and housing stability amongst survivors of IPV.

179. Wilson, Fauci & Goodman, 591.

180. Andrew J. Baxter et al., "Effects of Housing First approaches on health and well-being of adults who are homeless or at risk of homelessness: systematic review and meta-analysis of randomized controlled trials," *J. of Epidemiology & Community Health* 73, no. 5 (February 2019): 383–84.

181. Distinct from immediate *shelter*, which refers more to temporary, transitional, and congregate living housing.

182. Susan E. Collins et al., "Where harm reduction meets housing first: Exploring alcohol's role in a project-based housing first setting," *Int'l J. of Drug Policy* 23, no. 2 (March 2012): 111.

earlier approaches like the "Housing Readiness," "staircase," or "Treatment First" models, which required unhoused people to complete a sequence of steps to demonstrate their deservingness of permanent housing.[183] Those steps typically include sobriety, medication, and participation in mental health treatment before participants are deemed "housing ready."[184] Although Treatment First ("TF") had some success in housing individuals, housing advocates criticize the model as excluding the most vulnerable individuals experiencing homelessness, being overly punitive and dehumanizing, and removing individuals' autonomy.[185] Instead of TF, HF advocates argue that, "to achieve stability in other areas of life, one must first have stable housing."[186]

Notably, HF is not Housing Only; optional and complementary case management, mental health treatment, addiction treatment, childcare, and employment programs are crucial to keeping people with specialized needs housed.[187] Choice-based complementary care and services have been a built-in feature of HF since its inception. Dr. Sam Tsemberis, a psychologist and CEO of the nonprofit Pathways to Housing, developed HF in 1992 based on his experiences in mental health outreach.[188] The Pathways HF ("PHF") model emerged from a combination of "consumer-centric clinical approaches," such as trauma-informed care, psychiatric rehabilitation, respect for clients, and having client-members of the advisory board.[189] The PHF model had four major components: (1) program philosophy and practice values emphasizing consumer choice, (2) community based, mobile support services, (3) permanent, "scatter-site" housing, and (4) harm reduction.[190] Pathways selected each component based on its effectiveness in other disciplines.

One major difference between the PHF model and other approaches to permanent housing is that Pathways specifically looks for appealing, aesthet-

---

183. Julia R. Woodhall-Melnik & James R. Dunn, "A systematic review of outcomes associated with participation Housing First programs," *Housing Studies* 31, no. 3 (2016): 288–89.

184. Ibid.

185. Ibid.

186. Ibid.

187. Ibid.

188. Deborah K. Padgett, Benjamin F. Henwood, and Sam J. Tsemberis, *Housing First: Ending Homelessness, Transforming Systems, and Changing Lives* (New York: Oxford University Press, 2015), 4–5.

189. Ibid.

190. Ibid.

ically pleasing housing, to give clients (called consumers) one more reason to choose to stay housed.[191] Community-based mobile services, also developed in the 1970s, bring psychological services into communities rather than requiring people to travel to providers.[192] It seeks to reduce the need for inpatient hospitalization by providing ongoing support for people with serious mental illness.[193] Because HF does not require treatment for substance abuse or mental illness, such programs should try to reduce the risks of those behaviors.

B. Critiques of Housing First

Despite the empirical evidence, Housing First is not universally accepted. In fact, Robert Marbut, the former Executive Director of the United States Interagency Council on Homelessness ("USICH") is one of HF's staunchest critics,[194] stating, "I believe in Housing Fourth."[195] Marbut's Pinellas Safe Harbor Shelter in St. Petersburg, Florida was notorious for forcing residents to sleep outside in a flooded courtyard if they broke the rules, such as being rude, failing to clean up, or failing a drug test.[196] Although Marbut is certainly one of the most extreme critics, his views reflect a broader skepticism about HF. The most common arguments against HF are that HF enables substance abuse and negative behaviors, it is costly, and it does not reduce homelessness long-term.

Proponents of treatment first ("TF") housing programs argue that substance abuse will increase in HF programs if people have no drug tests or sobriety requirements and the privacy to partake.[197] However, the data indicate that this is not the case. In New York, a randomized controlled trial, considered to be the gold standard for experimental studies, found no significant difference

191. McCoy, Terrence. 2015. "Meet the outsider who accidentally solved chronic homelessness," *Washington Post*, Mat 16, 2015. https://www.washingtonpost.com/news/inspired-life/wp/2015/05/06/meet-the-outsider-who-accidentally-solved-chronic-homelessness/.

192. Padgett, Henwood, and Tsemberis, 4.

193. Ibid.

194. National Low Income Housing Coalition, *Memo to Members: Robert Marbut Removed as Executive Director of USICH* (February 22, 2021). https://nlihc.org/resource/robert-marbut-removed-executive-director-usich.

195. Ibid.

196. Arthur Delaney, "How A Traveling Consultant Helps America Hide the Homeless," *Huffpost* (March 9, 2015). https://www.huffpost.com/entry/robert-marbut_n_6738948.

197. Padgett, Henwood, and Tsemberis, 54.

in the use of alcohol and drugs between the HF and TF groups.[198] Although there was increased substance abuse and mental health treatment participation in TF groups (because they are mandatory), they were equally effective as not requiring treatment at all as a prerequisite for housing.[199] In addition, the housing retention rate for HF was significantly higher than TF groups.[200] Critics of HF point to this and say that "Housing First's record at addressing behavioral health disorders...is far weaker than its record at promoting residential stability."[201] However, eliminating substance abuse is simply not the goal of HF, permanent housing is.[202] This applies equally to the argument that HF does not save public systems money.[203] Assuming arguendo that HF is more expensive than the cost of sheltering, incarcerating, rehabilitating, and giving medical treatment to unhoused people (which is unsupported by data),[204] this does not negate the fact that HF is undoubtedly the best way to house people without being prohibitively costly.[205] Dr. Stefan Kertesz, a Birmingham, Alabama physician who works with unhoused veterans through the U.S. Department of Veterans Affairs, goes so far as to say that the notion that HF is only worth doing if it saves public money is "stupid and immoral logic."[206] Ultimately, critics who attack the potential substance abuse and cost-effectiveness effects of HF are missing the point: HF is the best way to solve the homelessness crisis and to restore people's dignity by facilitating access to housing in the quickest manner possible.

---

198. Ibid., 56.

199. Ibid., 54.

200. Ibid.

201. Stephen Eide, *Housing First and Homelessness: The Rhetoric and the Reality* (Manhattan Institute 2020), 4.

202. "PHF was not intended to end addiction.... [O]nce housing stability is so clearly in evidence, it seems obvious to look for other positives if they exist." Deborah K. Padgett, Benjamin F. Henwood, and Sam J. Tsemberis, *Housing First: Ending Homelessness, Transforming Systems, and Changing Lives* (New York: Oxford University Press, 2015), 54.

203. Stephen Eide, *Housing First and Homelessness: The Rhetoric and the Reality* (Manhattan Institute 2020), 4.

204. Research conducted in 2002 revealed that leaving people homeless costs, on average, over $40,000 per person annually. Padgett, Henwood, Tsemberis, 59.

205. Carlyn Zwarenstein, "Housing First and the Homelessness Crisis: What Went Wrong?" *Filter Magazine* (July 23, 2020).

206. Ibid.

Another criticism is that cities that implement Housing First policies have increasing numbers of individuals experiencing homelessness.[207] However, this is a gross overgeneralization of a nuanced issue. Los Angeles, the city often pointed to as a failure by HF critics,[208] has successfully housed thousands of individuals since the implementation of Measure H.[209] In fact, eighty-eight percent of people placed in permanent housing through agencies funded by the Los Angeles Homeless Services Authority (LAHSA) in 2018 did not return to homelessness as of June 2020.[210] Why, then, do LA County's homelessness numbers keep increasing? Even with significant gains in placing people into permanent housing in the last few years, it is simply not keeping pace with the number of people becoming unhoused. An estimated 82,955 people became unhoused during 2019 alone; in other words, while 207 people exit homelessness every day, 227 people become unhoused.[211] Ultimately, while HF is certainly an effective approach, it does not solve the greater systemic issues that cause people to become housing insecure in the first place.[212]

Advocates of HF recognize that the lack of available, affordable housing is a major barrier to ending homelessness even when HF is implemented. Part of this is due to a reduction in affordable units in major cities.[213] According to the National Low Income Housing Coalition, in 2017 there were only thirty-five available units of affordable housing for every 100 extremely low-income Americans.[214] In addition, the existing stock of affordable rental housing is being depleted. According to the National Housing Trust, the United States loses two affordable units for every one created, due to deterioration, abandonment, or

---

207. Stephen Eide, *Housing First and Homelessness: The Rhetoric and the Reality* (Manhattan Institute 2020), 10.

208. Ibid.

209. Los Angeles Homeless Services Authority. June 12, 2020. "2020 Greater Los Angeles Homeless County Shows 12.7% Rise in Homelessness Despite Sustained Increase in Number of People Rehoused." https://www.lahsa.org/news?article=726-2020-greater -los-angeles-homeless-count-results.

210. Ibid.

211. Ibid.

212. In a system where new entries into homelessness outpace housing placements, effective homeless prevention programs are paramount. For an in-depth discussion of homeless prevention, see Chapter 5.

213. National Low Income Housing Coalition, *A Brief Overview of Affordable Rental Housing* (2017) 7. https://nlihc.org/sites/default/files/AG-2017/2017AG_Ch01-S03_History -Of-Affordable-Housing.pdf.

214. Ibid., 8.

conversion to luxury units.[215] Another contributing factor is the difficulty in obtaining and keeping Section 8 housing vouchers. Wait lists can be years or even decades long,[216] and in major cities like New York and Los Angeles, the wait lists have been closed entirely for years.[217] Those who are lucky enough to receive a voucher have only ninety days to use it before it expires, which means that recipients in major renting cities may not find a willing landlord in time.[218] Starting in 2020, housing advocates are pushing President Joe Biden to make Section 8 an entitlement for all who are eligible,[219] and to better enforce the Fair Housing Act against landlords who discriminate against Section 8 renters.[220] Addressing all of these issues are crucial to ending homelessness in America and should be done in conjunction with the Housing First philosophy.

C. Implementing Housing First

As Housing First programs are increasingly implemented nationwide, researchers raise concerns regarding programs that stray from the original PHF design.[221] As Dr. Tsemberis noted, "the HF approach has since come to be defined in differing ways such that we reserve 'PHF' for the original

215. National Housing Trust. "What is Preservation?" Accessed April 11, 2021. https://www.nationalhousingtrust.org/what-preservation.

216. Margarita Lares, Director of the Housing Authority of Los Angeles County's Assisted Housing Division, reported in 2017 that the wait time in Los Angeles was eleven years. Julia Wick, "The Waiting List for Section 8 Vouchers In L.A. Is 11 Years Long," *LAist*, April 4, 2017. https://laist.com/2017/04/04/section_8_waiting_list.php.

217. New York City's Section 8 wait list has been closed since 2007. "Section 8," City of New York, updated March 1, 2021. https://perma.cc/SJT8-2J8F. In Los Angeles, the wait-list was closed for thirteen years before it opened and immediately closed again in 2017. "Section 8 Housing Choice Voucher Waiting List Lottery to Open on Monday," Housing Authority of the City of Los Angeles, October 2, 2017. https://perma.cc/4LCN-MC2D. Los Angeles opens its waiting list lottery in October 2022 for just under two weeks. https://www.lacda.org/section-8/shared-info/how-to-apply. This lottery does not equate to immediate housing but instead a chance at a spot on the wait list for housing.

218. Laura Sullivan and Meg Anderson, "Section 8 Vouchers Help the Poor—But Only If Housing Is Available," *NPR*, May 10, 2017. https://www.npr.org/2017/05/10/527660512/section-8-vouchers-help-the-poor-but-only-if-housing-is-available.

219. Matthew Yglesias, "Joe Biden's surprisingly visionary housing plan, explained," *Vox*, July 9, 2020. https://www.vox.com/2020/7/9/21316912/joe-biden-housing-plan-section-8.

220. Haag, Matthew. 2021. "'She Wants Well-Qualified People': 88 Landlords Accused of Housing Bias," *New York Times*, March 15, 2021, New York edition.

221. Patricia M. Chen, "Housing First and Single-Site Housing," *Social Sciences* 8, no. 4 (April 2019): 130; Padgett, Henwood, Tsemberis, 3.

model or direct and faithful replications. Not all HF programs follow PHF (hence the need for the distinction)."[222] Some researchers even developed fidelity assessments.[223] For example, the Pathways Housing First Fidelity Scale assesses thirty-eight items across five domains: housing choice and structure, separation of housing and treatment, service philosophy, service array, and program structure.[224] Other entities, such as the USICH, have HF checklists, which allow service providers to assess whether their "housing first" programs actually align with Housing First principles.[225] Similar to the PHF model, most assessments emphasize: (1) low-barrier to housing entry, (2) the separation of housing and treatment, (3) consumer choice, and (4) harm reduction.[226]

When designing a Housing First program, it is important to address each component with specificity in mind. For example, most people intuitively understand that low-barrier housing means housing that is relatively easier to obtain. Some programs may take this to mean low or no cost, which is certainly a good thing, but others find it more effective to have a comprehensive approach. A program that touts itself as low-barrier should consider the following: Is the office of the provider open after working hours or on the weekends? Must applicants visit the office multiple times or sit through long interviews to be enrolled? Does the program require current employment, credit or rental history, identification, a current address, or access to the internet? Do certain things such as a criminal conviction, undocumented status, or bad credit exclude people from eligibility? Must applicants speak or read English to easily apply?[227] All of these things can negatively affect a person's ability to access permanent housing, even if the rental cost is low. Other major factors to consider when utilizing an HF approach are scatter site vs. single-site housing, how the

222. Padgett, Henwood, Tsemberis, 3.

223. Patricia M. Chen, "Housing First and Single-Site Housing," *Social Sciences* 8, no. 4 (April 2019): 131.

224. Ana Stefancic, et al., "The Pathways Housing First Fidelity Scale for Individuals with Psychiatric Disabilities," *American J. of Psychiatric Rehabilitation* 16 (2013): 245.

225. United States Interagency Council on Homelessness, *Housing First Checklist: Assessing Projects and Systems for a Housing First Orientation* (September 2016): 2–3.

226. Patricia M. Chen, "Housing First and Single-Site Housing," *Social Sciences* 8, no. 4 (April 2019): 131; Ana Stefancic, et al., "The Pathways Housing First Fidelity Scale for Individuals with Psychiatric Disabilities," *American J. of Psychiatric Rehabilitation* 16 (2013): 245; United States Interagency Council on Homelessness, *Housing First Checklist: Assessing Projects and Systems for a Housing First Orientation* (September 2016): 2–3.

227. United States Interagency Council on Homelessness, *Housing First Checklist: Assessing Projects and Systems for a Housing First Orientation* (September 2016): 1.

program will find units (purchase property vs. work with landlords), and how the program will prioritize applicants if there is not enough housing available (Section 8, families with children, veterans, women, etc.).[228]

LIVED EXPERIENCE NARRATIVE

George Hill[229] is a veteran who experienced homelessness for 12 years following his discharge from the Marine Corps. He works as a peer support specialist for HUD-VASH, helping other veterans experiencing homelessness by sharing his story and offering advice.

On Experiencing Homelessness[230]

I became homeless in 1985 and I lived on the streets in San Diego and Los Angeles until August 3, 1998. So my "birth date," as we call it, is August 4, 1998 because that's when my life began. When I was homeless, that was not life. The misery is beyond what you can even imagine. I can't come up with enough adjectives to describe what it's like. The utter despair of homelessness is beyond words. Like, I never really committed to suicide, but there were times where I didn't care if I lived or died. [...]

I had been trained by the military to live with extreme heat, cold, hunger, and violence. And living on the streets is so much more violent than people are aware of. You won't ever hear about homeless people dying on the news unless they died horrifically. It is truly amazing how much death is around you when you're homeless. People don't realize that every time it rains—even a drizzle—someone you know is going to die. Everybody out there has a compromised immune system and no healthcare. Free clinics can only do so much and it's a major undertaking to try to make the trip and get seen while you're sick.

228. Melissa Osborne, "Who Gets 'Housing First'? Determining Eligibility in an Era of Housing First Homelessness," *J. of Contemporary Ethnography* 48, no. 3 (2019): 404.

229. Hill, George. Interview with Tammi Matsukiyo. March 31, 2021.

230. Mr. Hill's narrative has been reorganized into thematic sections and does not necessarily follow the structure of the interview. The "[...]" indicates that the separated paragraphs are taken from different moments of the interview. Furthermore, some grammatical edits have been made to clarify and contextualize his statements.

Shelters are there but they are just so undesirable. I only stayed in a shelter twice in twelve years. You couldn't bring any of your stuff into the shelter, so you had to leave it on the streets. At 5 o'clock you get in a line and wait a couple of hours. Then you get checked in and listen to an hour-long sermon. Around 8 you get something to eat, then shower, but there were bedbugs in the beds and they were filthy. Like I said, you couldn't bring any of your own blankets. Then you sleep and are woken up at 5 AM, eat breakfast, and by 6:30 to 7:00 AM you are on the streets again. Your stuff is gone. Then you do nothing all day until you can get back in line. I tried it once and hated it but decided to give it another try. The second time I got lice, so I never went back.

On Having PTSD

In the military we are warriors, and you have to be every part of that when you are in the service. To survive, you have to deal with the tragedies and not let it bother you. Well, it bothers some of us. When I was stationed at the DMZ[231] for Temporary Assigned Duty in 1979 and found out that people had been killing each other for years, I felt like a sitting duck—for three weeks it was kill or be killed. I didn't realize what that situation did to me, that I was traumatized. Back then, there was no training and nobody talked about the trauma. I am a Vietnam Era vet. The general public did not care about us when we came home, and most people in Congress didn't care either because their constituents didn't. […]

My PTSD went untreated for years. I spent twelve years in the wilderness with that. I didn't think I was suffering from PTSD because I didn't see combat. When I finally got diagnosed, the doctor explained it to me like this: when you feed a mouse to a pet snake, you have to put it in the cage. The mouse doesn't even have to see the snake in the cage to be afraid and act afraid. I was the mouse for three weeks straight before my TAD ended and I went back to Japan.

---

231. The Demilitarized Zone is a border barrier between North and South Korea. Between 1974–1979, there was at least one violent incident at the DMZ per year, and multiple North Korean tunnels were found under the DMZ. Congressional Research Service. "North Korean Provocative Actions, 1950–2007," Prepared by Hannah Fischer. Washington: Library of Congress, Apr. 20, 2007. https://fas.org/sgp/crs/row/RL30004.pdf.

On Veteran Homelessness

Experiencing homelessness as a veteran is different. You are so used to hardships and so done with institutions that you don't even want to engage with them. You develop a shell that is hard to penetrate. You also learn in the military that you are not to be a burden to anyone. I had family, but I refused to be a burden to them. [...]

If it weren't for the V.A., I'm sure I would be dead because I have no respect for gangs. When you are homeless, you are surrounded by gangs because that's who is selling narcotics to the homeless. Because of my military training, I wouldn't respect them—I would fight back.

The V.A. back then wasn't like it is today. The first time I went there for anything, it was because I had pneumonia in 1991. It was an El Niño year, so it was raining hard and I almost died. I made it to a clinic and the ambulance took me to the V.A. After they treated me, I walked right back out from the V.A. into the rain.

On the Turning Point

People ask, "what caused you to change?" and it wasn't even me. I was sitting and holding a bag of my stuff on the corner of 5th and Spring, waiting for my friend to get back from a check cashing place. I saw a man with rags tied on his feet and I thought, "Wow. That is terrible." Even though I was homeless, I never saw people with rags on their feet. He was covered in dirt—you could only see the skin on his joints where they had rubbed through. There are a lot of different people on skid row—people missing limbs, blind people--out of all of them, he reached his hand in his pocket and gave *me* a dollar. He said, "Here man, I feel sorry for you," and shuffled away. I was in shock and angry—how did *he* feel sorry for *me*? Something about that didn't sit right with me, so I realized I had to get help. From that moment, everything changed. I used that dollar and a few cents I had to get to the V.A. When I got to Westwood, they had already closed at 3:00 PM so I went next door to the Army National Guard and slept by the door. I woke up to the sprinklers hitting me, so I walked from Westwood to Santa Monica and slept on the pier. The next day, I walked to the VA and I was too late again, but I would not give up. On the third day I made sure to be there early, so I got in and learned about the New Directions program.

On New Directions

The V.A. told me that nobody signed up for New Directions because it was so structured, but I knew I needed that. In 1992, New Directions fought along with Representative Maxine Waters to acquire an abandoned building to house 170 people. I lived there for twenty months—I even got married there. The program gave me clothes, treated my medical conditions, fed us, and educated us. During my time, I went from learning one plus one to Calculus 3 because a teacher from the Los Angeles Unified School District came down to teach us. You didn't have to worry about anything but dealing with your own problems, so I was able to work on myself. That's when I got diagnosed with PTSD and my life changed. There, I founded the New Directions Veterans Choir for formerly homeless veterans.

When I was homeless, I would sing in the tunnels of MacArthur Park for hours and hours because it sounded like my own recording studio. When I was getting my life back together, I would sing in the stairwell at New Directions, too, and that's how we started the choir. The New Directions program helped me to live again, for lack of a better term. When I think about it, I was actually fortunate that I was a veteran because that meant that there was a place for me. What happens to people with nowhere to go?

III. Harm Reduction

A. Defining Harm Reduction

Harm reduction is a set of realistic and humane approaches that requires providers to meet their clients where they are. Harm reduction recognizes that abstinence, or the complete extinguishment of harmful health behaviors, is unrealistic and instead focuses on reducing the harmful effects of engaging in such behaviors.

Harm reduction arose as a grassroots effort to curb the spread of HIV and hepatitis B infections in the 1970s and 1980s,[232] although the principle was

---

232. Benjamin F. Henwood, Deborah K. Padgett, and Emmy Tiderington, "Provider Views of Harm Reduction Versus Abstinence Policies Within Homeless Services for Dually Diagnosed Adults," *J. of Behavioral Health Servs. & Research* 41 (2014): 81. https://doi.org/10.1007/s11414-013-9318-2.

practiced as far back as the early 1900s in narcotic maintenance clinics.[233] Traditional definitions describe harm reduction as practices that aim to minimize the negative legal, social, and health effects associated with drug use. Harm reduction is also used in different contexts in which there is a desire to reduce the negative effects of eating disorders, domestic violence, risky sexual behavior, and licit substance use, including tobacco, e-cigarettes, and alcohol.[234] As such, it may be more helpful to understand harm reduction as interventions aimed at reducing the effects of *harmful health behaviors*, separate from any goal of extinguishing said behaviors completely.[235]

Evolving far beyond its origins of syringe exchange, harm reduction is applied in a range of programs, including: housing,[236] access to food,[237] and policing approaches.[238] Further, the value of harm reduction, especially through the adoption of the Housing First model also discussed in this chapter, is widely recognized worldwide.[239] Harm reduction thus offers providers

---

233. Hawk et al., "Harm Reduction Principles for Healthcare Settings," *Harm Reduction J.* 14, no. 70 (2017). ttps://doi.org/10.1186/s12954-017-0196-4.

234. Ibid.

235. This broader understanding of harm reduction is more helpful in the context of homeless advocacy because while not every individual experiencing homelessness may engage in substance use, many individuals who are unhoused may experience, engage in, or otherwise be subjected to other harmful health behaviors. What is identified as the "traditional" definition of harm reduction is less helpful for practitioners and advocates because harm reduction in practice has expanded beyond reducing the individual and community harms of illicit substance abuse.

236. The more recent housing first approach (in contrast to the traditional "treatment first" approach) incorporates harm reduction. Benjamin F. Henwood, Deborah K. Padgett, and Emmy Tiderington, "Provider Views of Harm Reduction Versus Abstinence Policies Within Homeless Services for Dually Diagnosed Adults," *J. of Behavioral Health Services & Research* 41 (2014): 80–89. https://doi.org/10.1007/s11414-013-9318-2.

237. Christiana Miewald, Eugene McCann, Alison McIntosh and Cristina Temenos, "Food as Harm Reduction: Barriers, Strategies, and Opportunities at the Intersection of Nutrition and Drug-related Harm," *Critical Public Health* 28, no. 5 (2018): 586–95. https://doi.org/10.1080/09581596.2017.1359406.

238. Steve Herbert, Katherine Beckett, and Forrest Stuart, "Policing Social Marginality: Contrasting Approaches," *Law & Soc. Inquiry* 43, no. 4 (Fall 2018): 1491–1513. https://doi.org/10.1111/lsi.12287.

239. While this book is primarily focused on implementation of harm reduction in the United States, studies and articles of non-American scholars are valuable for illustrating the universal applicability of this principle and for gaining a more developed understanding of what harm reduction looks like in practice, especially in the wake of the COVID-19 pandemic (declared a public health emergency of international concern (PHEIC) by the World Health Organization (WHO) on January 30, 2020, and declared a national emergen-

a pragmatic approach to limit the negative consequences of harmful health behaviors by focusing on obtaining successful outcomes in other areas of need—such as obtaining housing security, access to nutritious food, legal services, and mental health services.

Empirical research studies show that harm reduction strategies are useful for practitioners to help affect behavioral change in clients and includes strategies such as safer use, managed use, abstinence, and housing first. In the context of homeless advocacy and services, for instance, harm reduction contributed to the housing first model, which has been championed as a successful permanent housing model amongst service providers.[240] In one study, consisting of 129 in-depth interviews with 41 providers, several housing first providers felt "liberated" because of the "freedom" of working with a client who could "be more honest about their substance use while staying engaged in services."[241] The goal for many of these providers was to foster open dialogue about substance use, and harm reduction allowed them to treat their clients "with respect[by] recognizing and pointing out that a stigma exists."[242] Thus, implementing harm reduction principles can foster positive relationships and promote not only increased program engagement but also meaningful choice for clients.

B. Harm Reduction as a Philosophy

The goal of harm reduction is to reduce the harms of substance use, not provide people access to drugs, as some misunderstand it. This popular misconception stems from the fact that harm reduction practices are not focused on reducing consumption per se but instead endorse the implementation of services such as syringe exchanges or supervised injection sites. Rather than condoning an individual's choice to engage in harmful health behaviors, harm

cy, beginning March 1, 2020, by President Donald J. Trump in Proclamation 9994 of March 13, 2020, 85 Fed. Reg. 15337 (Mar. 18, 2020)). See, for example, Amanda Roxburgh et al., "Adapting Harm Reduction Services During COVID-19: Lessons from the Supervised Injecting Facilities in Australia," *Harm Reduction J.* 18, no. 20 (2021). https://doi.org/10.1186/s12954-021-00471-x, and Marcus et al., "Harm Reduction in an Emergency Response to Homelessness during South Africa's COVID-19 Lockdown," *Harm Reduction J.* 17, no. 60 (2020). https://doi.org/10.1186/s12954-020-00404-0.

240. "Housing First" is discussed elsewhere in this chapter.

241. Benjamin F. Henwood, Deborah K. Padgett, and Emmy Tiderington, "Provider Views of Harm Reduction Versus Abstinence Policies Within Homeless Services for Dually Diagnosed Adults," *J. of Behavioral Health Servs. & Research* 41 (2014): 85. https://doi.org/10.1007/s11414-013-9318-2.

242. Ibid.

reduction accepts these behaviors as realities and seeks to limit the negative consequences associated with them. This subtle shift can be understood as harm reduction having a consequentialist justification—that is, it seeks to limit harmful *consequences* of behavior—in comparison to traditional abstinence models having a deontological justification—that is, seeking complete extinguishment of "morally questionable" behaviors.[243]

It may be helpful to understand harm reduction as not just a set of practices but also as a philosophy.[244] Harm reduction has been argued to have the deontological justification of respecting human dignity and autonomy,[245] justified as being necessary for social justice and equity,[246] and examined as an Aristotelian virtue ethic.[247] More specifically, proponents of embracing harm reduction as a philosophy[248] argue that the value of harm reduction lies in its

---

243. Deontological ethics is a complex moral philosophy topic. In the context of harm reduction practices working with unhoused people, this can be conceptualized by juxtaposing the abstinence model of drug treatment and rehabilitation as a condition for housing (and other markers of the "deserving" beneficiaries of social aid) with harm reduction that seeks to abolish the moral stigma associated with drug use. When the government-led War on Drugs initiative started in the 1970s using illegal drugs was seen as a "moral failing" and abstinence-based policies were considered "necessary to deter the morally bereft." Natalie Stoljar, "Disgust or Dignity? The Moral Basis of Harm Reduction," *Health Care Analysis* 28 (Oct. 2020) 343–51. https://doi.org/10.1007/s10728-020-00412-y. This stance and resulting negative impact on unhoused people spurred a turn to harm reduction, defining and implementing its practices.

244. This is a minority view of harm reduction. As mentioned above, although there is no universal definition of harm reduction, most definitions regard harm reduction as a pragmatic approach consisting of a learnable set of practices. This view, however, may limit the universal embracing of harm reduction; in fact, some scholars have argued that this consequentialist, utilitarian-type justification may be in fact harmful to harm reduction. Nicholas B. King, "Harm Reduction: A Misnomer," *Health Care Analysis* 28 (Nov. 2020): 324–34. https://doi.org/10.1007/s10728-020-00413-x.

245. Natalie Stoljar, "Disgust or Dignity? The Moral Basis of Harm Reduction," *Health Care Analysis* 28 (Oct. 2020) 343–51. https://doi.org/10.1007/s10728-020-00412-y.

246. The National Harm Reduction Coalition calls harm reduction a "movement for social justice" and a way to build "power and equity with people who use drugs." See https://harmreduction.org/ for more information.

247. Timothy Christie, Louis Groarke, and William Street, "Virtue Ethics as an Alternative to Deontological and Consequential Reasoning in the Harm Reduction Debate," *Int'l J. of Drug Policy* 19 (2008): 52–59. https://doi.org/10.1016/j.drugpo.2007.11.020.

248. The National Harm Reduction Coalition makes a distinction between Harm Reduction and harm reduction, the prior being a "philosophical and political movement focused on shifting power and resources to people most vulnerable to structural violence" and the latter being the "approach and fundamental beliefs in how to provide the services." "Homelessness and Harm Reduction," National Harm Reduction Coalition, revised 2020.

promotion of autonomy and dignity by increasing the number of meaningful options available and providing a non-judgmental, safe environment.[249] Thus, the accusation of harm reduction simply being a mode of giving people drugs fails to understand the philosophy of—or, perhaps more precisely, the motivations behind—harm reduction.[250]

Harm reduction also does not deny abstinence as an option, it just does not require abstinence to implement its approach.[251] For instance, nicotine patches are an example of a harm reduction strategy that could complement an abstinence model.[252] The key is to provide choices and options to people, wherever they are at.[253] In other words, different people require different support and solutions. Sometimes what people need varies by stage of life, or even by the day they present for services.

Harm reduction seeks to address the apparent failings of the abstinence model. Traditional housing models require immediate abstinence and adherence to strict rules—such as curfews, urine testing, daily supervision, or mandatory attendance to day treatment—in order to be and remain eligible

https://harmreduction.org/issues/harm-reduction-basics/homelessness-harm-reduction -facts/.

249. Natalie Stoljar, "Disgust or Dignity? The Moral Basis of Harm Reduction," *Health Care Analysis* 28 (Oct. 2020) 349. https://doi.org/10.1007/s10728-020-00412-y. Nicholas King has argued that the historical motivations of harm reduction are in fact *not* utilitarian in that harm reduction does not actually reduce harms, but rather is about rejecting ideas of moral depravity, stigma, and punitive Manichaeism, and embracing compassion and respect when serving individuals, regardless of their harmful health behaviors. "Harm Reduction: A Misnomer," *Health Care Analysis* 28 (Nov. 2020): 333. https://doi.org/10.1007 /s10728-020-00413-x.

250. One criticism of harm reduction, which is addressed below in "Critiques of Harm Reduction," is that it does not actually (empirically) improve health outcomes of individuals or reduce harms. Understanding harm reduction as a philosophy, however, can provide a deontological or ethical justification that rebuts this criticism. That is, harm reduction as a principle is valuable beyond its pragmatic applications.

251. See, for example, Benjamin F. Henwood, Deborah K. Padgett, and Emmy Tiderington, "Provider Views of Harm Reduction Versus Abstinence Policies Within Homeless Services for Dually Diagnosed Adults," *J. of Behavioral Health Services & Research* 41 (2014): 86. https://doi.org/10.1007/s11414-013-9318-2. Individuals who choose abstinence are accommodated in programs implementing harm reduction principles, such as in housing first. Harm reduction does not preclude abstinence as an option, it merely provides additional options to individuals who continue to engage in harmful health behaviors.

252. Natalie Stoljar, "Disgust or Dignity? The Moral Basis of Harm Reduction," *Health Care Analysis* 28 (Oct. 2020) 345. https://doi.org/10.1007/s10728-020-00412-y.

253. This concept of "meeting people where they are" is discussed as a foundational principle elsewhere in this chapter.

for temporary and permanent housing programs.[254] These continuing eligibility requirements, however, diminished engagement and successful housing retainment outcomes.[255] In contrast, harm reduction, as discussed above, is an alternative practice that has greater positive engagement in comparison to models contingent on the "all-or-nothing" abstinence proposition.

C. Critiques of Harm Reduction

One criticism of harm reduction is that it does not in fact improve health outcomes of individuals or reduce harms. For instance, one meta-analysis found non-statistically significant differences in improving recovery from drug use across five different empirical studies, although there appeared to be a *clinically* significant difference favoring harm reduction over abstinence due to the aggregate standardized mean difference.[256] However, as previewed earlier, understanding harm reduction as a philosophy can provide a deontological or ethical justification that rebuts this criticism. That is, harm reduction can be understood as a principle that is valuable in itself—important in that it promotes human dignity and autonomy and justice—beyond its pragmatic applications.

There is also disagreement as to whether harm reduction is a best practice. For instance, the Substance Abuse and Mental Health Services Administration (SAMHSA) under the U.S. Department of Health & Human Services (HHS) does not explicitly adopt harm reduction as a best practice, and instead advocates for "recovery-oriented care," which embraces a similar philosophy and but not necessarily the practices of harm reduction.[257] In contrast, the

---

254. Benjamin F. Henwood, Deborah K. Padgett, and Emmy Tiderington, "Provider Views of Harm Reduction Versus Abstinence Policies Within Homeless Services for Dually Diagnosed Adults," *J. of Behavioral Health Services & Research* 41 (2014): 81. https://doi.org/10.1007/s11414-013-9318-2.

255. Ibid.

256. Jill D. Parramore, "Group Treatment Effectiveness for Substance Use Disorders: Abstinence vs. Harm Reduction" (PhD diss., Old Dominion University, 2020).

257. "Recovery and Recovery Support," SAMHSA, last modified April 23, 2020. https://www.samhsa.gov/find-help/recovery. SAMHSA, however, does not currently appear to endorse either philosophy at this time (this is in contrast to an apparent press release in 2011, in which SAMSHA claimed that "abstinence is the safest approach for those with substance use disorders"; the webpage was last updated April 27, 2020, however, and was unable to be accessed). *See* Benjamin F. Henwood, Deborah K. Padgett, and Emmy Tiderington, "Provider Views of Harm Reduction Versus Abstinence Policies Within Homeless

National Health Care for the Homeless Council, which is funded by the Health Resources and Services Administration (HRSA) and HHS, posits that harm reduction is a best practice from the medical perspective and advocates its implementation in homeless services.[258]

D. Best Practices

Because there is no universal definition or understanding of harm reduction, implementation across programs and with different communities differs. There are, however, several programs that are effective in reducing individual and community harms: Housing First, syringe exchanges, supervised injection sites, wet houses, and overdose prevention through the use of naloxone.

Even if these programs do not actually reduce harm in a utilitarian sense, as addressed above, it is important to implement the philosophy of harm reduction—of respecting every individual's choice to promote dignity, autonomy, and justice—within a legal or advocacy practice when working with an extremely diverse and vulnerable population such as unhoused people. Definitional differences aside, understanding harm reduction as a philosophy not only tips the scales of its utility but also informs how legal advocates can use the practice in counseling and other client work. In other words, there is no need to wait until a client completes treatment to represent them or understand their communicated needs.

The National Harm Reduction Coalition provides fact sheets that are helpful in implementing harm reduction practices, including six (6) principles of harm reduction and pragmatic ways to implement said principles in the context of homeless services:[259]

1. **Health & Dignity:** Establishes quality of individual and community life and wellbeing as the criteria for successful interventions and policies.

Services for Dually Diagnosed Adults," *J. of Behavioral Health Services & Research* 41 (2014): 82, fn.20. https://doi.org/10.1007/s11414-013-9318-2.

258. "Harm Reduction," National Health Care for the Homeless Council. Accessed April 20, 2021. https://nhchc.org/online-courses/harm-reduction/.

259. "Homelessness and Harm Reduction," National Harm Reduction Coalition, revised 2020. https://harmreduction.org/issues/harm-reduction-basics/homelessness-harm-reduction-facts/.

- Affirming messages within space.
- Bathrooms accessible to both participants and staff members.

2. **Participant Centered Services:** Calls for nonjudgmental, non-coercive provision of services and resources to people who use drugs and the communities in which they live in order to assist them in reducing attendant harm.

  - Offering what participants say is most important (e.g., access to chargers, phones, computers).

3. **Participant Involvement:** Ensures participants and communities impacted have a real voice in the creation of programs and policies designed to serve them.

  - Creating message boards for participants to contribute feedback or share resources with others.
  - Elections for services and space changes.

4. **Participant Autonomy:** Affirms participants as the primary agents of change and seeks to empower participants to share information and support each other in strategies which meet their actual conditions of harm.

  - Having supplies and resources in spaces that are accessible without having to ask staff.
  - Allowing for participants to come/leave freely.

5. **Sociocultural Factors:** Recognizes that the realities of various social inequalities affect both people's vulnerability to and capacity for effectively dealing with potential harm.

  - Multilingual resources.
  - Posters that explicitly state that all people are welcome.
  - Variety of images in the space.

6. **Pragmatism & Realism:** Does not attempt to minimize or ignore the real and tragic harm and danger associated with drug use or other risk behaviors.

- Consider posting community agreements in public.
- Creating alternative spaces for people who need to move/be alone/pace.

To place two of these into the legal context, viewing legal representation as a form of participant centered services (#2 above) is essentially client-centered advocacy (a topic that follows in more detail below). As an "expert" advocate, one or more legal issues like eviction defense might stand out as most urgent in an initial intake, but if the client states that their custody issue, for example, is most important to them, then that might be what deserves initial primacy. The client is key in identifying their legal needs. It is also important to take sociocultural factors into account (#5). Advocates for unhoused people should ensure that the documents they ask their clients to acknowledge and sign are presented in the client's native language and that they understand the terms.

IV. Client-Centered Advocacy

Lawyers and other advocates seeking to end homelessness by representing unhoused people in addressing the hurdles they face in obtaining permanent housing should adopt a client-centered advocacy approach to such representation. This includes developing policies and practices that demonstrate an understanding of what it means to effectively represent clients who live in poverty.[260]

The client-centered advocacy approach focuses on the legal and non-legal aspects of the problem the client is seeking to address.[261] For unhoused people, that typically means helping to remove any hurdles to housing that exist, which may include past evictions; a criminal record that either affects eligibility for housing or the ability to earn an income or qualify for benefits sufficient to pay for such housing; or lacking necessary documentation to qualify for housing (a challenge particularly exacerbated for undocumented individuals).[262] As one can see, an advocate for unhoused people has the opportunity to practice many

---

260. "Pro Bono Clients: Strategies for Success: Assisting clients in poverty," ABA Brochure. https://www.americanbar.org/content/dam/aba/administrative/probono_public _service/as/brochure_probono.pdf.

261. David A. Binder, Paul Bergman & Susan C. Price, *Lawyers as Counselors: A Client-Centered Approach* 17–23 (1991).

262. In 2018, one of the contributors to this book, James Gilliam, launched a county-wide program in Los Angeles through which lawyers represent unhoused clients with

areas of law, given the myriad issues unhoused people must navigate to obtain and retain permanent housing.

Client-centered advocacy assumes that most clients are capable of thinking through the complexities of their problems. It also respects the autonomy of the unhoused person who "owns" the problem.[263]

The client-centered advocate guides the client, who actively participates in identifying their problems and in formulating and making decisions about potential solutions.[264] Though practices vary among advocates, a client-centered approach often includes the following attributes:

1. The lawyer helps identify problems from a client's perspective.

   An advocate will be most helpful to their client if they understand the problem from the client's point of view.

2. The lawyer actively involves a client in the process of exploring potential solutions.

   Here, it is important to ensure that the client considers the broadest range of options and considers the non-legal consequences of each potential solution.

3. The lawyer encourages a client to make those decisions which are likely to have a substantial legal or non-legal impact.

   Client-centered advocacy emphasizes the value and importance of clients playing the role of primary decision maker, given that the client is typically in a better position than the attorney to choose which potential solution is best. Only the client can decide how willing they are to run the risks and bear the costs of seeking a particular outcome.

4. The lawyer provides advice based on a client's values.

   Clients will demand to hear their advocate's advice; such advice should generally be based on the advocate's understanding of the client's values.

5. The lawyer acknowledges a client's feelings and recognizes their importance.

---

hurdles to housing. The top three issues unhoused clients reported as needing a lawyer to address were housing, enrollment in public benefits, and immigration issues.

263. Binder, Bergman, and Price, 17–23.

264. Ibid.

Legal problems do not exist in an emotional vacuum. By focusing on the client's feelings, as well as the facts, the advocate will be able to build rapport and help fashion solutions that best meet a client's needs.

6. The lawyer repeatedly conveys a genuine desire to help.

Perhaps the simplest of tips, looking a client in the eyes during an intake meeting and saying, "I am here to help you, and work together" will inure benefits to the attorney-client relationship long after that moment. Asserting your desire to help is an explicit form of reassurance that clients often find comforting and motivating.[265]

Lawyers who seek to inculcate these principles in their practice will need to possess good interpersonal skills, including active listening, empathy, genuineness, and probing.[266]

Moreover, advocates can adopt strategies when representing clients who live in poverty that will help build rapport and lead to better outcomes for the unhoused person.[267] Indeed, many unhoused clients will come from "generational poverty," and they may have developed mindsets that differ from most other clients.[268] As the American Bar Association (ABA) suggests, "awareness of these differences can improve an attorney's ability to provide effective representation." The ABA has suggested the following tips to help attorneys understand and effectively serve their clients who live in poverty, such as unhoused people and people who face imminent risk of homelessness.[269]

1. Build trust over time: Clients may be distrustful at first, based on prior experiences with the legal system. This may be particularly true for unhoused people who have been promised assistance over and over, only to see advocates disappear when funding lapses.

2. Be alert for roadblocks: Clients may have jobs, children, or a lack of transportation that makes it difficult to make it to appointments on time. Unhoused clients may need to work during the day to

---

265. Ibid.

266. Ibid.

267. "Pro Bono Clients: Strategies for Success: Assisting clients in poverty," ABA Brochure. https://www.americanbar.org/content/dam/aba/administrative/probono_public_service /as/brochure_probono.pdf.

268. Ibid.

269. Ibid. These six points from Pro Bono Clients have been adapted somewhat for the housing context.

find materials to recycle or may be uneasy leaving their belongings behind to come to an appointment with an attorney.

3. Listen carefully; communicate clearly: Keep your client focused on the legal issues and answer all your client's questions fully. It may be tempting to try to assist your client with all of their issues, like finding food. Focus on clearly communicating and problemsolving the legal issues. Then, provide the client with referrals to other resources they need. If it's possible to do "warm" or personalized referrals that can help expedite or remove barriers to their access to the resources all the better.

4. Help empower your client: Thoroughly explain the available options, offer advice on potential consequences, and let the client decide what's best for them. For example, an unhoused client may be offered housing in a remote area far removed from the services they need or the social support network they have developed; the client must determine whether to prioritize ending their homelessness or staying unhoused in their current locale.

5. Promote time and task management: While an unhoused client may face many daily challenges, including looking for food and water and constantly being on the move, it helps to emphasize the importance of keeping appointments as much as possible. Explain that this will help move the case forward. That said, an advocacy practice that reflects trauma-informed care will not punish an unhoused client for being tardy or missing an appointment.

6. Coach for courtroom success: Clients who are unfamiliar with legal proceedings may need assistance with understanding proper attire and courtroom demeanor. This may be a particular challenge for unhoused clients who may lack the appropriate wardrobe to appear in court.

7. Forestall future problems: Refer your client to other appropriate resources as warranted, such as for food and for clothes appropriate for the courtroom.

8. Become culturally attuned: See the world through your client's eyes to the extent possible. Learn about the problems your unhoused client faces daily, perhaps by visiting a shelter or attempting to

complete an application for public benefits.[270] Understanding the important "Philosophies of Care" that underly the homeless services delivery system will help an advocate see things from the client's perspective.

A. Best Practices

When establishing a legal advocacy project to represent unhoused people and people at imminent risk of homelessness, advocates should keep top of mind the principles of client-centered advocacy and the tips the ABA has proffered for working with clients in poverty and adopt low barrier, trauma-informed policies and procedures.

For example, advocates should be open to meeting with an unhoused client close to where they reside, rather than at the advocate's office. And such meetings may need to take place outside normal business hours to accommodate the time that an unhoused client may be able to safely leave their belongings.

When conducting an initial intake interview with an unhoused client, advocates should endeavor to capture as much information as possible in a format that will allow for it to be memorialized. Avoiding re-traumatization includes not asking a client to retell the traumatic events they have experienced repeatedly. Additionally, if the advocate is working alongside a provider servicing unhoused people that may have referred the client to legal services, ideally the advocate will obtain as much information about the client and the client's legal problem from the provider, to avoid having to ask the client the same questions they were already asked when they were assessed for homeless services.

---

270. Ibid.

THREE

Addressing the Impact of Homelessness on Diverse Communities

Activist and legal scholar Kimberlé Crenshaw first coined the term "intersectionality" in the late 1980s.[271] Crenshaw argued that a single-axis model of identity failed Black women because their experience is unique and not captured by examining gender and race as discrete identities. Crenshaw introduced the theory that different identities interact to create complex identities.[272] More recent intersectionality theories also speak to the structural component of discrimination.[273] Instead of focusing on categorizing individual identities, recent theories ask: what is society's reaction to this person? These theories identify power structures to determine whom to protect and how.[274]

---

271. Kimberlé Crenshaw, "Demarginalizing the Intersection of Race and Sex: A Black Feminist Critique of Antidiscrimination Doctrine, Feminist Theory and Antiracist Politics," *U. Chi. Legal F.* 1989: Iss. 1: 140.

272. Ibid.

273. Sandra Fredman, *Intersectional Discrimination in EU Gender Equality and Non-Discrimination Law. Luxembourg: Publications Office of European Union.* (Luxemboug: Publications Office of European Union, 2016, 31. http://ohrh.law.ox.ac.uk/wordpress/wp-content/uploads/2016/07/Intersectional-discrimination-in-EU-gender-equality-and-non-discrimination-law.pdf.

274. Ibid.

More recent intersectionality theories that conceive of discrimination as structural lend particular attention to historical disadvantages[275] experienced by a group of people. This method does not require for people to necessarily identify themselves into constructed and rigid categories, but rather recognizes that discrimination is linked to institutional factors. Our discussion regarding the disproportionate impact of homelessness on diverse communities keeps this method in mind. For example, a conversation regarding LGBTQ youth requires recognition of a historical, legislative blindness in providing legal protections to these individuals at school or within the welfare system, and therefore how these institutions accordingly fail LGBTQ youth and put them at risk of becoming unhoused.

This chapter examines six marginalized communities[276]: Black and indigenous people of color (BIPOC); other racial minorities (including Latinx people); women; individuals who identify as lesbian, gay, bisexual, transgender, queer, or questioning (LGBTQ); older adults; and veterans. In addition to being historically marginalized, these communities are also disproportionately unhoused. These examined categories are surely not exhaustive, and this analysis does not intend to suggest that an excessive proliferation of subjects or categories is necessary or that the needs of non-intersectional people experiencing homelessness are no different than those with multiple intersecting minoritized identities. Instead, this analysis highlights the need for advocates to refrain from homogenizing the unhoused community and to humanize unhoused people by asking, "Who is unhoused and why?"

---

275. Further discussion regarding historical disadvantages that lead to homelessness appears in Chapter 5.

276. Many of the terms in this chapter are ones that are changing to better reflect people's identities and preferences. For example, some may prefer "historically excluded" to "marginalized" to describe communities who were subject to colonial and racist practices in the United States. "Racial minorities" is used here but in many areas of the United States, races other than Caucasian make up most of the population; we continue its use here because groups continue to be "minoritized" in that they are treated as "less than" for purposes of rendering services for unhoused people (and in other ways not treated in this book).

I. BIPOC and Racial Minorities

A. Introduction and Statistics

Nationwide, racial minorities or people of color are disproportionately represented in the unhoused population. Black and Latinx[277] people are particularly overrepresented. Out of about 3.5 million people across the country who are unhoused, 42% are Black, 20% are Latinx, 4% are Native American or indigenous, and 2% are Asian.[278] These figures are not proportional to these groups' representation in the overall population: Black people make up 12% of the total population, Latinx people 12%, and Native American or indigenous people and Asian communities each make up 1% of the total population.[279] These statistics only reflect people living on the street, in shelters or transitional housing, or in areas unfit for human habitation. When considering people who have stayed temporarily in the homes of friends or family, the total reaches 7.4 million.[280]

Some studies reflect a starker difference between the impact of homelessness on racial minorities versus white people.[281] In a study covering six cities in Georgia, Ohio, Texas, California, New York, and Washington, 64.7% of the unhoused population were Black, 28% white, and 6.9% Latinx.[282] In the general population of the U.S., white people represent 73.8%, Black people 12.4%, and

---

277. Latinx is a gender neutral or nonbinary term describing people of Latin American origin or descent. The term is meant to be inclusive in this text, although it is acknowledged that many people of Latin American origin find the term academic and prefer "Latina/o."

278. Nat'l Law Ctr. on Homelessness & Poverty, *Racial Discrimination in Housing and Homelessness in the United States: A Report to the U.N. Committee on the Elimination of Racial Discrimination*, (2014), 3. https://nlchp.org/wp-content/uploads/2018/10/CERD _Housing_Report_2014.pdf.

279. Nat'l Law Ctr. on Homelessness & Poverty, *Racial Discrimination in Housing and Homelessness in the United States: A Report to the U.N. Committee on the Elimination of Racial Discrimination*, (2014), 3. https://nlchp.org/wp-content/uploads/2018/10/CERD _Housing_Report_2014.pdf.

280. Ibid.

281. Here, white refers to non-Latinx white people.

282. Jeffrey Olivet et. al, *Center for Social Innovation Supporting Partnerships for Anti-Racist Communities: Phase One Study Findings*, (2018), 4. https://perma.cc/7ZUH-5J8X. Though Latinx people seem to be underrepresented, researchers speculate that such figures may be an underestimate because recent immigrants or undocumented people may be doubled up or living in substandard housing to avoid shelters or services that put them at risk of deportation.

Latinx people make up 17.2%.[283] Out of unhoused young adults (from ages 18 to 24), 78% are Black, and more broadly, 89.1% are people of color.[284]

Moreover, in examining the lifetime prevalence of homelessness at late midlife both overall and for racial and ethnic groups, data from the Health and Retirement Study (HRS) shows that out of 6.2% of respondents who stated that they were unhoused at some point, lifetime prevalence of homelessness was significantly higher for minorities.[285] Black people are over three times more likely than white people to have experienced being unhoused once, even after adjustments to covariates such as education, veteran status, and geographic region.[286]

B. Discussion

Overall, racial minorities are disproportionately at risk of being unhoused due to obstacles in accessing an education that allows for economic mobility, obtaining housing, and family stabilization, as well as challenges due to exposure to the criminal justice system. All of these critical problems reflect a larger issue of systemic racism and discrimination against people of color.

1. Barriers to Economic Mobility

A lack of economic mobility or capital within social networks precipitates homelessness for many racial minorities. Economic mobility can be analyzed in two components: a financial dimension and a social dimension.

First, racial minorities face barriers to education, stable employment, and higher pay. In comparison to white males, Black males earn bachelor's degrees or higher at half the rate (15.6% to 32%).[287] In 2010, Black people with an associate degree experienced a higher unemployment rate (10.8%) than white people with a high school diploma (9.5%).[288] In the same year, a Black male employee with a bachelor's degree or higher was paid 25.4% less on average in weekly full-time salary in 2010 compared to a male white worker with the same

---

283. Ibid.

284. Ibid.

285. Vincent A. Fusaro et al., "Racial and Ethnic Disparities in the Lifetime Prevalence of Homelessness in the United States," *Demography* 55 (2018): 2122.

286. Ibid.

287. Inst. for Children, Poverty & Homelessness, *Intergenerational Disparities Experienced by Homeless Black Families*, (2012), 6. https://perma.cc/AXZ8-LVL2.

288. Ibid.

level of education.[289] More broadly, the median wealth of white households is about 20 times the wealth of Black households.[290] This factor is particularly relevant, given that access to additional funds allows for the transfer of inter-generational wealth,[291] which, in turn, enhances the economic circumstances of younger relatives through investments in children's education, inheritances, and monetary gifts. Homeownership also allows for the buildup of this wealth, thus demonstrating the compounding effect of discriminatory housing poli-cies and education and income disparities.

Second, the social dimension of economic mobility encapsulates the challenges people of color face because of fragile social networks. The lack of financial capital and resources in communities of color and the lack of emo-tional support networks means that individuals in these communities are less able to support each other.[292] For example, people may be willing to double up, take people in, or live in another person's home, but the person providing tem-porary housing may not have the financial capacity to help because he or she cannot afford the burden of additional consumption of resources (e.g., higher cost of food or utility bills).[293] This, in turn, can lead to strained relationships that further weaken community and social ties. Such housing arrangements may also threaten the primary lessor's own housing.

Access to a stable, living wage is further exacerbated because of the over-policing and mass incarceration of communities of color. Black men are seven times more likely to be imprisoned than white men, while Black women are eight times more likely than white women.[294] Compared to citizen offend-ers, non-citizen offenders are four times more likely to be incarcerated.[295] Non-citizen offenders are also more likely to suffer from abuses (such as strip searches) while in custody compared to citizen offenders.[296] Within the inmate population, recent homelessness is eleven times more common than among

---

289. Ibid.

290. Ibid.

291. There is further discussion of the role of race and access to home ownership in Chapter 1.

292. Jeffrey Olivet et al., *Center for Social Innovation Supporting Partnerships for An-ti-Racist Communities: Phase One Study Findings*, (2018), 12. https://perma.cc/7ZUH-5J8X.

293. Ibid.

294. Forrest Stuart et al., "Legal Control of Marginal Groups," *Ann. Rev. L. & Soc. Sci.* 11 (2015): 238.

295. Ibid.

296. Ibid.

the general population.[297] Compounding these challenges is the fact that cities across the country have legal practices that overwhelmingly police unhoused people, minorities, individuals with alcohol or substance abuse histories, and those engaged in informal economic enterprise.[298] Prior involvement in the criminal justice system or felony status bars many minorities experiencing homelessness from securing a stable, living-wage job, thus locking these individuals in a constant cycle of homelessness and criminalization.[299]

2. Barriers to Housing

Homelessness disproportionately impacts racial minorities because of longstanding racial disparities in access to affordable housing, vulnerability to foreclosure, and housing policies that lead to residential segregation. For example, racial minorities often struggle to find affordable housing because landlords refuse to accept housing vouchers or other housing assistance and income subsidies.[300] Sixty-two percent of housing voucher users in the U.S. are people of color.[301] In New York City, 3,000 housing advertisements displayed some limitation on the housing application based on the source of income.[302] In New Orleans, landlords deny housing vouchers about 82% of the time—75% of these landlords outright refuse to accept housing vouchers, while 7% mandate conditions that make it "virtually impossible for a voucher holder to rent the apartment."[303] Notably, in New Orleans, 99% of Housing Choice Voucher holders are Black.[304]

Another barrier to housing racial minorities face is discriminatory practices that make these communities more vulnerable to foreclosure. That is, racial minorities often lack access to sustainable mortgage credit. For instance, Fannie Mae and Freddie Mac, two Government Sponsored Enterprises (GSEs), bar people of color from accessing sustainable mortgage credit by "'unnecessarily

297. Ibid.

298. Ibid, 239.

299. Jeffrey Olivet et al., *Center for Social Innovation Supporting Partnerships for Anti-Racist Communities: Phase One Study Findings*, (2018), 13. https://perma.cc/7ZUH-5J8X.

300. Kaya Lurie, Breanne Schuster, and Sara Rankin, "Discrimination at the Margins: The Intersectionality of Homelessness & Other Marginalized Groups," *Homeless Rights Advocacy Project* (2015): 7–8. https://digitalcommons.law.seattleu.edu/hrap/8.

301. Ibid.

302. Ibid.

303. Ibid.

304. Ibid.

relying on credit profile factors' similar to credit risk by employing policies that 'divide loans into categories based on [factors such as] down payment (loan to value ratio), credit score, and product type.'"[305] "This type of policy imposes 'additional fees for purchasing a mortgage from the originating lender that rely on the amount of down payment provided and credit score of the borrower.'"[306] In addition, Black borrowers are 25–35% less likely to receive funding than a white borrower with similar credit, and if people of color are able to receive funding, these groups are more likely to get higher cost loans, be targeted for predatory lending, and lose their homes to foreclosure.[307] These policies disadvantage racial minorities and make it difficult to maintain housing.

In addition to income discrimination and discriminatory lending practices, federal housing policies create restrictions on affordable housing choices and promote residential segregation. For example, federal policies limit affordable housing choices or mobility for those in Section 8 Housing Choice Voucher programs.[308] Further, federal policies like the Low Income Housing Tax Credit encourage the development of affordable housing primarily in poor or predominantly minority neighborhoods.[309] As a result, people of color are disproportionately concentrated in poor, residential areas. These areas often have sub-standard housing conditions, limited employment opportunities, inadequate access to health care, under-resourced schools, and high exposure to crime and violence.[310] All of these factors contribute to a persistent cycle of poverty for communities of color. Renewal projects and gentrification may also contribute to residential segregation.[311] Notably, residential segregation negatively affects Black households to a greater extent than other minorities.[312]

3. Family Stabilization

Fragile social networks also relate to another pathway to homelessness and barrier to exit—family disintegration. Family disintegration often involves interaction with the child welfare, juvenile justice, and criminal justice sys-

---

305. Ibid., 10.

306. Ibid.

307. Ibid., 11.

308. Ibid., 9.

309. Ibid.

310. Ibid., 9–10.

311. Inst. for Children, Poverty & Homelessness, *Intergenerational Disparities Experienced by Homeless Black Families*, (2012), 6. https://perma.cc/AXZ8-LVL2.

312. Ibid.

tems.[313] Oftentimes, domestic violence precipitates family disintegration and increases the risk of homelessness, and multi-generational involvement in child welfare and foster care systems often occurs prior to and during experiences of homelessness.[314] For example, some states criminalize poverty by defining the inability to provide shelter for children as neglect. As a result, disproportionately poor and minority parents who are at risk of becoming unhoused or currently unhoused lose custody of their children and have their children forcefully removed from them. Children of unhoused parents have a higher likelihood of entering foster homes, and twelve percent of unhoused children are placed in foster homes, compared to 1% of their peers whose parents are not unhoused.[315]

Thus, a vicious cycle is perpetuated, as unhoused parents, oftentimes with weak social networks and previous encounters with these social service systems, lose their children to the foster care system, and placement in these systems, in turn, increases the child's likelihood of adult homelessness.[316] Beyond disrupting family bonds, interaction with the child welfare, juvenile justice, and criminal justice systems also impacts broader community bonds.[317] Communities of color are more likely to experience violence and incarceration, and are also more likely to lack the social networks and family bonds to cope with poverty and deprivation.

II. Women

A. Introduction and Statistics

Homelessness disproportionately impacts women in two primary ways. First, women are disproportionately represented in unhoused families. Across the country, 37% of people experiencing homelessness are members of

---

313. Jeffrey Olivet et al., *Center for Social Innovation Supporting Partnerships for Anti-Racist Communities: Phase One Study Findings*, (2018), 14. https://perma.cc/7ZUH-5J8X.

314. Ibid.

315. George Lipsitz, "In an Avalanche Every Snowflake Pleads Not Guilty: The Collateral Consequences of Mass Incarceration and Impediments to Women's Fair Housing Rights," *UCLA L. Rev.* 59 (2012): 1758.

316. Ibid., 1758–59.

317. Ibid., 1759.

unhoused families.[318] Of the sheltered adults[319] in families with children, 80% are women, while 20% of these adults are men.[320] Second, women who have faced domestic violence are disproportionately represented in the national unhoused population. Domestic violence is the third leading cause of homelessness, and 22 to 57% of women have cited domestic violence as the cause of them being unhoused.[321]

B. Discussion

1. Relationship Between Gender and Homelessness

As noted above, domestic violence is among the leading causes of homelessness for women. A 2005 study showed that in 24 cities, domestic violence was the primary cause of homelessness in half of the cities.[322] In San Diego, almost 50% of unhoused women are domestic violence survivors.[323] In Massachusetts, 92% of unhoused women reported severe physical and/or sexual assault at some time in their lives, while 1/3 were current or recent survivors of domestic violence.[324]

Several factors compound the risk of homelessness for domestic violence survivors. First, domestic violence survivors have more difficulty accessing

---

318. Kaya Lurie, Breanne Schuster, and Sara Rankin, "Discrimination at the Margins: The Intersectionality of Homelessness & Other Marginalized Groups," *Homeless Rights Advocacy Project* (2015): 12. https://digitalcommons.law.seattleu.edu/hrap/8.

319. In the context of this discussion, "sheltered" refers to an individual or family living in a supervised publicly or privately-operated shelter designed to provide a temporary living arrangement. "Unsheltered" refers to an individual or family whose primary nighttime residence is a public or private place not designed for or ordinarily used as a regular sleeping accommodation for human beings.

320. Lurie, Schuster, and Rankin, "Discrimination at the Margins," 12.

321. Ibid., 13.

322. Ibid.

323. American Civil Liberties Union, "Domestic Violence and Homelessness," last modified December 20, 2019. https://www.aclu.org/sites/default/files/field_document/factsheet_homelessness_2008.pdf. The phrase "domestic violence victim" is a phrase used by members of law enforcement and within a legal context or in courtroom proceedings. In effort to speak to a sense of empowerment these individuals may own over their experience, this discussion refers to people who have experienced domestic or intimate partner violence as "survivors." However, we recognize that ultimately, advocates should follow the lead of the person they are seeking to support. Whether a person identifies as a victim or a survivor is unique to that person's experience.

324. Ibid.

temporary shelter or financial support.[325] Perpetrators of domestic violence often isolate the survivors from family and friends, support networks, and their community. As a result, survivors of domestic violence are less likely to know about resources for temporary shelter, how to obtain money for moving expenses, and options for transitional housing.[326] Second, if survivors of domestic violence are able to transition from an abusive environment to a shelter, they face separation not only from the abuser but also from places of employment, children's schools, and any existing support networks and communities.[327] For instance, shelters may have age limits or restrictions on admittance of children, resulting in relocation of children to family members who live far from the children's schools.[328] If children are admitted to these shelters, these shelters may also be far removed from the school. Furthermore, some shelters have confidential locations to protect survivors from their abusers, but may also increase isolation.[329] Overall, moving to a shelter often disrupts or severs any existing relationships to necessary networks and communities. Further compounding this issue, domestic violence survivors have a short amount of time to get financial resources for new housing, with deadlines ranging from 14 to 30 days because these shelters are often temporary housing arrangements.[330]

Housing policies and discriminatory landlord policies often exacerbate the challenges domestic violence survivors face in accessing or retaining permanent housing. For example, "zero tolerance for crime" housing policies disadvantage domestic violence survivors by allowing landlords to evict tenants when violence occurs in the residence, regardless of whether the victim or the perpetrator caused the violence.[331] Landlords are often unwilling to rent to women who have experienced domestic violence. For example, in a New York

---

325. Margaret E. Johnson, "A Home With Dignity: Domestic Violence and Property Rights," *B.Y.U. L. Rev.* 1 (2014): 38.

326. Ibid.

327. Ibid., 9.

328. See Ms. Larae Cantley's lived experience testimonial in this chapter.

329. Margaret E. Johnson, "A Home with Dignity: Domestic Violence and Property Rights," *B.Y.U. L. Rev.* 1 (2014): 38.

330. Ibid., 43.

331. American Civil Liberties Union, "Domestic Violence and Homelessness," last modified December 20, 2019. https://www.aclu.org/sites/default/files/field_document/factsheet_homelessness_2008.pdf.

City study, 28% of landlords flatly refused to rent to domestic violence survivors or did not follow up after initial inquiries.[332] A Michigan study focused on women receiving welfare found that women who had experienced recent or current domestic violence were more likely to face eviction.[333] Though some federal protections exist, for the most part, domestic violence survivors are still vulnerable to evictions. In 2005, a federal law was adopted to prohibit discrimination against domestic violence survivors but was limited to inhabitants in Section 8 or public housing.[334] While some states have passed laws providing further protections, most provide narrow protections (e.g., protections only for survivors with a restraining order against the perpetrator) or none at all.[335]

In addition to experiences of domestic violence, disadvantageous work policies and inadequate income contribute to homelessness among women. First, a lack of required paid family and medical leave and no paid sick days disproportionately impacts mothers, who may lose pay when staying home to take care of family responsibilities.[336] Second, women are disadvantaged by a persistent gender wage gap—women make on average 77 cents for every dollar a man makes.[337] While 43% of women workers earn less than $15 per hour, only 1/3 of men earn at this rate.[338] Minority women experience the gender wage gap most severely. For example, Latinx women are paid 54 cents for every dollar paid to white men.[339] Native American women are typically paid 57 cents, while black women are typically paid 62 cents for every dollar paid to white men.[340] Asian women earn 90 cents for every dollar paid to white men.[341]

---

332. Ibid.

333. Ibid.

334. Ibid.

335. Ibid.

336. Kaya Lurie, Breanne Schuster, and Sara Rankin, "Discrimination at the Margins: The Intersectionality of Homelessness & Other Marginalized Groups," *Homeless Rights Advocacy Project* (2015): 15. https://digitalcommons.law.seattleu.edu/hrap/8.

337. Ibid.

338. Ibid.

339. National Partnership for Women & Families, "Quantifying America's Gender Wage Gap by Race/Ethnicity," last modified March 19, 2020. https://www.nationalpartnership.org/our-work/resources/economic-justice/fair-pay/quantifying-americas-gender-wage-gap.pdf.

340. Ibid.

341. Ibid.

These income disparities are further compounded for women with children—women with children are more likely to earn less than $15 per hour than their single-family peers.[342] Because of these economic disadvantages, women are more likely to be "forced to make difficult choices between housing, health care, food, paying bills, and saving for emergencies, which makes women particularly vulnerable to homelessness."[343]

2. Experience of Violence

Given the high levels of violent victimization women face before becoming unhoused, it is unfortunately predictable that women also report higher levels of violence than unhoused men. Common experiences of violence include domestic violence, intimate partner violence, stalking, physical violence and sexual assault.[344] The most significant risk factor for violent victimization as an adult is a pattern of physical, emotional, and sexual abuse as a child, thus highlighting the need to support children within the homeless services system.[345] Risk factors for violence among unhoused people include the severity of homelessness, substance or alcohol abuse, and survival crimes.[346] In Los Angeles, 46% of women report being attacked or physically assaulted while unhoused, with transgender women reporting higher rates at 63%.[347] Women also report a slightly higher rate than men in regards to encounters with law enforcement (as a witness, victim, or alleged perpetrator of a crime, or because police told them they must move along)—37% of women interacted with the police compared to 35% of men.[348]

Despite the dangers women face being unhoused, some may hesitate before choosing to reside in a shelter due to the hostility of bureaucratic shelter

---

342. Kaya Lurie, Breanne Schuster, and Sara Rankin, "Discrimination at the Margins: The Intersectionality of Homelessness & Other Marginalized Groups," *Homeless Rights Advocacy Project* (2015): 15. https://digitalcommons.law.seattleu.edu/hrap/8.

343. Ibid.

344. Los Angeles Homeless Services Authority. *Report and Recommendations of the Ad Hoc Committee on Women & Homelessness.* (Los Angeles: 2017), 17. https://www.lahsa.org/documents?id=1586-ad-hoc-committee-on-women-and-homelessness-report-and-recommendations.pdf.

345. Ibid.

346. Ibid.

347. Ibid.

348. Ibid.

systems.[349] Unhoused women often suffer from a lack of autonomy in shelter systems. Rather, shelter staff often enjoy a wide latitude of discretion and control.[350] For example, shelter staff determine residents' access to resources and manage entrance and exit of the shelter.[351] Shelters often have rules dictating activities, mealtime, and recreation.[352] Because shelter residents are fully reliant on the institution for basic necessities, these requirements are often demoralizing and infantilizing.[353]

In addition, these bureaucratic structures also often lack the resources to address the needs of domestic violence survivors, who often require resources to delve into the violent victimization experienced as a child or in an intimate partnership.[354] Rather than viewing domestic violence as a broader, shared societal concern, shelters often address domestic violence as an individualized problem.[355] For unhoused mothers permitted to enter a shelter with their child, they may be forced to forfeit their decision-making abilities and role as head of the household, as both mother and child are subjected to the rules and discipline of the shelter.[356] As a result, unhoused women are faced with the difficult choice of losing their autonomy by entering a shelter or risking the dangers of the streets with insecure access to shelter, food, and clothing.

3. Health Issues

A substantial number of unhoused women face health-related challenges, including serious mental illnesses, substance abuse disorder, and HIV/AIDs. Unsheltered women are disproportionately vulnerable to these health issues. In Los Angeles County, among the population of women aged 18 and above experiencing homelessness, more than one-third were chronically homeless (35%), with each of these health conditions more than twice as prevalent among the

---

349. Sarah L. DeWard and Angela M. Moe, "'Like a Prison!': Homeless Women's Narratives of Surviving Shelter," *The J. of Sociology & Social Welfare 37*, no. 1 (March 2010): 120. https://scholarworks.wmich.edu/jssw/vol37/iss1/7.

350. Ibid.

351. Ibid.

352. Ibid.

353. Ibid., 121.

354. Margaret E. Johnson, "A Home with Dignity: Domestic Violence and Property Rights," *B.Y.U. L. Rev.* 1 (2014): 44.

355. Ibid.

356. Ibid.

unsheltered population compared to the sheltered population of women.[357] For example, in comparison to 19% of sheltered females, 40% of unsheltered women indicated that they have a serious mental illness.[358] 22% of unsheltered women indicated that they have a substance use disorder, which is more than three times that of sheltered women at 7%.[359] Lastly, 1% of sheltered women had HIV/AIDS, compared to 3% of unsheltered women.[360] Overall, unsheltered women had a greater risk of poor physical and mental health, higher utilization of alcohol or non-injection drugs, and a greater likelihood of a history of physical assault.[361]

Unhoused women, especially unsheltered women, face challenges in protecting against unintended pregnancies, protecting the health of the baby and of self during the pregnancy, and finding ways to stay safe while generating income.[362] In addition, unhoused mothers face family separation when choosing to seek the support and resources of a shelter. Fifty-five percent of cities report that families may have to break up to be sheltered.[363] Unhoused children were often sent to families to avoid shelter life, and the National Center on Family Homelessness found that 1/5 of homeless children were separated from their families at some point.[364]

Unhoused mothers also are at a greater risk of mental and physical health issues. Over 92% of unhoused mothers have experienced severe physical and/or sexual abuse during their lifetime, with 63% reporting that the abuse was perpetuated by an inmate partner.[365] Unhoused mothers have three times the rate of posttraumatic stress disorder (PTSD) at 36% and twice the rate of drug and alcohol dependence at 41% compared to women without children.[366] Nationally, nearly half of unhoused mothers have had a major depressive episode

---

357. Los Angeles Homeless Services Authority. *Report and Recommendations of the Ad Hoc Committee on Women & Homelessness.* (Los Angeles: 2017), 7. https://www.lahsa .org/documents?id=1586-ad-hoc-committee-on-women-and-homelessness-report-and -recommendations.pdf.

358. Ibid.

359. Ibid.

360. Ibid.

361. Ibid., 17.

362. Ibid.

363. The National Center on Family Homelessness, "The Characteristics and Needs of Families Experiencing Homelessness," last modified August 1, 2013. https://files.eric .ed.gov/fulltext/ED535499.pdf.

364. Ibid.

365. Ibid.

366. Ibid.

since becoming unhoused.[367] In terms of physical health, unhoused mothers have ulcers at four times the rate of other women, and over one-third have reported suffering from a chronic physical health condition (such as asthma, chronic bronchitis, or hypertension).[368]

Health issues also arise from lack of access to secure and sanitary bathrooms and menstrual products. Though this challenge is common among unhoused women, who face the "double stigma of menstruation and homelessness,"[369] it is important to note that the issues of access to bathrooms and menstrual justice should be examined along the intersections of gender, race, class, gender identity, sexual orientation, age and ability.[370] So while this section analyzes this issue through the lens of the community of unhoused women, the challenges described here apply to menstruators broadly. Further, though this section only discusses menstrual justice and access to bathrooms as a health issue, a wider scope of menstrual justice would bring into focus the economic disadvantages, discrimination, harassment, and threats to personhood that menstruators face.

Constantly navigating a lack of safe, private bathroom access and the resources to buy clean menstrual products impacts unhoused women in two significant ways.

First, unhoused women face health risks because of lack of access to secure and sanitary bathrooms. Unhoused women often lack access to clean water and sanitation facilities during menstruation, and resources such as menstrual products, clean water, soap, and privacy are not commonly available in public bathrooms accessible to or near unhoused communities.[371] In addition, unhoused women risk assault and harassment when using public bathrooms.[372] Transgender individuals are particularly vulnerable to assault in these circumstances.[373] In response to the lack of secure and sanitary facilities, women often wait until daytime to change their menstrual products in a safe

367. Ibid.
368. Ibid.
369. Vora, Shailini, "The Realities of Period Poverty: How Homelessness Shapes Women's Lived Experiences of Menstruation," The Palgrave Handbook of Critical Menstruation Studies, edited by Chris Bobel et. al., Palgrave Macmillan, 25 July 2020.pp. 31–47. doi:10.1007/978-981-15-0614-7_4, p.33.
370. Margaret E. Johnson, "Menstrual Justice," *U.C. Davis L. Rev.* 53 (2019): 2.
371. Ibid., 70.
372. Ibid.
373. Ibid.

location in a shelter or soup kitchen, thus increasing their risk of toxic shock syndrome, infections, and other health complications.[374]

Second, unhoused women often face difficulties in purchasing menstrual products, either because of a lack of economic resources or because of a lack of access to stores that sell the products in bulk at lower prices.[375] Unhoused women may sometimes obtain these products at community organizations such as shelters, but these organizations may not have a steady supply of donations, or the menstrual products may be of a lower quality or less absorbent.[376] Menstrual products fall low on the list of priorities when unhoused women do receive money that can be used to feed themselves and/or their children.[377] Instead, unhoused women often attempt to use unsanitary items such as a dirty rag or t-shirt found in the streets[378] to staunch blood flow, which increases the risk of infections and diseases like cervical cancer.[379] If these individuals choose not to staunch blood flow, they increase the likelihood of spreading infections like HIV or hepatitis B and C through the menses.[380]

LIVED EXPERIENCE NARRATIVE

Larae Cantley[381] is a member of the Lived Experience Advisory Board (LEAB) within the Los Angeles Homeless Services Authority (LAHSA). LEAB is a leadership body consisting of members with current or past experiences of homelessness and who evaluate current systems of care and make recommendations for improvement. Ms. Cantley speaks on her experience as a black woman, a single mother, and a survivor of abuse.

---

374. Ibid.

375. Ibid., 60. To put the cost into perspective, women in the U.S. spend close to $18,171 in their lifetime on feminine products. "The Ultimate Guide to Feminine Hygiene," Duquesne University School of Nursing, 3 Dec. 2019. https://onlinenursing.duq.edu/master-science-nursing/the-ultimate-guide-to-feminine-hygiene/.

376. Johnson, 60.

377. Rafanelli, Amarica. "Rags Instead of Tampons. Here's What Period Poverty Looks Like in the US," Direct Relief, 22 July 2021. https://www.directrelief.org/2019/10/rags-instead-of-tampons-heres-what-period-poverty-looks-like-in-the-u-s/.

378. Ibid.

379. Johnson, 60.

380. Ibid.

381. Cantley, Larae, Interview with Bichnga Do, August 21, 2020.

On Being a Black Woman & Being Unhoused[382]

Yes [I do feel that black women are treated differently from other members in the homeless community]. There's very high rates of how black women and black girls are brought into the sex traffic world and victims of domestic violence due to this lack of access to a support structure, to a network, to knowing there's a way of being able to be treated [well]. A lot of our black girls don't know that they are worthy of being treated with respect, without being abused, without this idea that if I help you, then you are obligated to do whatever it is I say, otherwise your life is on the line, otherwise I'm going to beat you, or else I'll take your kid. I feel like there's a lot of that experienced by black women.

On the Perception of Unhoused People

Being a young black woman with multiple children...people have this perception that I was undereducated or uneducated, that I just spent my time laying on my back and having sex and making babies. People asked, "Why did you have the second child or the third child?" and not understanding that I was married to my abuser and this was part of the abuse.

It felt very volatile with so many people asking why I had so many children when prior to marrying my abuser, I was in school, I was working, and because of this abusive relationship everything has been threatened and taken away from me.

On Community Connections

I've come from the communities that are highly impoverished and lots of violence and gang association—lots of drug use and addiction. There's a lack of care for the resources that come here, how these resources are distributed, and the power of having some say-so in resources, where there's very little consideration for the health care and the education and the upkeep and the care of the community in and of itself.

[...]

---

382. Ms. Cantley's narrative has been reorganized into thematic sections and does not necessarily follow the structure of the interview. The "[...]" indicates that the separated paragraphs are taken from different moments of the interview. Furthermore, some grammatical edits have been made to clarify and contextualize her statements.

I reached out heavily to the church thinking that this was the only way for help and advice. When I open up and tell them about not having a stable home or having safety in this marriage. The social support of helping a young girl to see what a [healthy] relationship with people could look like was not available to me. It was more available to people who seem like they had their lives together. I would be excluded. There was no inclusion to share your life with us…and no opportunities to see that not everyone's home was abusive, and that this way of living was something you had to live through. I didn't know until I was at least 30 years old that I didn't have to live like this. [The church I went to] was not equipped with the partnerships [with social support services] to understand domestic violence or equipped with the connections to [these] services for people who are experiencing housing instability. Many people walked through those doors with housing instability, and the church was not equipped to give resources, to give information, to give connections or warm handoffs. They weren't educated enough about it to know that there were [sic] resources. Everyone would fend for themselves. There were people who we would call the aunties of the world who would want to take everyone in that they can.

On Domestic Violence

When I think about the instability, it started way back in my own childhood. My mom too is a survivor of domestic violence; my dad was constantly facing the criminal justice system. My dad was one to get swept up in the war on drugs, when all the drugs were released into my community, jobs were taken away, and my dad took the route of "The way I'm going to keep my family safe is joining the gang and the way I'm providing for my family is selling drugs." So, he was constantly in and out of the jails and constantly in and out of these situations where instability was my entire life.

[…]

Most of the housing instability [first] occurred back in the time with my parents when the violence occurred, and my sister was hurt. My sister had her intestines smashed and had to get it removed [and] that's where a lot of instability showed up. We were taken out of the home because my dad constantly went to jail and my mom didn't have the means to take care of finances. Lot of time my dad's drug money was taken and he was beaten by the police.

[...]

When I found out I was pregnant, that's when I signed up for housing in 1998 and immediately, I thought to myself how I could give this child a different way of life. That's when I started to seek out ways of being able to have my own idea of housing. So, I signed up for housing. What I did with my money was that I went to Palmdale, because that was the cheapest, most affordable living, and I put a down payment on an apartment. And I thought "How do I continue to pay rent?" And that's why I married my abuser because that was my thought: "His income was my income; we will be able to afford rent." And I wanted to give my children a different kind of life. So, the day after I graduated from high school, I moved out of my mom's home because she told me I couldn't move out until I graduated, and I already put that down payment down.

[...]

[When I moved in with my abuser] I didn't talk to many people, because there weren't many people to talk to. I think that's one of the main things about people in my community is that we don't have that social support that is talked about in surviving domestic violence. The [capacity to build] a healthy self-esteem is being connected to at least 5 healthy adults, and I didn't have that. I didn't have the connections and the transparency [regarding] the ways to get credit, get housing, didn't have any of those conversations existing in my reality. So I thought I would have the stability living with this guy. You know, in the beginning, everything is nice and cool, but as soon as he was unable to control his emotions he was lashing out and fighting. That was a lot of instability there. He was very similar to my dad, being a part of the gang and being a drug dealer. So, the instability seemed to stumble from [a] bad household with my mom to my own bad household with this new journey with my abuser.

[...]

In my domestic violence relationship, after putting down my down payment and having this place, [the cause of my homelessness] was an eviction. It was an eviction after I could no longer take out my child or check my mailbox and [my abuser] would come and he would go and it was fear that if I went anywhere, those people that he served drugs to in the community would tell him that. So, I never knew when he was coming or when he was going. And what he said to me was "I'm working these hours, security job hours, taking on two shifts," [so] I thought that these bills would be taken care of. I never thought that [sic] that the police would come knocking on my door, telling me that I had a few minutes to grab whatever I can and exit the premises.

Because I had no phone because [my abuser] didn't allow for any-thing like that, what I did was that I went to my dad's house, which was a very unsafe place because my dad still had connections with unhealthy people. I woke up to being sexually abused while everyone in the house was still asleep. So I got my kids and left from there. Through [my abuser] knowing my dad, he was able to keep [track of me].

I went to a shelter and while in the shelter, he would end up being near the shelter because the shelter would make me leave at a certain time, so when I walked out, he would be there [threatening me]. It was a challenge, so I had to leave. I ended up finding what you call, "boy-friends," but these weren't really boyfriends. They were actually people who sexually wanted something from me.... I left from the shelter, ended up in a relationship with a guy who had no idea to be with a women with children and it was basically one of those situations that if I had not controlled my children the way that he thought that I should control them or if I had not given sex—it was one of those "Oh, then you could leave" type things. It was a lot of that from my journey from 1998–2012 to getting housed.

[...]

I do feel like there was [a] sense of safety with how I was able to have some say-so in who I knew was going to be violent. When I was in [an unstable home] with my family, I never knew [who] was going to be violent, because of whatever was going on with my dad's life that I wasn't connected to.

On Experiencing the Criminal Justice System

[M]y mom, being a recovering addict...doing what she can, right, but her having all these barriers, all these challenges, all this trauma, she had never sought out domestic violence services. I would end up staying with her and ended up catching my first case of assault with a deadly weapon based on the fact that my mom had a mental breakdown and she wanted to fight with me and because I was staying in her home, I decided I was going to leave while she was having this mental breakdown. While I was leaving, she attacked me with the two by four and I tried my very best to keep her from hitting me with the two by four. Someone called the police and they said I had a [sic] weapon and the police, they came and fucked me up, ripped my clothes, my face was burnt from mace, and I was held in jail for a seventy-two hour hold in a men's jail. Wasn't able to shower, wasn't able to do too much in that thing, but when they found out that my mom's mental breakdown was the source of it, the judge said, "I don't even want to see her." They let me out of the actual court holding space without me seeing the judge ever. I don't really know how my record is impacted by being arrested for assault with a deadly weapon when there was no weapon that they were able to connect to me, there was no assault that they were able to connect to me, but because of the way of the police was being called and how the police addressed the situation, that's on my record.

Actually, both times of being arrested, were directly connected to instability. When I say instability, I was staying with a guy who I was able to contribute to the home through my cash aid, my Food Stamps—so that was one way that I found some support to where I was staying. I was able to contribute to food being put in the fridge, whether me and my children had access to it or not. It was my way of saying, "Thanks for letting us stay here." I was staying with a guy, I was giving my food assistance and also contributing my cash aid to the rent there. And he came in the middle of the night and asked me to attend to him sexually, and I chose not to. I left from the home in an angry rage after I had been drinking, and I got a DUI. Both times that I had any run-ins with arrests or the police, they were both connected to my being unstable. If I was stable in my own home and didn't live in a house under the pressure of who I was staying with, then I would most likely would have avoided those two moments in my life where I was arrested.

[…]

Not having my fee for the train but needing to get from one place to another. Needing get a place to another place. And the police [cited me for not paying the train fee], which made it difficult to get a driver's license. When the police showed up at the door to evict us, I was so emotionally distraught that I didn't know what the heck was happening with my life that I just did whatever he said. I already been instilled with so much fear about what the police do to people of color. My main go-to is to do whatever they say.

On Temporary Shelter

[When my children] were with the [abuser's] parents, the police escorted me to the shelter, I [told] the shelter, "I do have children," and they [told me that they only] have limited space. "So, whenever your children do come back with you, we'll have to figure out a new process. The new process was very different because you have a son who is of a certain age and he might not be able to stay with the family, we'll have to probably find a different placement for him." So, there was a whole new level of stress there. Between knowing when my children were going to be back [with] me and knowing that my son might be placed in a different placement and the treatment in the shelter, and the abuser constantly showing up in random places when I had to leave the shelter—between all of those things, I'm better off finding this boyfriend and sleeping over there with the children. That was [my] transition from shelter to boyfriend.

[...]

On Accessing Services

When it came to asking for help from the police, there were moments where they would ask "What do you want me to do?" Well first, how do I get safe [from my abuser]? There were so many moments where the dignity a human being has is stripped from them because of people's beliefs of why you are in this situation, why are you asking for my help, why are you even asking for my help? You put yourself here.

[...]

Most of the challenges [with social services] were around the divorce process [to divorce the abuser]. The court and the judge made it very difficult. I didn't want to tell the entire story of the abuse and being homeless, and I just wanted her to divorce me. It wasn't that simple—she made it very difficult [by asking] "Well, why aren't you asking for child support?" I just wanted to get away from him. I don't want to have to encounter him or have anything to do with him. The court would tell me to try and find him, and I'm still in housing instability with no idea where he is, and we have to come back and forth to this court for mediation. It was very uncomfortable and felt intrusive.

[...]

There was a time when I went into the DPSS building, and this was after my purse had been stolen. I went in to tell them, a few days from when my benefits would be released, knowing that if I didn't come in with something, which was some ability to put some food in the fridge, the place I was at would be in limbo. I let them know that my purse was stolen, and I needed access to my card. They were like, "Well, you need your ID." And I say, "Well, let's go back to my purse was stolen. So, I don't have an ID. I don't have my card, but I need to have access to funds in two days." They said, "We can't help you, you have no ID." Well, where do I start? I just sat in the lobby and cried because I did not know what would happen next. I was acknowledged by the supervisor. She said, "Why are you crying? This is not a normal thing." And I told her why, and then she took a look at my case and said, "In the past years, you've been checking a box that says you've been experiencing domestic violence. Have you been receiving any services?" I said, "No." I was supposed to have an entirely different case manager who was a specialist in domestic violence just because of [sic] my DPSS case by checking that box. That never happened to me. That woman, she was the catapult to getting me my services. If I had not broken down in that lobby and sat there and just sobbed, I would've been on another wild goose chase of harm and harm and harm and harm.

On Mental Health

I sought out domestic violence services, but that was more so when I had housing stability. When I got housing stability for myself, then I was able to actively seek out and participate in a mental health journey for myself. As a kid, I was admitted to a psychiatric hospital. Once in my twenties, I was admitted again. Right before I got housing, my plan was to live in a psychiatric hospital until I died. There was [a] long journey of mental instability. When I think of what mental health means to me, having this psychological and emotional balance, having some mental clarity to be in tune with oneself. I did not get that until after 30 years of living. I was constantly battling suicidal ideology. Seeking out help for mental health services required for me to have stability. As long as I was bouncing around a lot, I was super hyper-vigilant. I was diagnosed as [a] functional bipolar and [with] paranoia schizophrenia. I think the instability was the main thing when I was first released as a child, I was more afraid that I was going back into an environment then not knowing what was going to be next. So, when they released me back to my family, I knew it wasn't going to work. I knew I wasn't going to obtain any mental stability in that environment with the people who are still caught up in this cycle of living, where it was so dysfunctional. I just knew it wasn't going to help.

III. LGBTQ

A. Introduction and Statistics

Homelessness disproportionately affects LGBTQ individuals, and LGBTQ youth in particular. Approximately 1.6 million children and youth (ages 12–17) are unhoused each year without an accompanying parent or guardian.[383] Yet, though only 5–10% of American youth identify as LGBTQ, LGBTQ youth make up 20–40% of the unhoused youth population.[384] Though there are few studies identifying the number of LGBTQ youth who are racial minorities, those that do include such information show that LGBTQ unhoused youth are often also people of color.[385]

---

383. Nat'l l. Ctr. on Homelessness & Poverty & The Nat'l Network for Youth, *Alone Without a Home: A State-by-State Review of Laws Affecting Unaccompanied Youth*, (2012), 5. https://www.nlchp.org/Alone_Without_A_Home.

384. Kaya Lurie, Breanne Schuster, and Sara Rankin, "Discrimination at the Margins: The Intersectionality of Homelessness & Other Marginalized Groups," *Homeless Rights Advocacy Project* (2015): 18. https://digitalcommons.law.seattleu.edu/hrap/8.

385. Michelle Page, "Forgotten Youth: Homeless LGBT Youth of Color and the Runaway and Homeless Youth Act," *Nw. J. of L. & Soc. Policy* 12 (2017): 17.

B. Discussion

1. LGBTQ Youth: Relationship Between Gender Identity and Sexual Orientation & Causes of Homelessness for Youth

This section surveys the factors that can cause this disproportionate representation of LGBTQ youth in the unhoused community. One of the common causes of homelessness among LGBTQ youth is unsafe family and social environments because of their gender identity or sexual orientation. For instance, 46% of LGBTQ youth cite family rejection of their gender identity or sexual orientation as the reason they ran away from home and became unhoused.[386] Forty-three percent cited being forced out by their parents because of their gender identity or sexual orientation.[387] This discrimination extends to social programs as well. For example, because of a lack of legal protections for LGBTQ individuals, welfare workers can refuse to work with LGBTQ youth, including those forced out by their families, without fear of liability.[388] As a result, these individuals often are denied access to resources in these systems.

LGBTQ individuals who are successfully admitted into the welfare system face additional hurdles compared to their non-LGBTQ peers. LGBTQ individuals are overrepresented, but are more frequently rejected by foster families, adoptive parents, and group homes.[389] Other providers may force LGBTQ youth to denounce their orientation or identities to receive support, or they would place these youth in hostile homes.[390] Within these environments, LGBTQ youth might be forced to dress in ways that do not conform with their orientation or identities, be disciplined for any expression of their orientation or identities, and in some scenarios, be forced into conversion therapy programs.[391] The discrimination LGBTQ youth face within these systems may lead them to run away and face homelessness rather than live in such hostile environments.

---

386. Lurie, Schuster, and Rankin, 20.

387. Ibid.

388. Jordan B. Woods, "Religious Exemptions and LGBTQ Child Welfare," *Minn. L. Rev.* 103 (2019): 2344–45.

389. Ibid., 2348–49. James W. Gilliam, Jr., "Toward Providing a Welcoming Home for All: A New Approach to Address the Longstanding Problems Lesbian, Gay, Bisexual, and Transgender Youth Face in the Foster Care System," *Loy. L. Rev.* 37 (2004) 1037.

390. Woods, 2345; Gilliam, 1037.

391. Woods, 2349.

Even if LGBTQ youth do not run away, they are more likely to face housing instability once they age out of the welfare system. LGBTQ youth are much more likely than their non-LGBTQ peers to struggle to support themselves in the transition period to adulthood after leaving the welfare system.[392] Overall, for LGBTQ individuals, the welfare system often perpetuates the family and social instability that contributes to the disproportionate impact of homelessness in LGBTQ communities.

Barriers to education and poverty challenges also drive the disproportionate impact of homelessness on LGBTQ individuals,[393] which keep many LGBTQ individuals in vulnerable situations. LGBTQ youth have higher rates of harassment in school, which leads to problems such as fights, low grades, and high dropout rates.[394] Transgender youth may be barred from applying to school or higher education because of a lack of identification or because their I.D. does not match their name and gender.[395] Poverty is another major barrier LGBTQ youth face. LGBTQ youth often struggle with low income or no income.[396] Twenty percent of LGBTQ individuals living alone receive annual income of less than $12,000 compared to 17% of non-LGBTQ people living alone.[397] Transgender individuals are even more economically vulnerable—they are almost four times more likely than the general population to have annual incomes of less than $10,000.[398]

Lastly, anti-LGBTQ laws create barriers to housing and employment that also cause LGBTQ individuals to be unhoused disproportionately. These legal failures cause many LGBTQ individuals to be trapped in a devastating cycle of poverty. LGBTQ individuals lack legal protection from discrimination, meaning that they "can be fired, denied housing and credit, and refused medically necessary healthcare simply because they are LGBT[Q]," without

---

392. Woods, 2417.

393. Here, poverty challenges refer to not only challenges in sustaining a stable, living wage, but may also manifest in health issues (such as hunger and malnutrition), lack of access to education and other basic services, and social discrimination and exclusion. "Poverty Eradication," United Nations Department of Economic and Social Affairs, United Nations. https://www.un.org/development/desa/socialperspectiveondevelopment/issues/poverty-eradication.html.

394. Michelle Page, "Forgotten Youth: Homeless LGBT Youth of Color and the Runaway and Homeless Youth Act," *Nw. J. of L. & Soc. Policy* 12 (2017): 33.

395. Lurie, Schuster, and Rankin, 21.

396. Ibid.

397. Ibid.

398. Ibid.

any legal remedy.[399] As a result, federally funded programs may discriminate against LGBTQ individuals and deny access to housing. In states lacking protections for LGBTQ people, these individuals can be evicted without cause or warning.[400] LGBTQ individuals often face open hostility from landlords, real estate agents, and lenders during their housing search.[401] LGBTQ individuals, especially LGBTQ youth who may be too young to find traditional or stable employment, also face employment discrimination, leading them to turn to survival crimes, such as sex work, which funnel these individuals into the juvenile and criminal system.[402] With a prior criminal history, these individuals face further difficulties in obtaining stable employment and income and are further trapped in a cycle of poverty and homelessness.

2. Experience of Violence

Unhoused LGBTQ youth experience persistent and ongoing violence. Approximately 54% of unhoused LGBTQ youth have experienced sexual, physical, or emotional abuse by family members.[403] Once rejected from their families and on the streets, LGBTQ youth are much more likely than their non-LGBTQ peers to be survivors of abuse and violence on the streets. 30% of unhoused LGBTQ youth compared to 20% of their non-LGBTQ counterparts are robbed.[404] 28% of unhoused LGBTQ youth have endured physical assaults, in comparison to 18% of non-LGBTQ individuals.[405] LGBTQ unhoused youth experience sexual assault or rape at four times the rate of non-LGBTQ unhoused youth.[406] Compared to 35% of non-LGBTQ youth, nearly half of all unhoused LGBTQ youth are harassed by the police.[407]

Indeed, LGBTQ youth are also overrepresented in juvenile and criminal systems. Escaping from these unsafe environments leads to homelessness, and LGBTQ youth often commit survival crimes (such as sex work or theft), which

---

399. Ibid.

400. Ibid

401. Ibid.

402. Deborah Lolai, "'You're Going to Be Straight or You're Not Going to Live Here': Child Support for LGBT Homeless Youth," *Tulane J.L. & Sexuality* 24 (2015): 56.

403. Lurie, Schuster, and Rankin, 21.

404. Lolai, 52.

405. Ibid.

406. Ibid., 52–53.

407. Ibid. 53.

funnels these youth into the criminal system.[408] Aside from survival crimes, transgender youth may be criminalized based on "false personation" statutes. A transgender individual may tell a cop their preferred name rather than legal name out of fear of outing themselves to an openly hostile police system, which could be construed as "knowingly misrepresenting his or her actual name, date of birth, address to a police officer with intent to prevent such person from ascertaining such information."[409]

Within these systems, LGBTQ individuals disproportionately suffer from sexual assault and rape, to the extent that may even surpass the levels of violence these individuals would experience on the streets.[410] In many instances, prison officials and staff ignore reports of sexual assault and rape of LGBTQ inmates or fail to protect LGBTQ inmates from unwanted sexual advances.[411] Considering the abuse and trauma LGBTQ youth face within these systems, LGBTQ youth have difficulties upon release from juvenile or criminal detention and are usually at risk of becoming unhoused, upon which time they may be cycled back into the juvenile or criminal system.[412]

If unhoused LGBTQ individuals choose to seek support from shelters, they are still at risk of abuse. Unhoused LGBTQ individuals often still face violence from shelter staff or other shelter residents. Shelter residents are often segregated by the gender residents were assigned at birth.[413] Shelter staff often either openly discriminate and abuse LGBTQ individuals or ignore violence against LGBTQ shelter residents.[414] Shelters, much like other social support systems, are often run by religious organizations that may be openly hostile to LGTBQ youth and may refuse services to LGBTQ individuals or force LGBTQ individuals to denounce their orientation or sexuality to receive support.[415] Shelters may decline to provide accommodations to transgender residents because a small percentage of the general shelter population is transgender, but studies have shown that transgender people are overrepresented in unhoused populations in shelters.[416] As a result, unhoused LGBTQ individuals are often faced

---

408. Woods, 2387.
409. Lolai, 57.
410. Woods, 2408.
411. Lolai, 57.
412. Woods, 2408.
413. Lolai, 53.
414. Ibid.
415. Woods, 2344–45.
416. Lolai, 53.

with the choice between experiencing violence on the streets or within the shelter system.

3. Health Issues

Unsurprisingly, because of the violence and trauma that impact many unhoused LGBTQ people, this community also faces several health challenges. Homelessness often negatively shapes the subjectivities of LGBTQ youth, as studies show that unhoused LGBTQ youth internalize the idea that they are to blame for their living situation, which further worsens their self-esteem and sense of self-worth.[417] The impact of violence experienced within these various systems and on the streets also negatively impacts developmental processes, especially considering that these LGBTQ youth are often in the process of coming out or grappling with their identity.

Without other reliable options for support, many unhoused LGBTQ youth turn to substance abuse as a coping strategy, more so than their non-LGBTQ counterparts. Unhoused LGBTQ youth (from 13 to 21 years) are more likely than non-LGBTQ youth to use cocaine, crack, or methamphetamines.[418] In a study collating data across eight cities, 42% of unhoused LGBTQ youth binge drink, compared to 27% of non-LGBTQ youth.[419] Unhoused LGBTQ youth have higher rates of HIV infection but are more likely to report lack of access to testing and treatment for sexually transmitted infections.[420] LGBTQ individuals also suffer from a higher rate of mental health problems such as PTSD and depression in comparison to non-LGBTQ youth because of high rates of abuse.[421]

Despite these higher rates of abuse and violence against LGBTQ youth, they are less likely to receive care and treatment. Though only 9% of all unhoused youth have access to any mental health services, even less is available to LGBTQ individuals.[422] As a result, unhoused LGBTQ youth struggle with higher rates of suicide. For instance, 51% of transgender youths who have

---

417. Woods, 2408.

418. Michelle Page, "Forgotten Youth: Homeless LGBT Youth of Color and the Runaway and Homeless Youth Act," *Nw. J.L. & Soc. Policy* 12 (2017): 33.

419. Lolai, 58.

420. Ibid.

421. Ibid.

422. Ibid.

experienced family rejection have attempted suicide.[423] It is important to note that the mental health issues that LGBTQ individuals face are not a result of the inherent constitution of LGBTQ people, but because of a society that discriminates, stigmatizes, and enables abuse against the LGBTQ community.

As mentioned in the section on women and homelessness, LGBTQ individuals also face challenges in accessing safe and sanitary bathrooms. Generally, unhoused LGBTQ people face health concerns due to the frequency of maintenance of public bathrooms and their accessibility by the unhoused population.[424] Those with compromised immune systems are particularly vulnerable.[425] In addition, LGBTQ people face risks of harassment and assault in accessing bathrooms.[426] Without access to gender neutral bathrooms, transgender individuals are often penalized for using bathrooms.[427] LGBTQ individuals may also face the same issues of menstrual justice as women, as lack of access to bathrooms and hygiene products increase health problems related to menstruation, such as toxic shock syndrome, infections, and cervical cancer.[428]

IV. Older Adults

A. Introduction and Statistics

The indicators of people who become unhoused later in life differ from those who experience being unhoused younger than fifty years of age. And the group who are becoming unhoused as older adults (those 50 years and over) is growing. One in three sheltered (but otherwise unhoused) single adult males was 46–54 in 2010, a sharp increase in the proportion of this older population from 2000 (1 in 5) and 1990 (1 in 8).[429]

---

423. Ibid.

424. Margaret E. Johnson, "Menstrual Justice," *U.C. Davis L. Rev.* 53 (2019): 70.

425. Ron S. Hochbaum, "Bathrooms as a Homeless Rights Issue," *N.C. L. Rev.* 98 (2020): 243.

426. Johnson, 70.

427. Hochbaum, 243.

428. Johnson, 70.

429. Culhane, Dennis, Dan Treglia, Thomas Byrne, Kelly Doran, Eileen Johns, Mary-anne Schretzman, Stephen Metraux, and Randall Kuhn. 2019, *The Emerging Crisis of Aged Homelessness: Could Housing Solutions Be Funded by Avoidance of Excess Shelter, Hospital, and Nursing Home Costs?* p.1 https://www.aisp.upenn.edu/wp-content/uploads/2019/01/Emerging-Crisis-of-Aged-Homelessness-1.pdf.

A 55-year-old in 2010 was born in 1955. This post-WWII generation experienced multiple recessions during their adulthood, from the 1980s onward. Along with these broad societal financial setbacks came an increasing decline in the availability of affordable housing. Pairing these two stark realities reveals that one half of renters ages 50 and older in the United States pay more than 30 percent of their household income on rent. Paying this much for housing means cutting back on other expenses, including healthcare, transportation, and healthful food.[430] Low-income people who spend more than 30 percent of their income on rent are unable to save money, leaving them vulnerable to losing their housing when they face setbacks, such as a job loss, sickness, or death of a spouse or partner.[431]

There are varied reasons for older adults becoming unhoused. The "Health Outcomes for People Experiencing Homelessness in Older Middle Age" (HOPE HOME) study found that almost one-half of unhoused older adults had never experienced homelessness prior to the age of 50. The study found that participants with a first episode of homelessness after age 50 differed from those who were unhoused earlier in life and remained so in older middle age.[432] Those with early onset homelessness reported extraordinarily challenging childhoods, replete with significant adverse experiences that led to their developing mental health and substance use disorders early in life; many had limited formal education and had spent significant time incarcerated.

However, individuals with late onset homelessness had very different stories. "While almost all of these study participants had lived in poverty throughout their adult lives, they had long work histories, usually in low-paying, physically demanding work. These men and women reported that sometime, after age 50, they experienced a setback: the breakdown of a marriage, a job loss or illness (theirs, or their spouse or partner), or the death of their spouse, partner, or parent. With little savings, facing difficulty finding work as an older adult, and

430. *Housing America's Older Adults 2019*, prepared by the Joint Center for Housing Studies of Harvard University as a supplement to the state of the nation's housing report. https://www.jchs.harvard.edu/sites/default/files/reports/files/Harvard_JCHS_Housing _Americas_Older_Adults_2019.pdf.

431. Kushel, Margot, *Homelessness Among Older Adults: An Emerging Crisis, Generations J.*, Summer 2010. https://generations.asaging.org/homelessness-older-adults-poverty -health.

432. Brown, Rebecca T., Lori Thomas, Deborah F. Cutler, and Mark Hinderlie, "Meeting the Housing and Care Needs of Older Homeless Adults: A Permanent Supportive Housing Program Targeting Homeless Elders," *Seniors Hous. Care J.* 2013 January 1; 21(1): 126–135.

having little ability to compete in an unforgiving housing market, they faced homelessness for the first time."[433]

Within the population of older unhoused adults, there are gaps in data that, if filled, could help make accurate predictions of the need for services, legal or otherwise. UCLA's Williams Institute on Sexual Orientation and the Law estimates that 4.1% of American adults identify themselves as lesbian, gay or bisexual (whether they are open or closeted in larger society). Using these figures, the Institute estimates that LGBT people aged 65 or older number 1.5 million today and will grow to nearly 3 million by 2030. But it is unclear how many of these adults are unhoused, as there is no government data on LGBTQ older adults. Lesbians will likely be over-represented in these numbers, reflecting both general population trends and the decimation wrought by HIV/AIDS, which disproportionately affected gay men.

B. Discussion

1. Complex Healthcare Needs: Chronic Conditions and Disabilities

Unhoused older adults have medical ages that far exceed their biological ages due to the stresses and traumas that are part and parcel of living unhoused. Research shows that this group "experience[s] geriatric medical conditions such as cognitive decline and decreased mobility at rates that are on par with those among their housed counterparts who are 20 years older." The out of step bodily aging of unhoused adults "aged 50 and older have rates of chronic conditions similar to or higher than community-dwelling adults 15–20 years older including... geriatric conditions include[ing] memory loss, falls, difficulty performing activities of daily living, and urinary incontinence."[434]

Not only are these older adults impacted physically by their unhoused state, but their circumstances also make it less manageable to deal with their conditions and get adequate care. "Falls, loss of strength and mobility, and other common conditions of aging that impact mobility are more difficult to

---

433. Kushel, Margot. "Homelessness Among Older Adults: An Emerging Crisis," *Generations J.*, Summer 2010.

434. Brown, Rebecca T., Lori Thomas, Deborah F. Cutler, and Mark Hinderlie, "Meeting the Housing and Care Needs of Older Homeless Adults: A Permanent Supportive Housing Program Targeting Homeless Elders," *Seniors Hous. Care J.* 2013 January 1; 21(1): 126–135.

manage on the street and in homeless shelters. Homeless people are unable to modify their physical environment to match their physical limitations."[435] In addition to challenges arising out of not controlling their physical environments, unhoused people also often are required to travel significant distances to avail themselves of services such as food, housing, or social services, all made more difficult if they have physical disabilities or chronic conditions.

While disabilities come in many forms, those impacting mobility are more common in older adults. That, juxtaposed with the fact that "Less than one-half of 1 percent of existing housing is currently accessible to someone who uses a wheelchair,"[436] makes access to both services and appropriate shelter problematic. People with disabilities affecting mobility who do not require wheelchair use are affected as well: "In 2017, unassisted adults age 65 and over earning less than $15,000 per year were more likely than their higher-income peers to report difficulties with walking (42 percent vs. 33 percent) and with self-care (16 percent vs. 11 percent)."[437]

2. Dying Earlier

The average life span for an unhoused person is estimated to be 64 years, which is close to 15 years shorter than the average American.[438] This statistic reflects a harsh health reality for all ages of unhoused people, because both younger and older unhoused adults "experience premature mortality, but older adults are more likely to die from chronic conditions including cardiovascular disease and cancer...."[439] This suggests that preventive health care could be helpful in improving health outcomes for (all but particularly older) unhoused people.

---

435. Goldberg, Jennifer, Kate Lange, and Vanessa Barrington, *How to Prevent and End Homelessness Among Older Adults*, special report by Justice in Aging. p. 4–5. 2016. https://justiceinaging.org/wp-content/uploads/2016/04/Homelessness-Older-Adults.pdf.

436. Ibid. at 9.

437. *Housing America's Older Adults 2019*, prepared by the Joint Center for Housing Studies of Harvard University as a supplement to the state of the nation's housing report. p.10. https://www.jchs.harvard.edu/sites/default/files/reports/files/Harvard_JCHS_Housing_Americas_Older_Adults_2019.pdf.

438. Jeff Yungman, "The Graying of Homelessness," 39 No. 5 *Bifocal* 74 (2018).

439. Brown, Rebecca T., Lori Thomas, Deborah F. Cutler, and Mark Hinderlie, "Meeting the Housing and Care Needs of Older Homeless Adults: A Permanent Supportive Housing Program Targeting Homeless Elders," *Seniors Hous. Care J.* 2013 January 1; 21(1): 126–135.

Health care costs are high and "account for a higher percentage of older adults' expenses than for the general population, leaving them with less income to afford housing."[440] Medicaid may be available for those who are already unhoused, but when looking to help those who are at risk of becoming unhoused either for the first time or again, it is critical to examine the connection between housing and medical costs for older adults. Medicare is only available to people starting at age 65, a year older than the average life span of an unhoused person. Additionally, neither Medicare nor Medicaid provides much coverage for dental, hearing, or vision care.[441]

3. Discrimination in Other Categories (Race, Sexual Orientation and Gender Identity)

People face discrimination based on identities that affect their ability to secure housing of all kinds. This is true historically in the United States and continues to impact certain groups disproportionately, particularly older adults who have other intersecting identities. Various discriminatory practices in housing markets, "such as residential covenants and redlining (which restricted Black households from obtaining mortgages and enforced residential segregation), contributed to the enormous racial wealth gap between Black and white households."[442] This created a long enduring gulf between what housing options Black and white households can access in both the purchase and rental markets impacting generations of people and acutely affecting older adults.

To this day, older LGBT adults "may be denied housing, including residency in mainstream retirement communities, based on their sexual orientation and gender identity and expression."[443] Without these housing options, older LGBT adults can be pushed into homelessness and separated from loved ones or partners; they may feel pressure to re-enter or stay in the closet to obtain or maintain housing.[444]

---

440. Goldberg, Jennifer, Kate Lange, and Vanessa Barrington. 2016. *How to Prevent and End Homelessness Among Older Adults*, special report by Justice in Aging. p.2.

441. Ibid.

442. Kushel, Margot. "Homelessness Among Older Adults: An Emerging Crisis." *Generations J.*, Summer 2010.

443. *Improving the Lives of LGBT Older Adults*, special report by LGBT Movement Advancement Project (MAP). 2010. https://www.lgbtmap.org/file/improving-the-lives-of-lgbt-older-adults.pdf.

444. Ibid.

C. Avenues for Advocacy

There are numerous policy changes and areas in which to expand services that could positively impact older adults who are or who have been unhoused.

- Broadly expand housing interventions and funding. Look to this to decrease medical costs, improve quality of life for those at risk of becoming or remaining unhoused, and extending the life expectancy of people who are or have been unhoused for portions of their life. Without changes in housing for older adults, public resources will be spent on health and long-term care.

- Expand access to Housing Choice vouchers.[445]

- Expand safety net programs like Social Security and Supplemental Security Income (SSI). Specifically, SSI's benefit amount should be increased to reflect inflation since 1972, and Social Security's special minimum benefit should increase to improve income security of those with low lifetime earnings.[446]

- Expand Medicaid eligibility for older adults and fill coverage gaps like dental and vision care.[447]

- Link permanent supportive housing facilities to providers trained in geriatric health.[448] In addition to being the ethical outcome, "permanent supportive housing programs have demonstrated improved health outcomes and decreased health care costs among chronically homeless persons with a range of disabilities."[449]

- Increase eviction prevention.[450]

---

445. Kushel.

446. Goldberg, Jennifer, Kate Lange, and Vanessa Barrington, 2016. *How to Prevent and End Homelessness Among Older Adults*, special report by Justice in Aging. p.6.

447. Ibid., 7.

448. *Housing America's Older Adults 2019*, prepared by the Joint Center for Housing Studies of Harvard University as a supplement to the state of the nation's housing report. p.10.

449. Brown, Rebecca T., Lori Thomas, Deborah F. Cutler, and Mark Hinderlie, "Meeting the Housing and Care Needs of Older Homeless Adults: A Permanent Supportive Housing Program Targeting Homeless Elders," *Seniors Hous. Care J.* 2013 January 1; 21(1): 126–135.

450. Jeff Yungman, The Graying of Homelessness, 39 No. 5 Bifocal 74 (2018). See Chapter 5 for an in-depth discussion of homeless prevention programs.

- "Pass non-discrimination acts (NDAs) or ordinances at the state or local level. NDAs can provide legal recourse for LGBT elders who experience discrimination in a variety of settings, including senior citizen centers, low-income housing, hospitals, nursing homes, assisted living facilities, senior centers, etc."[451]

V. Veterans

A. Introduction and Statistics

Veterans comprise approximately 15% of the unhoused adult population living in shelters, whereas only about 10% of the adult population has served in the armed forces.[452] Berenson succinctly explains the myriad of factors that contribute to the prevalence of veterans among the unhoused population:

Many veterans find the transition from the structure and fast pace of military life back to the relatively unstructured and slower pace of civilian life to be difficult. Large numbers of veterans also suffer from mental health issues, including Post Traumatic Stress Disorder (PTSD), Traumatic Brain Injuries (TBI), and Major Depression.... Even under the best of circumstances, these illnesses can be difficult to diagnose. Combining that fact with a military culture that frowns on admitting weakness and seeking out help means that many veterans suffering from these illnesses will not receive a proper diagnosis. And even for those veterans with proper diagnoses, accessing available resources to deal with these issues can be difficult. Veterans suffering from undiagnosed and/or untreated mental health issues are likely to "self-medicate" through the use of alcohol and/or illegal drugs, thus often adding substance abuse to their list of problems. Of course, veterans suffering from these issues also find themselves having difficulty in maintaining employment and family relationships, and frequently encountering the criminal justice system. All of these factors may contribute to veterans' descent into homelessness.[453]

---

451. *Improving the Lives of LGBT Older Adults*, special report by LGBT Movement Advancement Project (MAP). 2010.

452. Steven Berenson, "Homeless Veterans and Child Support," 45 *Fam. L.Q.* 173, 174 (2011).

453. Ibid.

Between 2011 and 2021, there was overall national progress for unhoused veterans: "Since 2011, the number of veterans experiencing homelessness has dropped by 43.3 percent. But since 2019, the number has increased 0.5%."[454] But progress stalled in 2019 and, even prior to 2019 was uneven across gender and racial lines, and even by age. Approximately 9 out of 10 veterans experiencing homelessness are men. Over the course of the past decade, the total number of unhoused male veterans declined by 3%. In contrast, the number of unhoused female veterans rose 3%.[455] And despite a decline in the overall number of veterans experiencing homelessness, the total number of unhoused African American veterans remained the same, at least between 2018 and 2019.[456] Across all genders and races within the veteran community, 19.2 percent of veterans experiencing homelessness were 62 or older in 2017, up from 8.8% in 2009.[457]

In 2020, seven states had over 1,000 unhoused veterans: 11,401 in California, 2,436 in Florida, 1,948 in Texas, 1,607 in Washington, 1,329 in Oregon, 1,251 in New York, and 1,044 in Colorado.[458]

B. Discussion

1. Re-Entry into Civilian Life: Job Training

When a veteran transitions out of the military, preparing to enter the civilian job market is a primary pain point. To address this, a federal statute mandates creating programs to provide job training, counseling, and place-

---

454. *Veterans*, updated April 2021. National Alliance to End Homelessness. https://endhomelessness.org/homelessness-in-america/who-experiences-homelessness/veterans/.

455. Ibid.

456. *Veteran Homelessness: Overview of State and Federal Resources*, prepared by the National Conference of State Legislatures, 2021. https://www.ncsl.org/research/military-and-veterans-affairs/veteran-homelessness-an-overview-of-state-and-federal-resources.aspx.

457. *Housing America's Older Adults 2019*, prepared by the Joint Center for Housing Studies of Harvard University as a supplement to the state of the nation's housing report. p.10. https://www.jchs.harvard.edu/sites/default/files/reports/files/Harvard_JCHS_Housing_Americas_Older_Adults_2019.pdf.

458. Total Veterans Experiencing Homelessness Point-in-Time Count data tool https://www.usich.gov/tools-for-action/map/#fn[]=100&fn[]=200&fn[]=400&fn[]=600&fn[]=800&all_types=true&year=2020. For a more detailed breakdown of communities with unhoused veterans, see https://endhomelessness.org/homelessness-in-america/who-experiences-homelessness/veterans/.

ment services to expedite the reintegration of unhoused veterans into the labor force.[459] There is a need for certain of these programs to be tailored to women and other unhoused veterans with children, including ones that include job training, counseling, and placement services and also child care services.[460] And some are, but the level of financial allocation towards these programs, the accountability of grantees providing the services, and the outreach within the unhoused veteran population prove to be ongoing challenges.

2. Re-Entry into Civilian Life: Mental Health and Other Disability Support

There are multiple programs available to the unhoused veteran community that aim to support those who require mental health or other disability support alongside their housing needs. For temporary support, there is care from domiciliaries across the country.[461]

For longer term solutions, there are HUD-VASH vouchers. The program is a collaboration between HUD and Veterans Affairs Supportive Housing wherein veterans are given a housing choice voucher which is then paired with the V.A. case management and supportive service to help the veteran sustain the house and support recovery from physical or mental health problems.[462] There are also regular statutory mandates to supplement these broader programs for more particularized populations, including those who were involved in the criminal justice system after their time in service. For example, 38 U.S.C. § 2022 requires the Mental Health Service and the Readjustment Counseling Service of the Veterans Health Administration to develop a coordinated plan for joint outreach by the two Services to veterans at risk of homelessness, including particularly veterans who are being discharged or released from institutions after inpatient psychiatric care, substance abuse treatment, or imprisonment.

---

459. 38 U.S.C. § 2021.

460. Ibid.

461. U.S. Department of Veterans Affairs, VA Homeless Programs: Domiciliary Care for Homeless Veterans Program. https://www.va.gov/homeless/dchv.asp.

462. *Veteran Homelessness: Overview of State and Federal Resources*, prepared by the National Conference of State Legislatures. 2021.

3. Unmet Needs: Legal Needs Generally

In data collected from thousands of active-duty service members, national guardsmen and veterans in March 2020, 35% of veterans stated that they would like legal services, as did 32% of active-duty service members.[463] There was a relatively lower self-reported need for housing and shelter resources (18% for veterans and 26% of active-duty service members, respectively).[464] As of January 4, 2021, the federal government is allowing for legal services for unhoused veterans and veterans at risk of homelessness.[465] The extent to which this mandate, and paired funding, will meet the unmet legal needs of veterans nationally is unknown. It will require, at minimum, building a larger pipeline of advocates versed in how legal issues uniquely affect veterans.

4. Unmet Needs: Child Support

Many veterans need particularized legal assistance for child support. This matter received the second highest score for unmet needs for unhoused veterans.[466] Accrued child support arrears can negatively impact a veteran's ability to obtain or afford permanent housing.

5. Unmet Needs: Housing Support

In addition to HUD-VASH, the Supportive Services for Veteran Families (SSVF) program provides case management and supportive services to very low-income veterans to prevent the imminent loss of a Veteran's home or identify a new, more suitable housing situation for the individual and his or her family. SSVF also works with unhoused veterans and their families with the goal of rapidly re-housing them.[467]

---

463. Euto, L., R. Maury, N. Armstrong, B. Stone, & R. Linsner, May 2020, p.5. *Coronavirus (COVID-19) Climate Snapshot Poll: Top Resource Needs of Veterans and Active Duty Service Members*, special report by Institute for Veterans and Military Families.

464. Ibid.

465. 38 U.S.C. § 2022A.

466. Steven Berenson, "Homeless Veterans and Child Support," 45 *Fam. L.Q.* 173, 176 (2011).

467. *VA Programs for Homeless Veterans*, U.S. Department of Veterans Affairs, February 18, 2021. https://www.va.gov/homeless/for_homeless_veterans.asp.

C. Avenues for Advocacy

- Provide adequate funding for programs allowed for or mandated by statute that meets the need for the number of unhoused veterans. Account for additional funding to create tailored programs or fund subgrantees working with historically marginalized communities and women veterans. Examples of programs provided for by statute that should be fully funded include:

  - Case management services to improve the retention of housing by veterans who were previously homeless.[468]

  - Programs to provide job training, counseling, and placement services to expedite the reintegration into the labor force of unhoused veterans.[469]

  - Increase awareness of legal services and increase funding for them. An example of a helpful resource on how to find veteran-specific legal assistance is: https://www.statesidelegal.org/finding-legal-help.

- Learn and create best practices from state and county initiatives that have either vastly reduced or eliminated homelessness for veterans.[470] Two state level examples of state legislation to be emulated include:

  - The Maryland General Assembly passed HB 12, which expands the eligibility for veterans to reside at veterans' homes supervised by the V.A. Eligibility was expanded to include veterans who received an honorable discharge from active service with a uniformed service.[471]

  - In Washington state, HB 1754 allows religious organizations to host unhoused people on outdoor encampments. The bill decrees and prohibits counties from specifically limiting a re-

---

468. 38 U.S.C. § 2013.

469. 38 U.S.C. § 2021.

470. U.S. Department of Veterans Affairs, VA Homeless Programs: Ending Veteran Homelessness. https://www.va.gov/homeless/endingvetshomelessness.asp.

471. *Veteran Homelessness: Overview of State and Federal Resources*, prepared by the National Conference of State Legislatures. 2021.

ligious organization's availability to host on its property while reducing or waiving permitting fees.[472]

- Continue funding HUD-VASH and its wraparound services. Allow all "homeless or chronically homeless" veterans to be eligible—not just those who are VA health care eligible. Limiting voucher eligibility to those veterans who are VA health care eligible excludes a group of veterans with discharge statuses that they received unjustly, often due to a lack of recognition of their PTSD, by mislabeling them as having a personality disorder, or because they were discharged due to their sexual orientation through the discriminatory and now defunct policy of "Don't Ask, Don't Tell."

- Peer support plays a prominent role in many successful veteran re-entry interventions and programs. Build in funding for staff that can provide veteran-to-veteran mentorship and guidance to federal and state grants.

- Continue to host stand downs at local levels, collaborative events often organized by local Veterans Affairs Medical Centers with support from community agencies, other government agencies, and community groups that serve unhoused people.

---

472. Ibid.

FOUR

The Criminalization of Homelessness

I n 2010, Steve Jacobs-Elstein was arrested as he exited his parked car, which was among the few possessions he owned before he became unhoused. The law Steve was arrested under was Los Angeles Municipal Code (LAMC) section 85.02, which prohibited the use of a vehicle as living quarters. Although Steve assured the officers that he slept in a nearby shelter and not in his car, he was still arrested. Just three years before, Steve owned a home and a legal temp company that he ran for almost ten years. Then, in the 2007 economic crash, Steve lost everything. He began to suffer from severe anxiety and depression, and three years later, his sole possessions consisted of a small SUV, two computers, and some clothes. Because he could not afford storage, he kept everything he owned in his car. Before his arrest under LAMC section 85.02, Steve had no criminal record.[473]

Steve challenged the constitutionality of LAMC section 85.02 in the Ninth Circuit case *Desertrain v. City of L.A.*,[474] and the court ruled that the law was unconstitutional. But Steve's story is not unique, and neither is the type of law under which he was arrested. Laws criminalizing unhoused people or homelessness refer to those "that prohibit or severely restrict one's ability to engage in necessary life-sustaining activities in public, even when that person has no

---

473. *Desertrain v. City of L.A.*, 754 F.3d 1147, 1150–1152 (9th Cir. 2014).
474. *Desertrain*, 754 F.3d at 1150–1152.

reasonable alternative."[475] Upwards of 187 cities across the United States have laws that criminalize various aspects of homelessness.[476] The most prevalent of these laws include prohibitions on the following activities: camping and sleeping in public; sitting and lying down in public; sleeping in vehicles; loitering and vagrancy; begging and panhandling in public; and even food sharing by organizations that want to distribute food to unhoused people.[477]

Laws criminalizing homelessness are on the rise. The National Law Center on Homelessness and Poverty (NLCHP) tracked the same 187 cities between 2006 and 2019 to observe the relative increase or decrease in laws criminalizing homelessness, and the research "reveals that laws punishing the life-sustaining conduct of homeless people have increased in every measured category since that time, and in some cases dramatically so."[478] Despite some legal victories since 2015, criminalization policies have continued to rise at a rate of growth correlated with the rise in homelessness nationwide.[479]

Based on its study of 187 cities, NLCHP found the following increases in criminalization laws between 2006 and 2019: a 92% increase in city-wide camping bans; a 70% increase in area-specific camping bans;[480] a 50% increase in city-wide sleeping bans; a 29% increase in area-specific sleeping bans; a 78% increase in laws prohibiting some form of sitting or lying down in public; a 213% increase in laws restricting living in vehicles; a 137% increase in city-wide laws prohibiting begging or panhandling; a 13% increase in area-specific laws prohibiting begging or panhandling; a 103% increase in laws prohibiting loitering, loafing, or vagrancy; and a 28% increase in laws prohibiting area-specific loitering, loafing, or vagrancy. Additionally, between 2016 and 2019, there was a 42% increase in laws prohibiting or restricting food sharing.[481]

---

475. Sara K. Rankin, "Punishing Homelessness," 22 *New Crim. L. Rev.* (2019): 106–07.

476. National Law Center on Homelessness & Poverty, *No Safe Place: The Criminalization of Homelessness in U.S. Cities.* (July 2014): 7. http://www.nlchp.org/documents /No_Safe_Place. [Hereinafter "*No Safe Place*"].

477. *No Safe Place*, 7–8.

478. National Law Center on Homelessness & Poverty, *Housing Not Handcuffs: Ending the Criminalization of Homelessness in US Cities* (December 2019), 37–38. [Hereinafter "*Ending the Criminalization of Homelessness*"].

479. *Ending the Criminalization of Homelessness*, 37–38.

480. "Area-specific" or "place-specific" bans refer to bans on certain activities within a specified area of a city, for example, a downtown commercial center or a certain park.

481. *Ending the Criminalization of Homelessness*, 38–46.

Because these laws tend to prohibit activities that are essential to human survival, such as eating and sleeping, and because unhoused people have nowhere else to fulfill these necessary activities, even the existence of unhoused people becomes criminalized. While the animus behind these laws is not always explicit, they are enacted to deter unhoused people from settling in cities, despite the fact that such laws are more expensive and less effective than other solutions.[482] Many cities prefer enacting laws that criminalize unhoused people to providing social services and long-term solutions, because they fear that by implementing social programs, they will attract unhoused people to their cities.[483] Cities that use criminalization as a solution to homelessness often forgo offering long-term assistance to unhoused people, choosing instead to banish them in the hopes that they will move on to other areas. As a result of this lack of services, many municipalities see a rise in tent cities and homeless encampments, demonstrating the ineffectiveness of criminalization solutions.[484]

The obvious solution to homelessness is housing, but it can take years for communities to build enough permanent supportive housing units to house everyone who needs it. Until cities and communities establish robust systems to support the unhoused and place them into permanent housing, criminalizing people who are unhoused will only make the problem worse. Making people constantly pick up all their belongings and move makes it more difficult for unhoused people to connect to case managers, more difficult to hold down a job, and more difficult to keep track of important documents.

Current conditions make encampments inevitable. Within the reality of lack of housing, rather than criminalizing people who reside there, cities should offer services such as bathrooms, hand-washing stations, and trash pickup to make encampments more livable for the unhoused residents and their housed neighbors. Cities should also offer more safe camping and safe parking sites for unhoused people to set up their tents, RVs, or vehicles in which to sleep without fear of breaking the law or harassment by law enforcement.

---

482. Rankin, "Punishing Homelessness," 104.

483. Ibid., 124–125.

484. Ali, Farida, "Limiting the Poor's Right to Public Space: Criminalizing Homelessness in California," 21 *Geo. J. on Poverty L. & Pol'y* (2014): 197.

I. Impact of Criminalizing Unhoused People

Not only are laws that criminalize behaviors that unhoused people inevitably engage in ineffective at combating homelessness and its causes, but they can also actually make the problem of homelessness worse for individuals already struggling to survive. An arrest or citation for violating one of these ordinances can lead to bars on housing (including shelters), employment, and certain social benefits and programs.[485] Citations issued for crimes such as jaywalking, sitting or sleeping in public, loitering, and littering (to name only a few) come with fines attached that often go unpaid due to the reality that many unhoused people have no steady source of income.[486] Unpaid citations can result in warrants for arrest, and ultimately, jail.[487] Many unhoused people who never previously had a criminal record are subjected to arrests and charges for failure to pay citation fines.[488]

The cycle proceeds as follows: First, the citation will likely require a court appearance and usually also includes a cost-prohibitive fine. Then, if the unhoused person misses the hearing or is unable to pay the fine, they risk being arrested. Once arrested, most unhoused people will lack the financial resources and support network to post bail or to be released on their own recognizance, leading to lengthy pre-trial detention periods. Rather than sit in jail awaiting trial, many unhoused people will accept a plea, which results in a criminal record.

Moreover, once an unhoused person is convicted, they are less likely to receive probation because they lack an address; they also lack the financial resources to pay the fees that are associated with being placed on probation. Hence, an unhoused person who gets convicted of violating these types of ordinances faces even more penalties, including additional time in jail, potentially losing their job or opportunity to vote, and losing access to their public benefits.

---

485. Rankin, "Punishing Homelessness," 107–109.

486. *See generally* Stuart, Forrest. *Down, Out, and Under Arrest: Policing and Everyday Life in Skid Row* (Chicago: University of Chicago Press, 2016).

487. Stuart; Coalition on Homelessness, *Punishing the Poorest: How the Criminalization of Homelessness Perpetuates Poverty in San Francisco,* (2015): 33–34. [Hereinafter "*Punishing the Poorest*."].

488. Vitale, Alex S., "The Safer Cities Initiative and the Removal of the Homeless: Reducing Crime or Promoting Gentrification on Los Angeles' Skid Row," *Criminology and Public Policy* 9, no. 4 (November 2010): 867–874.

The ongoing impact of holding a criminal record creates additional barriers to housing and employment, thus both directly and indirectly putting people with criminal records at even greater risk of becoming unhoused and making it more difficult for unhoused people to break the cycle of homelessness and obtain housing.

Police also systematically harass unhoused people in some areas, such as Los Angeles County's Skid Row district, which is (as of 2020) home to approximately 4,662[489] unhoused individuals.[490] Police in these areas are known to use pressure tactics, such as threats of fines and arrests, to push individuals into residential rehabilitation programs against their will.[491] These rehabilitation programs, many of which religious organizations operate, mandate random drug testing, curfews, and require participants to attend bible studies and employment training classes.[492] This type of paternalistic policing is often the product of government crime intervention programs, such as Los Angeles County Police Department's now obsolete *Safer Cities Initiative* (SCI), which intensified policing in areas with large unhoused populations.[493]

SCI, which ran from 2006 to 2015, put eighty additional officers on the .85 square mile of Skid Row, and resulted in nine thousand arrests and twelve hundred citations in its first year alone.[494] In one fourteen-month period recorded during that time, there were 1,200 arrests for unpaid citations alone, meaning that individuals were criminalized for failing to pay fines for civil infractions.[495] The program, considered a "broken windows"[496] approach to crime prevention, is heavily criticized as failing to reduce crime in the area, while making it even more difficult for individuals to escape being unhoused, due to the long-term

---

489. Los Angeles Homeless Services Authority (LAHSA), *2020 Greater Los Angeles Homeless Count—Skid Row*, (July 2020): https://www.lahsa.org/documents?id=4700-2020 -greater-los-angeles-homeless-count-skid-row.pdf.

490. Rankin, "Punishing Homelessness," 104.

491. Ibid.

492. Ibid.

493. Ibid.

494. Ibid.

495. Ibid.

496. Broken windows policing refers to the practice of policing economically depressed areas more heavily on the presumption that the "mere presence of street homeless in the public sphere has the effect of unraveling the social order, leading to an increase in crime and thereby driving middle- and upper-class consumers out of downtown areas and into the suburbs." Donald Saelinger, "Nowhere to Go: The Impacts of City Ordinances Criminalizing Homelessness," *Geo. J. on Poverty L. & Pol'y* 13, Iss. 3 (2006): 553.

impact of having a criminal record and inability to pay fines.[497] SCI is now recognized as less of a crime prevention program and more of a tactic to remove unhoused people from public view and wipe the blight of encampments from the streets of L.A.[498] Similar tactics have been used to remove unhoused people from commercial areas in Denver, San Francisco, Seattle, and Baltimore.[499]

II. Employment

The criminalization of homelessness significantly impacts employment opportunities for the unhoused. Researchers estimate that the unemployment rates among unhoused people range from 57% to over 90%, compared to the 3.6% for the general United States population.[500] In some respects, this may not seem too surprising; after all, it makes sense that someone who lacks a stable income may have trouble maintaining housing. However, there is another perspective to this statistic that often goes undiscussed. Unemployment is usually seen as a major cause of homelessness, but the ideas of homelessness as a major cause of unemployment and the criminalization of homelessness as a barrier to (re-)employment need to be explored in greater depth. See Chapter 6 for further discussion of criminal records as employment barriers.

As the following materials illustrate, advocates have found great success bringing constitutional challenges to the types of ordinances that drive the cycle of homelessness. Indeed, the First, Fourth, Eighth, and Fourteenth Amendments have all proven effective in limiting the negative impacts these types of ordinances threaten to exact on unhoused residents.

---

497. Vitale, 867–874.

498. The Council of Economic Advisors, *The State of Homelessness in America* (September 2019): 19,

https://www.whitehouse.gov/wp-content/uploads/2019/09/The-State-of-Homelessness-in-America.pdf.

499. Vitale, 870, fn 17.

500. Gabriel, Ian, Elly Schoen, Victoria Ciudad-Real, and Allan Broslawsky. "Homelessness and Employment." Homelessness Policy Research Institute, August 24, 2020.

III. Anti-Homeless Ordinances & Constitutional Challenges

Laws that criminalize homelessness generally take the form of city and municipal ordinances. Legal practitioners and advocates refer to these laws as "anti-homeless" laws because they are crafted to target and deter unhoused people from settling or remaining in certain areas.[501] Officially termed "quality of life" laws,[502] anti-homeless laws prohibit activities like camping and sleeping in public, sitting and lying down in public, sleeping in vehicles, loitering and vagrancy,[503] begging and panhandling, and food sharing in certain public places.[504] Activities that are traditionally seen as public nuisances, such as drinking and smoking in public, walking a dog without a leash, littering, etc.,[505] also fall under the category of quality of life laws, and in some areas, laws that prohibit camping or loitering are passed as nuisance statutes.[506] Because anti-homeless laws generally prohibit doing activities in public that are legal to do in the privacy of one's home, they naturally have a disproportionate impact on unhoused people who are forced to do nearly every activity in public places.[507] Conflating life sustaining activities, such as sleeping and eating, with general nuisance issues, like littering, demonstrates a failure to recognize that being unhoused is not voluntary.

Some lawmakers consider these types of laws necessary to balance the rights of unhoused people against the quality and safety of the larger com-

---

501. *No Safe Place*, 24.

502. Berkeley Law Policy Advocacy Clinic, *California's New Vagrancy Laws: The Growing Enactment and Enforcement of Anti-Homeless Laws in the Golden State* (February 2015): 6.

503. It is important to note that the use of terms like vagrancy or loitering indicate criminality. These terms tend to have negative connotations and are associated with criminal behavior. Advocates must push back against these characterizations, but the language reflecting the ordinances is used here because the authors would like to have cohesion for the sake of clarity. The conduct that anti-homeless ordinances have described as loitering or vagrancy is in most cases not criminal; for example, in one anti-vagrancy statute, loitering is defined as remaining "in any one place with no apparent purpose." *City of Chicago v. Morales*, 527 U.S. 41 (1999).

504. *No Safe Place*, 16–26.

505. *Punishing the Poorest*, 6.

506. *No Safe Place*, "Prohibited Conduct Chart." Appendix.

507. *Punishing the Poorest*, 6–7.

munity.[508] Anti-homeless laws are commonly justified as falling within the public interest of maintaining the general welfare of the entire society.[509] For example, laws prohibiting sitting down or sleeping on public sidewalks are often explained as necessary to maintain the public interest in unobstructed walkways.[510]

While these laws may arguably benefit a part of society, they harmfully impact unhoused people by seeking to remove them from public view without providing viable alternatives.[511] In some cases, even the officials enforcing these laws have begun to publicly voice the inadequacy of criminalization as a solution to homelessness.[512] For example, one former head of the Los Angeles Police Department's (LAPD) homelessness effort said of the LAPD's approach, "What we're trying to do is our best to serve and solve a complex problem that is far beyond what we have been given the tools and mechanics to fix."[513]

Beyond being ineffective, the de facto criminalization of homelessness via laws that appear facially neutral—written in a non-discriminatory manner—but have a disproportionate impact on unhoused people,[514] raises serious constitutional concerns. The United States Constitution affords certain protections, enumerated in the Bill of Rights, and legal advocates have successfully challenged anti-homeless ordinances on numerous different constitutional grounds.

Legal advocates and organizations have mobilized the First, Fourth, Eighth and Fourteenth Amendments to challenge different classes of anti-homeless ordinances. For example, anti-panhandling ordinances have been challenged under the First Amendment as violating freedom of speech and freedom of expression.[515] Anti-loitering and anti-vagrancy[516] laws have also been chal-

---

508. Holland, Gale and Zhang, Christine. 2018. "Huge increase in arrests of homeless in L.A.—but mostly for minor offenses," *Los Angeles Times,* February 4, 2018.

509. *No Safe Place,* 16.

510. See e.g., Los Angeles Municipal Code (LAMC), Ch. IV, §41.18.

511. *Punishing the Poorest,* 6–9.

512. Holland & Zhang, *Los Angeles Times,* February 4, 2018.

513. Ibid., *quoting* Cmdr. Todd Chamberlain.

514. Rankin, "Punishing Homelessness," 103 ("By virtue of their sustained visibility in public space, chronically homeless people are the primary target of ordinances punishing homelessness").

515. *Loper v. New York City Police Dep't,* 999 F.2d 699 (2d Cir. 1993); *Blair v. Shanahan,* 775 F. Supp. 1315 (N.D. Cal. 1991), vacated on other grounds, 919 F. Supp. 1361 (N.D. Cal. 1996); *Benefit v. Cambridge,* 679 N.E.2d 184 (Mass. 1997).

516. *Loper,* 999 F.2d at 704.

lenged on First Amendment grounds, as have laws prohibiting camping in public, sleeping in public, and sleeping in vehicles.[517] Laws regarding how, when, and where religious and homeless advocacy organizations can feed unhoused people, and penalizing organizations and individuals that violate these laws, have been challenged under the First Amendment as violating freedom of speech and religious expression.[518]

The Fourth Amendment has been used to challenge the warrantless search and seizure of unhoused people's belongings, and to regulate law enforcement behavior when they enforce laws that prohibit storing belongings in public spaces through practices like street sweeps, which involve the removal and destruction of unhoused people's property from public spaces. Such practices violate the fundamental rights of unhoused people when certain procedural requirements are not met.[519] Warrantless searches of unhoused people's belongings and temporary shelter have also been challenged as unlawful searches under the Fourth Amendment.

Laws criminalizing sleeping and sitting in public, known as "sit-lie" laws, have been successfully challenged under the Cruel and Unusual Punishment Clause of the Eighth Amendment on the basis that they criminalize the status of being unhoused and punish involuntary behavior that is inherent to the human condition.[520] Other laws criminalizing status, such as certain "disorderly persons" laws,[521] that criminalize individuals for loitering within city

---

517. *Stone v. Agnos*, 960 F.2d 893 (9th Cir. 1992).

518. *Big Hart Ministries Ass'n Inc. v. City of Dallas*, 2011 WL 5346109 (N.D. Tex. Nov. 4, 2011).

519. *Lavan v. City of L.A.*, 693 F.3d 1022, 1024 (9th Cir. 2012).

520. *Pottinger v. Miami*, 810 F. Supp. 1551 (S.D. Fla. 1992); *Bell v. City of Boise*, 709 F.3d 890 (9th Cir. 2013); *Jones v. City of Los Angeles*, 444 F.3d 1118 (9th Cir. 2006), *vacated*, 505 F.3d 1006 (9th Cir. 2007) (finding that enforcing criminal ordinances against sleeping or lying on public streets violates the Eighth Amendment because it criminalizes the status of homelessness).

521. Las Vegas, Nev., City Code Tit. VI, Ch. 1, § 11 provides:
Persons within the limits of the City who have the physical ability to work, not having visible means of support, living idly, or who are found loitering or loafing about the streets, alleys or public places of the City, or who are found loafing or loitering habitually in or about the dramshops, tippling houses, saloons, barrooms, roadhouses, night clubs, gambling houses or places resorted to by persons for purposes of prostitution or immoral purposes, shall be deemed disorderly persons and shall be guilty of a misdemeanor.

limits, have been challenged and found unconstitutional under the Due Process Clause.[522]

A. Bringing a Constitutional Challenge

There are several ways a constitutional challenge to an anti-homeless ordinance can be brought before a court. A law can be challenged "as applied," meaning its constitutionality is being challenged as applied to a particular plaintiff or plaintiffs,[523] or plaintiffs can bring a "facial challenge" to the law, meaning that the constitutionality of the law as it applies to everyone is being challenged and no application of the statute can be legal.[524] A criminal defendant can challenge the constitutionality of a law under which they are prosecuted, as applied in that individual's case.[525] Plaintiffs impacted by a law can also challenge it proactively, before any criminal liability attaches, by bringing a civil suit against the government body enforcing the law.[526]

1. Standing

A plaintiff must have standing to challenge a law. Standing determines whether a plaintiff is entitled to have the court consider a particular issue and requires a sufficient connection between the plaintiff and the harm the law causes.[527] To have standing, a plaintiff must show the following: that he or she has suffered or will imminently suffer an injury; that the injury be "fairly traceable" to the defendant's conduct; and that a favorable decision is likely to redress the injury.[528] Injury to a fundamental right or individual liberty is gen-

---

522. *Parker v. Mun. Judge of Las Vegas*, 83 Nev. 214, 427 (1967) (law criminalizing "disorderly person" deemed an unconstitutional violation of due process because it makes the status of poverty a crime); *see also Reno v. Second Judicial Dist. Court*, 83 Nev. 201, 427 P.2d 4 (1967) ("disorderly conduct" law overturned as a violation of due process because it allowed arrests of individuals based on having an "evil reputation").

523. *See e.g. Jones v. City of L.A.*, 444 F.3d 1118 (9th Cir. 2006), *vacated*, 505 F.3d 1006 (9th Cir. 2007).

524. *Joel v. City of Orlando*, 232 F.3d 1353, 1360 (11th Cir. 2000).

525. E.g. *Jones*, 444 F.3d 1118.

526. *Big Hart Ministries*, 2011 WL 5346109.

527. *Warth v. Seldin*, 422 U.S. 498 (1975).

528. *Clapper v. Amnesty International*, 133 S. Ct. 1138, 1147 (2013).

erally sufficient to establish standing. In addition, a plaintiff seeking injunctive relief must show a likelihood of future harm if the injunction is not granted.[529]

2. Standard of Review

Courts subject any law that is challenged as unconstitutional to an initial test—called the "standard of review"—to determine what "level of scrutiny" is to be applied to determine the constitutionality of the law. There are three levels of scrutiny that a court considering the constitutionality of a law can apply—rational basis review, intermediate scrutiny, and strict scrutiny.[530] The level of scrutiny to be applied depends on the right that the law violates. Scrutiny is used to balance individual rights and the government's interest in passing the law.

As explained below, anti-homeless ordinances challenged under equal protection are generally subjected to *rational basis* review, because courts do not consider unhoused people to be a suspect class, nor do courts see such laws as infringing on any fundamental rights.[531]

Rational basis is the lowest level of scrutiny and is applied to laws that do not infringe on fundamental rights or target a suspect class.[532] A law will survive rational basis review if the law is rationally related to a legitimate government purpose.[533] Under rational basis review, the individual seeking relief must prove that the contested law does not serve a legitimate governmental purpose.[534] Because courts are highly deferential to governmental interests, constitutional challenges to these types of laws—which maintain that they are enacted in the public interest—prove difficult to overcome.[535]

Under intermediate scrutiny, a law will be upheld if it is *substantially related to an important government purpose.*[536] This means that the government's purpose in enacting the law must be more than legitimate; it must also be important to achieving the government's goal.[537] Under intermediate scru-

---

529. *Jones,* 444 F.3d at 1127; *Los Angeles v. Lyons,* 461 U.S. 95 (1983).
530. See Erwin Chemerinsky, Constitutional Law 529 (2001).
531. *Joel,* 232 F.3d at 1357 (11th Cir. 2000).
532. Ibid.
533. Ibid.
534. Ibid.
535. *Joel,* 232 F.3d at 1358.
536. *Loper,* 999 F.2d at 703.
537. Ibid.

tiny, the burden of proof shifts to the government, which means the law will be struck down if the government fails to show that the law is serving an important government purpose.[538]

Strict scrutiny is the most rigorous standard of review, and the most difficult for the government to overcome. Courts generally apply strict scrutiny in instances where a statute is challenged under equal protection as discriminatory on the basis of a "suspect" classification—race, religion, national origin, and alienage, or if the law infringes on a fundamental right.[539] Under strict scrutiny, the burden is on the government to show that the law is *necessary to achieve a compelling government purpose.*[540] The government must show that the law is the least restrictive means of achieving its goal, which requires the law to be narrowly tailored to further the government's compelling interest.[541]

To date, no court has recognized unhoused people as a suspect class, and the United States Supreme Court has held that classifications based on wealth are not suspect.[542] However at least one court[543] has suggested that the argument has some merit, writing, "[t]his court is not entirely convinced that homelessness as a class has none of these 'traditional indicia of suspectness.' It can be argued that unhoused people are saddled with such disabilities or have been subjected to a history of unequal treatment or are so politically powerless that extraordinary protection of the homeless as a class is warranted."[544] Likewise, sleeping out of doors has not been recognized as a fundamental right.[545]

Constitutional challenges to anti-homeless ordinances are not all successful, but understanding how legal advocates have approached these laws, and what has and has not worked, is an extremely important component of the legal advocate's toolbox. The sections below will delve into the Constitutional issues in greater detail and provide a comprehensive overview of the seminal cases challenging laws that criminalize homelessness.

---

538. *Edenfield v. Fane*, 507 U.S. 761, 770 (1993).

539. *Pottinger*, 810 F. Supp. at 1578.

540. *Burson v. Freeman*, 504 U.S. 191, 198 (1992).

541. *Grutter v. Bollinger*, 509 U.S. 306, 326 (2003).

542. *Pottinger*, 810 F. Supp. at 1578 (*citing Kadrmas v. Dickinson Public Schools*, 487 U.S. 450, 458 (1988)).

543. *Pottinger*, 810 F. Supp. at 1578.

544. Ibid.; *see also Joel*, 232 F.3d at 1357.

545. *Joel*, 232 F.3d at 1357.

B. Eighth Amendment Challenges: Punishing Unhoused People for Involuntary Acts

The Eighth Amendment to the U.S. Constitution provides that "excessive bail shall not be required, nor excessive fines imposed, nor cruel and unusual punishments inflicted."[546] The last section of the amendment is known as the Cruel and Unusual Punishment Clause, and it imposes substantive limits on the type of conduct that can be criminalized and punished.[547] It functions to restrict the criminal process in three ways: "First, it limits the kinds of punishment that can be imposed on those convicted of crimes; second, it proscribes punishment grossly disproportionate to the severity of the crime; and third, it imposes substantive limits on what can be made criminal and punished as such."[548] The Eighth Amendment "seeks 'to limit the power of those entrusted with the criminal-law function of government.' If the state transgresses this limit, a person suffers constitutionally cognizable harm as soon as he is subjected to the criminal process."[549]

The Cruel and Unusual Punishment Clause has been used to successfully challenge anti-homeless ordinances that ban essential activities, like sleeping and sitting, because they criminalize behavior that is necessary to sustain human life and therefore offer no choice to unhoused people other than to break the law.

Ordinances that criminalize sleeping and sitting represent some of the harshest kinds of anti-homeless ordinances, because they convey the message that if you are unhoused, your very existence is unwelcome. A lack of adequate numbers of shelter beds in many cities means that unhoused people have no alternative but to sleep in public spaces.[550] Additionally, because unhoused people have nowhere to eat and rest during daylight hours, they are invariably forced to do these things in public spaces.[551]

---

546. U.S. Const. amend. VIII.

547. *Jones,* 444 F.3d at 1128.

548. *Ingraham v. Wright,* 430 U.S. 651, 667 (1977).

549. *Jones,* 444 F.3d at 1129.

550. National Law Center on Homelessness & Poverty, *Housing Not Handcuffs: A Litigation Manual.* https://nlchp.org//wp-content/uploads/2018/10/Housing-Not-Handcuffs-Litigation-Manual.pdf, 6. [Hereinafter "*A Litigation Manual.*"]

551. National Alliance to End Homelessness, *State of Homelessness: 2020 Edition.* https://endhomelessness.org/homelessness-in-america/homelessness-statistics/state-of-homelessness-2020/.

Prohibitions on camping, sleeping, sitting, and lying in public take various forms, but are commonly justified under public health and safety grounds. In 2019, of the 187 cities surveyed by the National Law Center on Homelessness and Poverty, seventy-two percent had laws prohibiting camping in public, fifty-one percent had laws prohibiting sleeping in public, and fifty-five percent had laws prohibiting sleeping or lying down in public.

In the following cases, the Eighth Amendment was used to challenge anti-sleeping, anti-camping, and anti-sitting laws that leave unhoused people no choice but to break the law.

1. The Criminalization of Status

In the 1962 case *Robinson v. California*,[552] the United States Supreme Court first recognized that criminalizing *status*—that is, punishing people for traits rather than for their actions—is an unconstitutional violation of the Eighth Amendment. What is now known as the "status crimes doctrine" provides that the Eighth Amendment prohibits subjecting an individual to criminal punishment based on his or her status.

In *Robinson*, the Supreme Court considered whether a California state law making it a criminal offense to "be addicted to the use of narcotics" was constitutional. In finding that the law violated the Cruel and Unusual Punishment Clause of the Eighth Amendment, the Court explained that targeting an individual based on his or her "status" of being addicted to a narcotic would be akin to making it "a criminal offense for a person to be mentally ill, or a leper, or to be afflicted with a venereal disease."[553] Recognizing that drug addiction is an illness, the Court determined that "a law which made a criminal offense of such a disease would doubtless be universally thought to be an infliction of cruel and unusual punishment in violation of the Eighth and Fourteenth Amendments."[554]

Several years later, the United States Supreme Court refined the status crimes doctrine in *Powell v. Texas*,[555] a case concerning a Texas law that penalized being drunk in public. In arguing that the status crimes doctrine should apply, Powell claimed that his chronic alcoholism compelled him to drink excessively and that this condition made him unable to control the behavior

---

552. *Robinson v. California*, 370 U.S. 660 (1962).
553. *Robinson*, 370 U.S. at 666.
554. Ibid., 666–67 (internal citations omitted).
555. *Powell v. Texas*, 392 U.S. 514 (1968).

of drinking in public. In other words, his status as a chronic alcoholic involuntarily compelled him to drink in public. As such, he argued that the law, which made it a crime to be drunk in public, punished his *status* as a chronic alcoholic and should therefore be struck down as unconstitutional under the Eighth Amendment.

The Court ultimately rejected Powell's argument, making a distinction between the offense of being drunk in public and being a chronic alcoholic. The Court held that the Texas law was not punishing "mere status, as California did in *Robinson*" but instead regulated public behavior that threatened the public interest in health and safety, which was "a far cry from convicting one from being an addict, being a chronic alcoholic, being 'mentally ill, or a leper.'"[556]

But in a concurrence that is now widely accepted as the correct interpretation of the status crimes doctrine, Justice Byron White carved out an exception that has since been used to argue the merits of Eighth Amendment challenges to anti-homeless ordinances that make homelessness a crime:

> The fact remains that some chronic alcoholics must drink and hence must drink somewhere. Although many chronics have homes, many others do not. For all practical purposes the public streets may be home for these unfortunates, not because their disease compels them to be there, but because, drunk or sober, they have no place else to go and no place else to be when they are drinking. This is more a function of economic station than of disease, although the disease may lead to destitution and perpetuate that condition. For some of these alcoholics I would think a showing could be made that resisting drunkenness is impossible and that avoiding public places when intoxicated is also impossible. As applied to them this statute is in effect a law which bans a single act for which they may not be convicted under the Eighth Amendment—the act of getting drunk.[557]

Robinson and *Powell* paved the way for several crucial cases that used their combined reasoning to extend the status crimes doctrine to anti-homeless ordinances that punish involuntary acts that are the unavoidable consequence of being unhoused.[558] Anti-homeless ordinances that criminalize publicly

---

556. *Powell v. Texas*, 392 U.S. 514, 532.

557. Ibid., 551.

558. *Pottinger v. Miami*, 810 F. Supp. 1551 (S.D. Fla. 1992); *Jones v. City of L.A.*, 444 F.3d 1118 (9th Cir. 2006); *Martin v. City of Boise*, 920 F.3d 584, 617 (9th Cir. 2019).

engaging in life-sustaining activities when there are no alternatives available to avoid breaking the law punish the status of homelessness. In such cases, individuals are forced to make a choice between breaking the law on the one hand, and foregoing life-sustaining activities on the other.

2. The Status Crimes Doctrine Applied to Anti-Homeless Ordinances

Pottinger v. Miami (1992) was the first case to combine the *Robinson / Powell* status crimes doctrine and apply it to an anti-homeless ordinance.[559] In *Pottinger,* a class of plaintiffs challenged several city laws that criminalized various forms of sleeping, standing, sitting and lying down in public places. The plaintiffs argued that their status as unhoused people was "involuntary and beyond their immediate ability to alter." [560] The conduct for which plaintiffs were being punished was "inseparable from their involuntary homeless status," and therefore in violation of the Cruel and Unusual Punishment Clause of the Eighth Amendment.[561] The U.S. District Court for the Southern District of Florida found the plaintiffs' argument compelling:

> For plaintiffs, resisting the need to eat, sleep or engage in other life-sustaining activities is impossible. Avoiding public places when engaging in this otherwise innocent conduct is also impossible. Moreover, plaintiffs have not argued that the City should not be able to arrest them for public drunkenness or any type of conduct that might be harmful to themselves or to others. To paraphrase Justice White, plaintiffs have no place else to go and no place else to be. This is so particularly at night when the public parks are closed. As long as the homeless plaintiffs do not have a single place where they can lawfully be, the challenged ordinances, as applied to them, effectively punish them for something for which they may not be convicted under the eighth amendment--sleeping, eating and other innocent conduct. Accordingly, the court finds that defendant's conduct violates the eighth amendment ban against cruel and usual punishment and therefore that the defendant is liable on this count.[562]

---

559. *Pottinger,* 810 F. Supp. 1551.
560. Ibid.
561. Ibid., 1561.
562. Ibid., 1565.

In *Jones v. City of L.A.* (2006), the Ninth Circuit Court of Appeals considered whether a Los Angeles sit-lie law punished the status of being unhoused.[563] The six plaintiffs in *Jones* challenged Los Angeles Municipal Ordinance § 41.18(d),[564] which criminalized the conduct of sitting, lying, or sleeping on public streets and sidewalks at any time of day. At the time, § 41.18(d) was considered one of the most restrictive municipal laws regulating public spaces in the United States because it provided no exception or carve-out limiting the hours of enforcement, and therefore made criminality under the law unavoidable.[565]

The six plaintiffs in *Jones*—Edward Jones, Patricia Vinson, George Vinson, Thomas Cash, Stanley Barger, and Robert Lee Purrie—were residents of the Los Angeles Skid Row area, and each of them were cited or arrested for violating the law at times when no shelter beds were available, giving them no option than to go without sleep or violate the law.

They argued that the law violated the constitutional rights of individuals who were unable to obtain shelter and therefore compelled them to break the law, and by enforcing the ordinance "twenty-four hours a day against persons with nowhere else to sit, lie, or sleep, other than on public streets and sidewalks, the City is criminalizing the status of homelessness in violation of the Eighth and Fourteenth Amendments to the U.S. Constitution." As such, they sought to enjoin the city from enforcing this city-wide, blanket ban on these activities between the hours of 9:00 p.m. and 6:30 a.m.

The *Jones* court made clear that "the state may not criminalize 'being'; that is, the state may not punish a person for who he is, independent of anything he has done," nor can it "punish a person for certain conditions, either arising from his own acts or contracted involuntarily, or acts that he is powerless to avoid."[566]

> The City could not expressly criminalize the status of homelessness by making it a crime to be homeless without violating the Eighth Amendment, nor can it criminalize acts that are an integral aspect of that status. Because there is substantial and undisputed evidence that the number of homeless people in Los Angeles far exceeds the number of available shelter beds at all times, including on the nights of their

---

563. *Jones v. City of L.A.*, 444 F.3d 1118 (9th Cir. 2006), *vacated*, 505 F.3d 1006 (9th Cir. 2007).

564. L.A., Cal., Mun. Code § 41.18(d).

565. *Jones*, 444 F.3d at 1123.

566. *Jones*, 444 F.3d at 1133.

arrest or citation, Los Angeles has encroached upon Appellants' Eighth Amendment protections by criminalizing the unavoidable act of sitting, lying, or sleeping at night while being involuntarily homeless. A closer analysis of *Robinson* and *Powell* instructs that the involuntariness of the act or condition the City criminalizes is the critical factor delineating a constitutionally cognizable status, and incidental conduct which is integral to and an unavoidable result of that status, from acts or conditions that can be criminalized consistent with the Eighth Amendment....[567]

The *Robinson* and *Powell* decisions, read together, compel us to conclude that enforcement of section 41.18(d) at all times and in all places against unhoused people who are sitting, lying, or sleeping in Los Angeles's Skid Row because they cannot obtain shelter violates the Cruel and Unusual Punishment Clause. As unhoused people, Appellants are in a chronic state that may have been acquired "innocently or involuntarily." Whether sitting, lying, and sleeping are defined as acts or conditions, they are universal and unavoidable consequences of being human. It is undisputed that, for unhoused people in Skid Row who have no access to private spaces, these acts can only be done in public. In contrast to Leroy Powell, Appellants have made a substantial showing that they are "unable to stay off the streets on the night[s] in question...."[568]

Similarly, applying *Robinson* and *Powell*, courts have found statutes criminalizing the status of vagrancy to be unconstitutional. For example, *Goldman v. Knecht* declared unconstitutional a Colorado statute making it a crime for "'any person able to work and support himself'" to "'be found loitering or strolling about, frequenting public places,...begging or leading an idle, immoral or profligate course of life, or not having any visible means of support.'" 295 F. Supp. 897, 899 n.2, 908 (D. Colo. 1969). These cases establish that the state may not make it an offense to be idle, indigent, or homeless in public places.[569] Nor may the state criminalize conduct that is an unavoidable consequence of

---

567. Ibid, 1132.

568. Ibid., 1136.

569. This last paragraph in *Jones* recognizes that the status crimes doctrine has been successfully used to challenge vagrancy and "disorderly persons" laws. While this avenue for challenging vagrancy ordinances won't be addressed in detail here, it is important to note that Eighth Amendment challenges to such laws can be a successful approach.

being homeless—namely sitting, lying, or sleeping on the streets of Los Angeles's Skid Row. As Justice White stated in *Powell*, "punishing an addict for using drugs convicts for addiction under a different name."[570]

The Ninth Circuit granted the injunction against enforcing the ordinance, stating that if the number of unhoused people outnumbered available shelter beds, the ordinance could not be enforced. After the *Jones* decision, the plaintiffs and the City of Los Angeles reached a settlement providing that the ordinance would not be enforced between the hours of 9:00 p.m. and 6:00 a.m.[571] The case was ultimately remanded and vacated pursuant to the settlement but remains an important case in Eighth Amendment status crimes jurisprudence.[572]

In *Martin v. City of Boise* (2019), the Ninth Circuit again considered the criminalization of status in the context of two Boise ordinances—an anti-camping ordinance[573] and a disorderly persons ordinance[574]—both of which limited plaintiffs' ability to sleep in public. Once again, the court found that the Eighth Amendment prohibits the imposition of criminal penalties for sitting, sleeping, or lying outside on public property, when the lack of available alternatives forces unhoused people to break the law.[575]

The holding in Martin, like that of Jones, was limited to instances in which the number of unhoused people outnumbered the available shelter beds but established a precedent in the Ninth on the kinds of anti-sleeping, anti-camping, and anti-sitting laws cities can enact without violating the Eighth Amendment. As the next section illustrates, advocates should consider how these types of cases may turn out if the jurisdiction provides enough shelter beds for all the unhoused people in the community.

3. Unsuccessful Eighth Amendment Challenges

In *Joel v. City of Orlando* (2000),[576] the Eleventh Circuit Court of Appeals rejected plaintiff's argument that an Orlando anti-camping ordinance[577] vio-

---

570. *Jones*, 444 F.3d at 1137.
571. *A Litigation Manual*, 34.
572. *Jones*, 505 F.3d 1006.
573. Boise City Code § 9-10-02.
574. Boise City Code § 6-01-05.
575. *Martin v. City of Boise*, 920 F.3d 584, 617 (9th Cir. 2019).
576. *Joel*, 232 F.3d at 1361–62.
577. Section 43.52 of the Orlando City Code.

lated the Cruel and Unusual Punishment Clause of the Eighth Amendment. Joel, an unhoused man who was arrested for violating the ordinance, argued that the City's enforcement guidelines demonstrated that "a person's unhoused status, combined with sleeping, constitutes a criminal offense."[578] The court rejected Joel's argument and distinguished the case from *Pottinger* and *Jones* on the basis that those cases relied on the lack of sufficient shelter space that forced unhoused people to choose between breaking the law and going without sleep, thus criminalizing their status.[579] The facts in *Joel,* on the other hand, established that a large shelter within city limits had never run out of shelter beds, and therefore, the ordinance did not criminalize involuntary behavior.[580]

In *Tobe v. City of Santa Ana,*[581] the California Supreme Court upheld an anti-camping ordinance, despite evidence that:

> The ordinance was the culmination of a four-year effort by Santa Ana to expel homeless people. There was evidence that in 1988 a policy was developed to show "vagrants" that they were not welcome in the city. To force them out, they were to be continually moved from locations they frequented by a task force from the city's police and recreation and parks departments; early park closing times were to be posted and strictly enforced; sleeping bags and accessories were to be disposed of; and abandoned shopping carts were to be confiscated. Providers of free food were to be monitored; sprinklers in the Center Park were to be turned on often; and violations of the city code by businesses and social service agencies in that area were to be strictly enforced.[582]

The court rejected plaintiffs' argument that the ordinance punished the status of being unhoused, stating "it is far from clear that none had alternatives to either the condition of being homeless or the conduct that led to homelessness and to the citations."[583]

---

578. *Joel,* 232 F.3d at 1361–62.
579. Ibid., 1363.
580. Ibid.
581. *Tobe v. City of Santa Ana,* 9 Cal. 4th 1069, 1082 (1995).
582. Ibid.
583. Ibid., 1105.

C. First Amendment Challenges: Punishing Speech & Charity

The First Amendment protects freedom of speech, freedom of religion, and the right to assembly.[584] This protection encompasses the public expression of ideas in all its forms—including printed, spoken, symbolically represented, or otherwise—even when those ideas are considered offensive to others.[585]

Although the First Amendment protects the right to free expression in public spaces, the government may still regulate that freedom to some extent. Assessing the constitutionality of the First Amendment restrictions the government places on public property is referred to as the "forum-based" approach.[586] Under the forum-based approach, any law regulating speech or expression in a "public forum," is subject to the highest level of scrutiny by the courts.[587] Public forums are spaces that are traditionally recognized as available for public expression—like parks, streets, and sidewalks.[588] These spaces "have immemorially been held in trust for the use of the public and, time out of mind, have been used for purposes of assembly, communicating thoughts between citizens, and discussing public questions."[589] The level of scrutiny applied to laws that regulate speech in public forums depends on whether the regulation is "content-based" or "content-neutral."

To be content-neutral, a speech restriction must be both "viewpoint" neutral—the regulation cannot be based on the ideology of the message—and "subject matter" neutral, meaning that the regulation can't be based on the topic involved.[590] Content-neutral speech regulations are subjected to intermediate scrutiny, which allows for reasonable time, place, and manner restrictions on speech, as long as the restrictions are "narrowly tailored to serve a sig-

---

584. "Congress shall make no law respecting an establishment of religion, or prohibiting the free exercise thereof; or abridging the freedom of speech, or of the press; or the right of the people peaceably to assemble, and to petition the government for a redress of grievances." U.S. Const. amend. I.

585. *Street v. New York*, 394 U.S. 576 (1969); *Spence v. Washington*, 418 U.S. 405 (1974).

586. *Loper*, 999 F.2d at 703.

587. Ibid.

588. Ibid., 703, (*citing Hague v. CIO*, 307 U.S. 496, 515 (1939)).

589. *Loper*, 999 F.2d at 703 (*quoting* Hague, 307 U.S. at 515) (internal quotations omitted).

590. *McLaughlin v. City of Lowell*, 140 F. Supp. 3d 177, 185 (D. Mass. 2015).

nificant government interest, and leave open ample alternative channels of communication."[591]

Content-based speech regulations restrict speech based on the message, ideas, subject matter, or content.[592] Content-based speech regulations are subject to the highest level of scrutiny, strict scrutiny, because as the United States Supreme Court has recognized,

> Government action that stifles speech on account of its message, or that requires the utterance of a particular message favored by the Government, contravenes this essential right. Laws of this sort pose the inherent risk that the Government seeks not to advance a legitimate regulatory goal, but to suppress unpopular ideas or information or manipulate the public debate through coercion rather than persuasion. These restrictions "raise the specter that the Government may effectively drive certain ideas or viewpoints from the marketplace."[593]

Under strict scrutiny review, the government must prove that the regulation is *necessary to serve a compelling state interest* and that it is narrowly drawn to achieve that end.[594]

Laws regulating protected speech or expression can also be challenged as unconstitutionally vague or overbroad. A law is unconstitutionally vague if it is so ambiguous that a reasonable person cannot tell what expression is forbidden and what is allowed, and it is unconstitutionally overbroad if it regulates more speech than the constitution allows.[595] A law that limits free expression can be challenged under the overbreadth doctrine "in cases where every application creates an impermissible risk of suppression of ideas, such as an ordinance that delegates overly broad discretion to the decision maker, and in cases where the ordinance sweeps too broadly, penalizing a substantial amount of speech that is constitutionally protected."[596]

When a restriction reaches so broadly that it deters expression the First Amendment protects, it can be challenged as overbroad.[597] First Amend-

---

591. *Loper*, 999 F.2d at 703.

592. *Police Dept. of Chicago v. Mosley*, 408 U.S. 92, 95–96 (1972).

593. *Turner Broad. Sys. v. FCC*, 512 U.S. 622, 641 (1994).

594. *Loper*, 999 F.2d at 703.

595. *Kolender v. Lawson*, 461 U.S. 352, 357 (1983).

596. *Forsyth Cty. v. Nationalist Movement*, 505 U.S. 123, 129–30 (1992).

597. *Diamond S.J. Enter. v. City of San Jose*, 430 F. Supp. 3d 637, 644 (N.D. Cal. 2019).

ment overbreadth and vagueness challenges "seek to strike restrictions that may chill protected speech. Uncertain meanings inevitably lead citizens to steer far wider of the unlawful zone than if the boundaries of the forbidden areas were clearly marked."[598]

The First Amendment has been used to challenge ordinances that prohibit activities that fall under the umbrella of free expression. These activities include panhandling, food sharing, certain conduct that falls under the term "vagrancy," and in some cases sitting or sleeping. Anti-panhandling laws have been successfully challenged on the basis that they regulate the "content" of the speech—that is they regulate speech based on its message, ideas, subject matter, or content.[599] Anti-vagrancy laws have been successfully challenged as constitutionally overbroad limitations on expression.[600] The following cases illustrate how the First Amendment has been used to challenge a wide array of anti-homeless ordinances.

1. Panhandling

Prohibitions on panhandling and begging remove the sole means of support for some individuals. These laws take various forms and generally prohibit begging in specific zones of commercial activity, like downtown areas, or within a certain proximity to the entrance of commercial businesses.[601] Some anti-panhandling laws regulate the way donations can be solicited, for example, by only allowing silent solicitations through the use of signs.[602]

Panhandling was recognized as a form of protected speech for several decades, meanwhile, courts often upheld content-neutral anti-panhandling ordinances as valid time, place, and manner restrictions.[603] However, in the seminal *Reed v. Town of Gilbert* case,[604] the Court redefined the distinction between content-neutral and content-based speech restrictions, and, as a result, courts across the country struck down anti-panhandling laws as unconstitutional regulations of protected speech.

---

598. Ibid., 644.

599. *Mosley*, 408 U.S. at 95–96.

600. *Loper*, 999 F.2d 699.

601. *No Safe Place*, 20.

602. *Norton v. City of Springfield*, 806 F.3d 411 (7th Cir. 2015).

603. Ocelyn Tillisch and Drew Sena, "Begging for Change: Begging Restrictions Throughout Washington," *Seattle Univ. Homeless Rights Advocacy Project* (May 2018): 27–28.

604. *Reed v. Town of Gilbert*, 576 U.S. 155 (2015).

Reed v. Town of Gilbert refined what constitutes content-based speech. *Reed* had nothing to do with panhandling—it concerned a law that placed different restrictions on outdoor signs based on the type of information conveyed. A small church challenged the practice as discriminatory because it subjected churches and other non-profits to stricter regulations than other categories of signs. Prior to *Reed*, some courts had held that a law did not regulate the content of speech as long as it was neutral with respect to viewpoint and ideas—in other words, as long as the government did not adopt a regulation of speech because it disagreed with the message conveyed.[605] *Reed* changed that. According to *Reed*, "Government regulation of speech is content based if a law applies to particular speech because of the topic discussed or the idea or message expressed."[606] Under this interpretation, a court must consider whether a regulation of speech "on its face" draws a distinction based on the message a speaker conveys by considering whether it "applies to particular speech because of the topic discussed or the idea or message expressed."[607]

Reed has since paved the way for courts to strike down anti-panhandling laws as unconstitutional restrictions of content-based speech, and courts have "consistently recognized the protected, expressive nature of panhandling."[608] *Norton v. City of Springfield* was the first case to do so.[609] The plaintiffs in *Norton* alleged that the City of Springfield's anti-panhandling law, which prohibited oral solicitations for "an immediate donation of money" but allowed signs and solicitations for money later, constituted a form of content discrimination. On reconsideration after the *Reed* decision was issued, the court agreed, stating "Springfield's ordinance regulates 'because of the topic discussed.'" [See the *Practitioner Narrative* at the end of this chapter for an interview with Adele Nicholas, the civil rights attorney who litigated *Norton v. Springfield*.]

After *Reed* and *Norton*, the National Law Center on Homelessness and Poverty (NLCHP), in concert with the ACLU, sent demand letters to counties and municipalities in Illinois and across the country, notifying them that their ordinances restricting panhandling were unconstitutional under the First Amendment.

The following is an excerpt from a July 17, 2019 letter from the NLCHP, the ACLU of Illinois, and the Chicago Coalition on Homelessness to the City

605. *Otterson v. City of Springfield*, 768 F.3d 713 (7th Cir. 2014).
606. *Reed*, 576 U.S. at 163.
607. *Reed*, 576 U.S. at 155.
608. *McLaughlin*, 140 F. Supp. 3d at 184.
609. *Norton v. City of Springfield*, 806 F.3d 411, 412 (7th Cir. 2015).

of O'Fallon regarding two ordinances that prohibited panhandling in several manners and locations:

> Since the landmark *Reed v. Gilbert* case in 2015, every panhandling ordinance challenged in federal court—at least 25 of 25 to date—including many with features similar to the ones in O'Fallon ("the City"), has been found constitutionally deficient or resulted in the repeal of that ordinance. At least 31 additional cities—including eight municipalities in Illinois in the past year alone—have repealed their panhandling ordinances when informed of the likely infringement on First Amendment rights. The City's ordinances not only almost certainly violate the constitutional right to free speech protected by the First Amendment to the United States Constitution, but it is also bad policy, and numerous examples of better alternatives now exist which the City could draw on. We call on the City to immediately repeal the Ordinances and instead consider more constructive alternatives or risk potential litigation.
>
> The Ordinances overtly distinguish between types of speech based on "subject matter...function or purpose." The Ordinances define panhandling as an in-person solicitation in a public place for "an immediate donation of money, goods or any other form of gratuity", except for requests that involve "passively standing or sitting with a sign or other indication that one is seeking donations." Section 111.02. The Ordinances prohibit panhandling in locations including bus stops, on public transportation, in sidewalk cafes, during times after sunset and before sunrise, and in a group of two or more persons. Section 111.09. The Ordinances also prohibit individuals from soliciting contributions while standing on median strips or in roadways. Section 74.07. The Ordinances are content-based because they restrict the content of a person's speech—asking for money. They are not neutral because other types of speech, such as political campaigning, catcalling, evangelizing, or asking for signatures are not restricted.
>
> As a result, the Ordinances impose "content-based" restrictions on speech that are presumptively unconstitutional. Courts use the most stringent standard – strict scrutiny—to review such restrictions. The Ordinances cannot survive strict scrutiny because neither do they serve any compelling state interest, nor are they narrowly tailored.
>
> First, the Ordinances serve no compelling state interest. Distaste for a certain type of speech, or a certain type of speaker, is not even a *le-*

gitimate state interest, let alone a *compelling* one. Shielding unwilling listeners from messages disfavored by the state is likewise not a permissible state interest. As the Supreme Court explained, the fact that a listener on a sidewalk cannot "turn the page, change the channel, or leave the Web site" to avoid hearing an uncomfortable message is "a virtue, not a vice."

Second, even if the City could identify a compelling state interest, there is no evidence to demonstrate that the Ordinances are "narrowly tailored" to such an interest. Theoretical discussion is not enough: "the burden of proving narrow tailoring requires the County to prove that it actually *tried* other methods to address the problem." The City may not "[take] a sledgehammer to a problem that can and should be solved with a scalpel."

Though "public safety" is an important state interest, the Ordinances are not narrowly tailored to serve it. For example, the City can protect pedestrian safety with other regulations, such as those prohibiting pedestrians from crossing the roadway at any point other than a crosswalk (Section 74.03). As a result, the Ordinance cannot be said to further public safety.

The location restrictions in the Ordinances, which outlaw panhandling at locations including intersections, median strips, bus stops, and sidewalk cafes, are also unconstitutional. Unsurprisingly, every court to consider a regulation that, like the Ordinances, bans requests for money within an identified geographic area has stricken the regulation.

The Ordinances also restrict the manner in which people can ask for an in-person donation, including by prohibiting panhandling in a group of two or more persons. Courts have not hesitated to strike regulations that regulate the manner in which a person can ask for a donation, even where the regulation was supposedly justified by a state interest in public safety. And for good reason: restricting people's behavior on account of their speech is almost always too over-reaching to be narrowly tailored to any compelling governmental interest.

For these reasons, among others, the Ordinances cannot pass constitutional muster.[610]

---

610. Letter from the ACLU of Illinois, Chicago Coalition for the Homeless, and the National Law Center on Homelessness and Poverty, Re: City of O'Fallon Ordinances 74.07 and 111.09 on Solicitations and Panhandling. (July 17, 2019) (internal citations omitted).

Demand letters like the one excerpted above are an important component of legal advocacy work because they provide a way to ensure that local and state governments comply with constitutional standards as they evolve, without the need to bring cost-prohibitive litigation in multiple jurisdictions.

A plethora of cases since *Norton* have successfully applied *Reed* to challenge the constitutionality of anti-panhandling ordinances.[611] Although *Reed* has made it much more difficult for governments to pass anti-panhandling ordinances, laws that permit content-neutral time, place, and manner restrictions still fall within the scope of permissible exceptions. Additionally, cities often pass "aggressive panhandling" ordinances to "circumvent judicial scrutiny by enacting aggressive begging laws under the veil of targeting aggressive behavior rather than protected speech."[612]

Aggressive panhandling laws "hinge on subjective perceptions of the person being solicited for help—for example, a person might be guilty of aggressive begging if someone listening to them feels intimidated, regardless of the means and manner of the solicitation."[613] While these laws are nominally enacted to deter threatening or intimidating behavior, they are often enforced against individuals engaging in harmless behavior. These laws can encompass behavior as innocuous as soliciting donations from an individual who is standing in line to enter a business[614] or a request for donations from a person who has already declined to donate.[615] In at least one case, sitting and holding a sign requesting donations was included as prohibited behavior under an aggressive panhandling statute.[616] Although *Reed* has made it more difficult for these types of aggressive panhandling laws to withstand scrutiny,[617] such laws remain an area of concern for the unhoused and the advocates who represent them.

---

611. *See, e.g., Thayer v. City of Worcester*, 144 F. Supp. 3d 218, 233–34, 237–38 (D. Mass. 2015) (finding the city's aggressive begging ordinance restricted content-based speech); *McLaughlin*, 140 F. Supp. 3d at 182 (finding the town's aggressive panhandling restrictions to be unconstitutional under the First Amendment); *Browne v. City of Grand Junction*, 136 F. Supp. 3d 1276, 1292 (D. Colo. 2015) (finding that under *Reed* the city's aggressive panhandling ordinance was content-based); *City of Lakewood v. Willis*, 37 P.3d 1056 (Wash. 2016) (finding that two provisions of anti-panhandling ordinance restricted content-based speech).

612. Tillisch & Sena, 27–28.

613. Ibid., 3.

614. Farida Ali, "Limiting the Poor's Right to Public Space: Criminalizing Homelessness in California," 21 *Geo. J. Poverty Law & Pol'y* (2014): 197.

615. *McLaughlin*, 140 F. Supp. 3d at 182.

616. Ibid.

617. *See e.g. McLaughlin*, 140 F. Supp. 3d at 177.

2. Food Sharing

Ordinances restricting individuals and organizations from food sharing with unhoused people limit access to food for those in need of it and penalize through fines and criminalization unhoused people and the organizations that provide free food.[618] These ordinances generally include a zoning component limiting the time, place, or manner in which organizations can feed the poor,[619] a restrictive permitting component,[620] or a public health and safety component, citing concerns with sanitation.[621] Food sharing ordinances have been connected to government strategies aimed at deterring unhoused people from remaining or settling in certain areas, with the rationale that if access to life-sustaining resources is limited, unhoused people will be forced to relocate to other areas.[622] Advocates have used the First Amendment with varying degrees of success to challenge these types of ordinances.

Permitting requirements add another layer to First Amendment challenges to the extent that they constitute a "prior restraint" on speech, which exists when speech is "conditioned on the prior approval of the speaker."[623] Permitting requirements[624] can be seen as a prior restraint on speech, and courts place a "heavy presumption" against the validity of a prior restraint because there is a strong risk of government censorship.[625] But the United States Supreme Court has recognized that "to regulate competing uses of public forums," the

---

618. *Big Hart Ministries*, 2011 WL 5346109.

619. *Stuart Circle Parish v. Board of Zoning Appeals of the City of Richmond*, 946 F. Supp. 1225 (E.D. Va. 1996).

620. *McHenry v. Agnos*, 983 F.2d 1076 (9th Cir. 1993).

621. *Big Hart Ministries*, 2011 WL 5346109 at *2 (the stated purpose of the Texas food-sharing ordinance was "to safeguard public health and provide to consumers food that is safe, unadulterated, and honestly presented").

622. *No Safe Place*, p. 24.

623. See *Forsyth*, 505 U.S. at 130.

624. Special event and free speech permits are issued at the city or county level, and the issuing department varies by state, county, and city. Often, police departments issue these permits (this is the case in Los Angeles and the Orlando), and sometimes more than one department (in L.A., the Dept. of Public Works issues permits as well). Other examples of departments that also issue permits: The Parks, Recreation and Community Resources Advisory Commission, along with city staff and the Special Events Subcommittee (Hermosa Beach); the Department of Parks and Recreation (Ventura); The Film and Special Events Department (Miami, FL); Community Service Department (Naples, FL); Special Events Office and Dept. of Parks and Recreation (Reno, NV); Police Dept (Huntsville, AL); Special Event Dept. (Montgomery, AL).

625. *Bantam Books, Inc. v. Sullivan*, 372 U.S. 58, 71 (1963).

government "may impose a permit requirement on those wishing to hold a march, parade, or rally."[626]

Permitting schemes themselves must meet certain constitutional requirements; importantly, "any permit scheme controlling the time, place, and manner of speech must not be based on the content of the message, must be narrowly tailored to serve a significant governmental interest, and must leave open ample alternatives for communication."[627] Additionally, "a law subjecting the exercise of First Amendment freedoms to the prior restraint of a license must contain narrow, objective, and definite standards to guide the licensing authority."[628] A government regulation that allows arbitrary application is inconsistent with this principle. If a permitting scheme "involves appraisal of facts, the exercise of judgment, and the formation of an opinion by the licensing authority, the danger of censorship and of abridgment of our precious First Amendment freedoms is too great to be permitted."[629]

a. Food Sharing as an Exercise of Religious Freedom

In *Stuart Circle Parish v. Board of Zoning Appeals of the City of Richmond*, a Fourth Circuit Court of Appeals considered the constitutionality of a Richmond, Virginia zoning ordinance that limited "feeding and housing programs for the homeless within churches to no more than thirty unhoused people for up to seven days between the months of October and April."[630]

Stuart Circle Parish, a partnership of six churches of different denominations, operated a "Meal Ministry" that offered "worship, hospitality, pastoral care, and a healthful meal to the urban poor of Richmond" every Sunday. Plaintiffs sought to permanently enjoin the city from enforcing a zoning ordinance that limited feeding and housing programs for unhoused people, thus interfering with their Meal Ministry activities.[631] To the plaintiffs, the Meal Ministry was the "physical embodiment of a central tenet of the Christian faith, ministering to the poor, the hungry and the homeless in the community" and the City had not shown a "compelling state interest for burdening the exercise of this central tenet by the members and pastors of the six churches which compromise Stuart Circle Parish."[632]

---

626. *Forsyth*, 505 U.S. at 130.
627. Ibid., 130.
628. *Shuttlesworth v. Birmingham*, 394 U.S. 147, 150–151 (1969).
629. *Forsyth*, 505 U.S. at 130–31.
630. *Stuart Circle Parish v. Board of Zoning Appeals*, 946 F. Supp. 1225 (E.D. Va. 1996).
631. Ibid., 1228–29.
632. Ibid.

Plaintiffs contended that enforcement of the code constituted a violation of their rights to the free exercise of religion as protected by the First Amendment and by the Religious Freedom Restoration Act, which "provides that a government shall not substantially burden a person's exercise of religion unless it demonstrates that application of the burden is in furtherance of a compelling governmental interest and is the least restrictive means of furthering that interest."[633] The court agreed, holding that plaintiffs would suffer irreparable injury without injunctive relief because they would otherwise be prevented from engaging in the free exercise of their religion.[634]

b. Food Sharing as an Exercise of Free Speech and Free Expression

However, not all First Amendment challenges to food-sharing restrictions have been successful. In *First Vagabonds Church of God v. City of Orlando*, the Eleventh Circuit Court of Appeal upheld a municipal ordinance restricting the number of times any person or political organization was allowed to feed large groups of individuals in centrally located parks.[635]

Plaintiffs, Orlando Food Not Bombs and First Vagabonds Church of God, fed large groups of unhoused people two nights a week in downtown Orlando's Lake Eola Park. After receiving complaints from local residents, the city enacted a food-sharing ordinance that required any organization or individual feeding large groups in the Greater Downtown Park District to obtain a permit before doing so, and it limited any individual or group to two permits a year for any park within the district. A large group feeding was defined as any "event intended to attract, attracting, or likely to attract twenty-five (25) or more people[] ... for the delivery or service of food."[636] The City of Orlando enacted the ordinance "to spread the burden that feedings of large groups have on parks and their surrounding neighborhoods."[637]

Plaintiffs argued that the ordinance as applied was an unconstitutional violation of their First Amendment right to free speech and free expression and that their conduct of feeding large groups in public parks was protected. The court assumed that the conduct of feeding individuals in the park was expressive and "entitled to some protection under the First Amendment."[638] But it

---

633. Ibid.
634. Ibid., at 1234.
635. *First Vagabonds Church of God v. City of Orlando*, 638 F.3d 756 (11th Cir. 2011).
636. Ibid., at 759.
637. Ibid., at 758.
638. Ibid., at 760.

found that the ordinance did not violate the First Amendment based on the following reasoning:

> Even when we assume that the feeding of homeless persons is expressive conduct, the ordinance, as applied to Orlando Food Not Bombs, is a reasonable time, place, or manner restriction.... Orlando Food Not Bombs does not contend that the ordinance is content based. The ordinance leaves open ample channels of communication; Orlando Food Not Bombs is not prevented by the ordinance from conducting as many political rallies, demonstrations, distributions of literature, or any other expressive activities as it likes at Lake Eola Park. The ordinance also narrowly furthers the substantial interest of the City in managing its parks and "be[ing] fair to individual neighborhoods" by spreading the burden of the large group feedings.[639]

As such, the court found that the ordinance was "a valid regulation of expressive conduct."[640]

3. Vagrancy and Sleeping Laws

The First Amendment has also been used to challenge vagrancy and sleeping ordinances, to varying degrees of success. Courts have clearly accepted that panhandling constitutes a protected form of speech, yet the line is not so clear when it comes to protecting conduct that only incidentally conveys a message, such as the message of poverty an individual sleeping in a park might express to those passing by. Generally, courts reject First Amendment challenges to anti-vagrancy and anti-sleeping ordinances,[641] but in some contexts, such challenges are successful.

4. Overbroad Regulation of Protected Speech

In *Loper v. New York City Police Dep't*,[642] the Second Circuit Court of Appeals struck down a New York penal statute that criminalized the conduct of loitering for the purpose of begging on the basis that it constituted an over-

---

639. Ibid., 761–62.

640. Ibid., at 762.

641. *Stone v. Agnos*, 960 F.2d 893 (9th Cir. 1992) (sleeping is not protected speech under the First Amendment); *Whiting v. Town of Westerly*, 942 F.2d 18 (1st Cir. 1991) (finding sleeping in public was not expressive conduct protected by the First Amendment); *Roulette v. City of Seattle*, 850 F. Supp. 1442, 1449 (W.D. Wash. 1994).

642. *Loper*, 999 F.2d at 704.

broad regulation of protected speech. Under the statute, which was in effect city-wide, "a person is guilty of loitering when he loiters, remains or wanders about in a public place for the purpose of begging."[643]

The plaintiffs in *Loper* represented a class of plaintiffs "consisting of all 'needy persons who live in the State of New York, who beg on the public streets or in the public parks of New York City,'" and challenged the law on the basis that it was overbroad and in violation of the First Amendment.[644]

The City Police defended the law, explaining it as an "essential tool to address the evils associated with begging on the streets of New York City."[645] They characterized panhandling as criminal conduct that would eventually lead to more serious forms of crime, and suggested that areas frequented by "beggars" and crime are indicative of a decaying social order.[646] The City Police argued that the statute served the compelling government interest in "preventing the fraud, intimidation, coercion, harassment and assaultive conduct that is said frequently to accompany begging by individual street solicitors who do not solicit on behalf of any organization."[647]

The court, however, could find no compelling government interest in a law "excluding those who beg in a peaceful manner from communicating with their fellow citizens."[648] In striking down the law, the court determined that "the total prohibition on begging in the city streets imposed by the statute cannot be characterized as a merely incidental limitation, because it serves to silence both speech and expressive conduct on the basis of the message."[649] The court found the law unconstitutionally overbroad and determined that a "statute that prohibits loitering for the purpose of begging must be considered as providing a restriction greater than is essential to further the government interests listed by the City Police, for it sweeps within its overbroad purview the expressive conduct and speech that the government should have no interest in stifling."[650]

---

643. N.Y. Penal Law § 240.35(1) (McKinney 1989).

644. *Loper*, 999 F.2d at 704 (*quoting Loper v. New York City Police Dep't*, 802 F. Supp. 1029, 1033 (S.D.N.Y. 1992)).

645. *Loper*, 999 F.2d at 701.

646. *Loper*, 802 F. Supp. at 1034–35.

647. *Loper*, 999 F.2d at 705.

648. Ibid.

649. Ibid.

650. Ibid., 705–06.

Loper demonstrates that anti-vagrancy ordinances clearly connected to protected speech can be successfully challenged under the First Amendment, but the holding and application are extremely narrow. As *Roulette v. City of Seattle*, discussed below, demonstrates, courts are hesitant to recognize a First Amendment right to expressive conduct that does not intentionally convey a message. [651]

5. The Limits of Expressive Conduct

In *Roulette v. City of Seattle*, a U.S. Federal District court[652] and the Ninth Circuit Court of Appeals[653] rejected a First Amendment challenge to a Seattle sidewalk ordinance that prohibited an individual from sitting or lying on any public sidewalk within the downtown or commercial area, between the hours of 7 a.m. and 9 p.m. The plaintiff class, comprised of unhoused people, advocates, and several political groups, claimed the ordinance restricted the ability to engage in expressive conduct and that sitting itself can convey a message. The plaintiffs argued that "the mere silent presence of an unkempt and disheveled person sitting or lying on a sidewalk can be expressive conduct protected by the First Amendment because it communicates a message about the person's need for assistance and society's failure or inability to address that need."[654]

The Ninth Circuit dismissed the First Amendment challenge out of hand, on the basis that sitting or lying on the sidewalk does not constitute a protected form of speech or expression. According to the court, sitting or lying on the sidewalk is not "integral to, or commonly associated with, free expression,"[655] and although plaintiffs might intend to engage in expressive conduct while sitting or lying on Seattle's sidewalks, sitting or lying was not a "necessary part of their communicative endeavors" and therefore did not constitute protected speech.[656] The court also found it unnecessary to subject the ordinance to a First Amendment standard of review, because that the ordinance did not "by

---

651. *See Roulette*, 850 F. Supp. at 1449; *Stone v. Agnos*, 960 F.2d 893 (9th Cir. 1992) (plaintiff raised a First Amendment challenge to an anti-sleeping law after he was arrested for sleeping in public; court rejected that sleeping is a form of expression protected by the First Amendment).

652. *Roulette*, 850 F. Supp. at 1449.

653. *Roulette v. City of Seattle*, 97 F.3d 300 (9th Cir. 1996).

654. *Roulette*, 850 F. Supp. at 1449.

655. *Roulette*, 97 F.3d at 304.

656. *Roulette*, 850 F. Supp. at 1449.

its terms" seek to regulate speech or expressive conduct, but merely prohibited sitting or lying on the sidewalk.[657]

The majority made clear that extending First Amendment protections to the conduct of sitting on the sidewalk was far too broad, even though such conduct might incidentally convey a message, and it admonished that recognizing such conduct as expressive would render every action of unhoused people protected under the First Amendment.

While the majority was clearly dismissive of extending First Amendment protections to the type of conduct vagrancy ordinances target, the dissent in *Roulette* suggests that there may be room for such an argument in the future. The *Roulette* dissent makes several compelling arguments to justify the conclusion that the ordinance placed an "unconstitutional burden on free expression in Seattle's key public forums."[658] The dissent took issue with the majority's failure to apply an intermediate scrutiny First Amendment analysis to an ordinance that clearly constituted a content-neutral, time, place, and manner restriction.[659]

In applying its own analysis, the dissent found the majority's conclusion insufficient in three ways: First, the dissent questioned the City's claim that there was a significant governmental interest in passing the sidewalk ordinance to preserve the economic vitality of Seattle's commercial areas, stating, "we should hesitate to accord great weight to 'a perceived public interest in avoiding the aesthetic discomfort of being reminded on a daily basis that many of our fellow citizens are forced to live in abject and degrading poverty.'"[660] Second, although the city claimed it enacted the ordinance to promote public safety, the orderly movement of pedestrians, and to protect the local economy, the ordinance was not narrowly tailored to meet this end.[661] And finally, highlighting that "an alternative forum is inadequate if the speaker is not permitted to reach his intended audience," the dissent argued that the ordinance's restriction on sitting or lying on the sidewalks of Seattle's central commercial districts, deprived unhoused people and their advocates of the use of some of Seat-

---

657. *Roulette*, 97 F.3d at 303–04.

658. Ibid., 311 (Pregerson, J., dissenting).

659. Ibid.

660. Ibid., 309 (Pregerson, J., dissenting), citing *Streetwatch v. National R.R. Passenger Corp.*, 875 F. Supp. 1055, 1066 (S.D.N.Y. 1995) (ruling that Amtrak could not continue to eject people from Pennsylvania Station in New York City simply because they are homeless or appear homeless).

661. *Roulette*, 97 F.3d at 308–09 (Pregerson, J., dissenting).

tle's most dense and diverse public forums, an audience that could be found nowhere else in the city.[662]

Roulette instructs that freedom of expression under the First Amendment must be based on conduct that is intended to send or communicate a message, and not conduct that might incidentally convey a message. For the time being, *Roulette*'s holding may represent the limit of the First Amendment's applicability to freedom of expression in the context of anti-vagrancy ordinances, but the dissent's reasoning presents an alternative approach that may be appropriate as First Amendment jurisprudence evolves.

6. Free Exercise of Religion

Under the Free Exercise Clause of the First Amendment,[663] any law that restricts the free exercise of religion and "substantially burdens the exercise of sincerely held religious beliefs" is subject to strict scrutiny.[664] When such a law is challenged under the First Amendment, the government must show that the law serves a compelling government interest and that it is narrowly tailored to meet that interest.[665] Individuals challenging a law under the Free Exercise Clause need only show that their beliefs are "sincerely held" and regarded as religious by the individual. [666] There is no requirement that the belief be "acceptable, logical, consistent, or comprehensible to others."[667]

In *Fifth Ave. Presbyterian Church v. City of N.Y.*, advocates successfully used the Free Exercise Clause of the First Amendment[668] to challenge enforcement of a New York anti-sleeping law. The plaintiff, Fifth Ave. Presbyterian, a Manhattan church, sought injunctive relief to prevent the City from forcibly removing

---

662. Ibid., 311 (Pregerson, J., dissenting), citing *Bay Area Peace Navy v. United States*, 914 F.2d 1224, 1229 (9th Cir. 1990).

663. "Congress shall make no law respecting an establishment of religion, or prohibiting the free exercise thereof; or abridging the freedom of speech, or of the press; or the right of the people peaceably to assemble, and to petition the government for a redress of grievances." U.S. Const. amend. I.

664. A law restricting free exercise that is "neutral and of general applicability" is subject to rational basis.

665. *Fifth Ave. Presbyterian Church v. City of N.Y.*, 293 F.3d 570, 574 (2d Cir. 2002), citing *Church of Lukumi Babalu Aye v. City of Hialeah*, 508 U.S. 520, 546 (1993).

666. *Fifth Ave. Presbyterian*, 293 F.3d at 574, quoting *Patrick v. Lefevre*, 745 F.2d 153, 156–57 (2d Cir. 1984).

667. Ibid.

668. "Congress shall make no law respecting an establishment of religion, or prohibiting the free exercise thereof...." US Const. amend. 1

unhoused people from the Church's outdoor landing and steps , even though they were sleeping there with the Church's consent. The Second Circuit Court of Appeal accepted the Church's contention that its "outdoor sanctuary forms an integral part of its religious mission and that the police's removal of the homeless interferes with the Church's ministry and homeless outreach program."[669]

Taken together, these cases show how the First Amendment can be used in a variety of ways to successfully advocate for the rights of unhoused people.

D. Fourth Amendment Challenges: Property and Privacy

The Fourth Amendment protects individuals against unreasonable governmental search and seizure and provides that the "right of the people to be secure in their persons, houses, papers, and effects, against unreasonable searches and seizures, shall not be violated."[670] Fourth Amendment protections extend to "warrantless" searches and seizures, and in cases where an exception to the warrant requirement does not apply.[671] However, not all warrantless governmental intrusions are considered unlawful under the Fourth Amendment.[672] For a warrantless search or seizure to be unlawful, it must be "unreasonable."[673] The reasonableness of a search is determined by the area and location of the items searched and the location of the property seized.[674]

The Fourth Amendment is rooted in the notion that the privacy of the home is a sanctuary from governmental intrusion, and the United States Supreme Court has made clear that "[a]t the very core of the Fourth Amendment stands the right of a man to retreat into his own home and there be free from unreasonable governmental intrusion."[675] However, the traditional scope of the Fourth Amendment's protections focus on activities conducted inside rather than outside the home and without consideration that a home might not

---

669. *Fifth Ave. Presbyterian*, 293 F.3d at 574.

670. *Kolender*, 461 U.S. at 363.

671. *Mincey v. Arizona*, 437 U.S. 385, 390 (1978), citing *Katz v. United States*, 389 U.S. 347, 357 (1967) ("The Fourth Amendment proscribes all unreasonable searches and seizures, and it is a cardinal principle that 'searches conducted outside the judicial process, without prior approval by judge or magistrate, are per se unreasonable under the Fourth Amendment—subject only to a few specifically established and well-delineated exceptions.'").

672. *Katz*, 389 U.S. at 347.

673. *Kyllo v. United States*, 533 U.S. 27, 31 (2001) ("With few exceptions, the question whether a warrantless search of a home is reasonable and hence constitutional must be answered no.").

674. *Katz*, 389 U.S. at 347.

675. *Kyllo*, 533 U.S. at 31 (quoting *Silverman v. United States*, 365 U.S. 505, 511 (1961)).

include a house, severely limiting for unhoused people the right to the basic protections the Fourth Amendment provides.[676]

Unhoused people's vulnerability and status in society, which in part stem from the fact that they do not have access to private spaces, makes them particularly susceptible to having their Fourth Amendment rights violated. The Fourth Amendment is implicated in cases involving sweeps of homeless encampments, warrantless searches of unhoused people and their belongings, and the warrantless seizure of property and of unhoused people themselves.[677]

Street sweeps of homeless encampments are commonplace, as are laws against storing personal belongings in public, making unhoused people extremely vulnerable to losing what little property they own.[678] Cities commonly rely on camping bans, prohibitions on the obstruction of public walkways, and laws prohibiting the public storage of belongings to legitimize the practice of street sweeps and destruction of belongings.[679] While public sanitation and safety are legitimate government interests, constitutional protections limit how the government achieves those ends. However, without procedures in place to ensure that unhoused people and their belongings are treated lawfully, government practices frequently violate the Fourth Amendment.

Legal advocates are essential to ensuring that government policies and ordinance enforcement procedures comply with constitutional requirements. As the cases below demonstrate, legal advocates have been successful in using the Fourth Amendment to enforce compliance with minimum constitutional standards.[680]

---

676. David A. Sklansky, "Back to the Future: Kyllo, Katz, and Common Law," 72 *Miss. L.J.* (2002): 143, 192 (commenting on the uneven distribution of Fourth Amendment's protection of privacy rights, writing "rich people have bigger and more comfortable homes than poor people; it is therefore much easier for rich people than for poor people to stay home when engaged in activities they wish to keep private. Granting homes more privacy than other places therefore tilts Fourth Amendment protection in favor of the rich and against the poor, who are forced to conduct much of their lives outside of their residences.").

677. In some instances, police have adopted the practice of illegally seizing and forcibly removing unhoused people from downtown areas and relocating them to remote locations where they are then left. See e.g. *Clements v. City of Cleveland*, No. 94-CV-2074 (N.D. Ohio 1994); *Johnson v. Freeman*, 351 F. Supp. 2d 929 (E.D. Mo. 2004) (unlawful seizure of unhoused people).

678. *No Safe Place*, 26.

679. Ibid.

680. See e.g. *Allen v. City of Pomona*, No. 16-cv-1859 (C.D. Cal. filed Mar. 18, 2016); *Lavan v. City of L.A.*, 693 F.3d 1022, 1028 (9th Cir. 2012); *Pottinger*, 810 F. Supp. at 1571.

1. Search or Seizure

"A 'search' occurs when an expectation of privacy that society is prepared to consider reasonable is infringed. A 'seizure' of property occurs when there is some meaningful interference with an individual's possessory interests in that property."[681] Whether the challenged government conduct is a *search* or a *seizure* is an important distinction, because each is analyzed under a different constitutional test.

Courts generally apply a "reasonable expectation of privacy test" to determine whether a warrantless search has violated the Fourth Amendment. Under this test, courts first consider whether an individual has "manifested a subjective expectation of privacy in the object of the challenged search," and second whether society is "willing to recognize that expectation as reasonable."[682] A warrantless search is considered unlawful when an individual has both a subjective and objective expectation of privacy in the area being searched.

In determining whether a warrantless seizure of property is lawful, courts look at whether the government has engaged in "some meaningful interference" with an individual's possessory interest in the property.[683] Put another way, "the Fourth Amendment protects possessory and liberty interests even when privacy rights are not implicated."[684]

While these principles are straightforward in the context of a traditional home, the lines blur when the area searched or the thing seized is outside of the traditional scope of what is meant by "home" or when people claim a right to privacy within that public space. While the reasonable expectation of privacy test is dominant, Fourth Amendment jurisprudence also includes a trespass element that has been "understood to embody a particular concern for government trespass upon the areas it enumerates," including persons, houses, papers, and effects.[685]

The Supreme Court has held that the reasonable expectation of privacy test does "not erode the principle that, when the Government does engage in physical intrusion of a constitutionally protected area in order to obtain information, that intrusion may constitute a violation of the Fourth Amend-

---

681. *United States v. Jacobsen*, 466 U.S. 109, 113 (1984).

682. *United States v. Sandoval*, 200 F.3d 659, 660 (9th Cir. 2000) (citing *California v. Ciraolo*, 476 U.S. 207, 211 (1986).

683. *Lavan*, 693 F.3d at 1028.

684. Ibid.

685. *United States v. Jones*, 565 U.S. 400, 406 (2012).

ment."[686] This means that although the "expectation of privacy test" originally extended the traditional reach of the Fourth Amendment to areas outside the home, there is no requirement for courts to apply this test when the "subject of the search was persons, houses, papers or effects."[687] The caveat is that many courts have determined that the place searched is "highly relevant to the fourth amendment analysis because 'expectations of privacy in some places are afforded greater constitutional legitimacy than in others.'"[688]

This all may sound confusing because it is. Courts commonly confuse these distinctions, as seen in the cases that follow. Courts are inconsistent in how they interpret the extent to which the Fourth Amendment applies to individuals claiming a privacy right in public spaces, which is particularly relevant in the context of homeless advocacy.

Because an unhoused individual's temporary shelter is not considered a "home" in the traditional sense, and because unhoused people are forced to store their belongings in public, courts have grappled with how and to what extent Fourth Amendment protections apply to the property and shelter of unhoused people.[689] Some jurisdictions have found that Fourth Amendment protections do not extend to the shelter and belongings of individuals living on public property without permission.[690] Other jurisdictions have found that Fourth Amendment protections do extend to property and temporary shelters located on public property, regardless of whether the individual has permission to camp in a particular location.[691] Some courts base their determination

---

686. *Jones*, 565 U.S. at 407 (internal citations omitted, quoting *United States v. Knotts*, 460 U.S. 276, 286 (1983)).

687. *United States v. Duenas*, 691 F.3d 1070, 1080–81 (9th Cir. 2012), quoting *Katz v. United States*, 389 U.S. 347 (1967).

688. *State v. Mooney*, 218 Conn. 85, 94–95 (1991); see also *United States v. Ruckman*, 806 F.2d 1471, 1473 (10th Cir. 1986).

689. See e.g. *Ruckman*, 806 F.2d 1471.

690. *Amezquita v. Hernandez-Colon*, 518 F.2d 8 (1st Cir. 1975) (finding the destruction of the squatters' homes did not violate the Fourth Amendment, because they were trespassing, had been told to leave, and therefore had no reasonable expectation of privacy); *Ruckman*, 806 F.2d at 1472–73 (finding an individual had no reasonable expectation of privacy in a cave because "a trespasser on federal lands and subject to immediate ejectment.... Ruckman's subjective expectation of privacy [was] not reasonable in light of the fact that he could be ousted by [Bureau of Land Management] authorities from the place he was occupying at any time."); c.f. *Sandoval*, 200 F.3d at 661 (defendant's subjective expectation of privacy in his tent led to the determination that his expectation of privacy was objectively reasonable, despite the fact that he was trespassing on government land).

691. *Sandoval*, 200 F.3d at 660; *Lavan*, 693 F.3d at 1022.

on whether the property in question can be considered abandoned, making Fourth Amendment protections inapplicable.[692]

The following cases demonstrate how courts have treated Fourth Amendment challenges to the warrantless searches of the shelter, belongings, and bodies of unhoused people, and the warrantless seizure of property.

2. Unlawful Seizure: Seizure as a Property, Not Privacy Issue

In *Lavan v. City of Los Angeles*, a group of nine plaintiffs, all unhoused residents of the Skid Row area in Los Angeles, sued under the Fourth and Fourteenth Amendments for injunctive relief against the City's practice of seizing and destroying the unabandoned belongings of residents while they attended to necessary tasks such as eating, showering, and using restrooms.[693] On appeal from the City, the Ninth Circuit affirmed that the City violated the Fourth Amendment rights of the plaintiffs when it seized and immediately destroyed their personal property, which included items such as personal identification documents, birth certificates, medications, family memorabilia, toiletries, cell phones, sleeping bags, and blankets. These items were stored in clearly marked mobile containers that social service organizations provided to Skid Row residents for the purpose of storing and transporting belongings. According to the statement of facts:

> On separate occasions between February 6, 2011 and March 17, 2011, [plaintiffs] stepped away from their personal property, leaving it on the sidewalks, to perform necessary tasks such as showering, eating, using restrooms, or attending court. [Plaintiffs] had not abandoned their property, but City employees nonetheless seized and summarily destroyed [plaintiffs'] EDARs[694] and carts[695], thereby permanently depriving [them] of possessions ranging from personal identification documents and family memorabilia to portable electronics, blankets,

---

692. *United States v. Edwards*, 644 F.2d 1, 2 (5th Cir. 1981).

693. *Lavan*, 693 F.3d at 1024.

694. "EDARs are small, collapsible mobile shelters provided to unhoused people by Everyone Deserves a Roof, a nonprofit organization. EDARs are intended to address the chronic shortage of housing faced by unhoused people in Los Angeles. Former Los Angeles City Mayor Richard Riordan spent the night of Saturday, November 6, 2010 in an EDAR on Skid Row to demonstrate how the shelters could be used by the homeless population residing there." *Lavan*, 693 F.3d at 1025 n.4.

695. The carts were provided by the Los Angeles Catholic Worker organization and bore distinctive features identifying them as such. *Lavan*, 693 F.3d at 1025.

and shelters. City did not have a good-faith belief that [plaintiffs'] possessions were abandoned when it destroyed them. Indeed, on a number of the occasions when the City seized [plaintiffs'] possessions, [plaintiffs] and other persons were present, explained to City employees that the property was not abandoned, and implored the City not to destroy it. Although "the City was in fact notified that the property belonged to Lamoen Hall[696] and others, . . . when attempts to retrieve the property were made, the City took it and destroyed it nevertheless."[697]

In defense of this practice, the City maintained that the seizure and disposal of plaintiffs' property was authorized under a local ordinance[698] prohibiting individuals from leaving property on "any parkway or sidewalk."[699] The City argued that the Fourth Amendment did not apply to the seizure and destruction of plaintiffs' property, because there was no reasonable expectation of privacy in belongings left unattended on public sidewalks.

However, the court held that the "expectation of privacy" standard does not apply in the context of the warrantless seizure of property, because "the Fourth Amendment protects possessory and liberty interests even when privacy rights are not implicated."[700] A warrantless seizure is unreasonable when there is some "meaningful [governmental] interference with an individual's possessory interest" in their property.[701] "[B]y seizing and destroying [plaintiffs'] unabandoned legal papers, shelters, and personal effects, the City meaningfully interfered with [their] possessory interests in that property. No more is necessary to trigger the Fourth Amendment's reasonableness requirement."[702]

Additionally, the court held that the "violation of a city ordinance does not vitiate the Fourth Amendment's protection of one's property. Were it otherwise, the government could seize and destroy any illegally parked car or unlawfully unattended dog without implicating the Fourth Amendment."[703]

Lavan is an important case in homeless advocacy because it distinguishes the Fourth Amendment's protection against unreasonable searches from its

---

696. Lamoen Hall was one of the plaintiffs named in the suit.
697. *Lavan*, 693 F.3d at 1025.
698. Los Angeles Municipal Code § 56.11,
699. *Lavan*, 693 F.3d at 1026.
700. Ibid., 1027–28.
701. Ibid., 1028.
702. Ibid., 1030.
703. Ibid.

protection against unreasonable seizures. That is, the *Lavan* court suggests that even in the context of a search, the property analysis should apply when that search involves "persons, houses, papers, [or] effects."[704] This separation of privacy interests from property interests underscores that, while it may be unreasonable to expect privacy in public spaces, the right to control property remains unaffected.

For example, compare *Lavan* with *Pottinger v. Miami* (the same *Pottinger v. Miami* discussed in the Eighth Amendment context). In *Pottinger*, the District Court for the Southern District of Florida considered whether the seizure and destruction of plaintiffs' property was unreasonable under the Fourth Amendment. The *Pottinger* court subjected the seizure of plaintiffs' property to both a property and a privacy analysis but focused on "whether an individual has a legitimate privacy interest in property that is seized in a public area."[705]

Plaintiffs were found to have a subjectively reasonable expectation of privacy because they "maintain[ed] their belongings—e.g., bags or boxes of personal effects and bedrolls—in a manner strongly manifesting an expectation of privacy."[706] The organization and arrangement of property "in a manner that suggests ownership, for example, by placing their belongings against a tree or other object or by covering them with a pillow or blanket," was an additional factor that made the property of unhoused people clearly distinguishable from abandoned property, which the Fourth Amendment does not protect.[707]

The *Pottinger* court recognized that whether society recognizes an expectation of privacy as reasonable depends on whether the person occupying the property is a trespasser or is rightfully allowed to be there, and whether the property is left in such a state that it is readily accessible and exposed to the public.[708] However, it emphasized that while those factors were "relevant as helpful guides," "they should not be undertaken mechanistically" but merely "aid in evaluating the ultimate question in all fourth amendment cases—whether the

---

704. Ibid. ("[E]ven if we were to analyze the reasonableness of the City's search of Plaintiffs' belongings, we would still apply the Fourth Amendment's requirement that the search be reasonable—irrespective of any privacy interest—because the City searched Plaintiffs' 'persons, houses, papers, [or] effects.'").

705. *Pottinger*, 810 F. Supp. at 1571.

706. Ibid.

707. Ibid.

708. Ibid.

defendant had a legitimate expectation of privacy, in the eyes of our society, in the area searched."[709]

The court ultimately chose not to base plaintiffs' privacy rights on their status as trespassers and looked instead to cases that had recognized a right to privacy in closed containers, finding that the right to privacy for unhoused people in their personal effects is specific to their unique circumstances. The court wrote: "the interior of the bedrolls and bags or boxes of personal effects belonging to unhoused people in this case is perhaps the last trace of privacy they have. In addition, the property of unhoused people is often located in the parks or under the overpasses that they consider their homes.... [U]nder the circumstances of this case, it appears that society is prepared to recognize plaintiffs' expectation of privacy in their personal property as reasonable."

Lavan and *Pottinger* demonstrate that courts can use different reasoning to come to the same conclusion. The cases below demonstrate that courts are equally inconsistent in the realm of unlawful search of unhoused people's property.

3. Unlawful Search

An array of factors that vary by jurisdiction determine the extent to which the Fourth Amendment protects unhoused people and their property against warrantless searches. Some courts have found that the Fourth Amendment does not apply to the property of unhoused people, especially if the individual was asked to vacate the area on previous occasions.[710] Courts also look at whether an individual has a "legitimate expectation of privacy in the invaded place"[711] and whether the property subject to the search is abandoned.[712]

4. Trespass

In *United States v. Sandoval*, the Ninth Circuit considered whether the warrantless search of Sandoval's makeshift tent, located on Federal Bureau of Land Management (BLM) land, violated the Fourth Amendment. The court found that the search was unreasonable and in violation of the Fourteenth Amendment. In doing so, the court rejected the government's main argument—that Sandoval

---

709. Ibid., 1572.

710. *Sandoval*, 200 F.3d at 659; *People v. Nishi*, 207 Cal. App. 4th 954 (2012).

711. *State v. Mooney*, 218 Conn. 85, 98 (Conn. March 19, 1991), quoting *Rakas v. Illinois*, 439 U.S. 128, 143 (1978).

712. *Pottinger*, 810 F. Supp. at 1551.

could not have a reasonable expectation of privacy in the shelter because it was located on public property and Sandoval was not authorized to camp there.[713]

The court determined that the "the reasonableness of Sandoval's expectation of privacy [does not] turn on whether he had permission to camp on public land. Such a distinction would mean that a camper who overstayed his permit in a public campground would lose his Fourth Amendment rights, while his neighbor, whose permit had not expired, would retain those rights."[714] Although Sandoval did not have permission to camp in the area, "he was never instructed to vacate or risk eviction, and... whether Sandoval was legally permitted to be on the land was a matter in dispute."[715]

It was clear to the court that Sandoval had a subjective expectation of privacy—the tent was in a secluded, overgrown area that was well hidden from view, the tent itself was enclosed on all four sides, and its interior could not be viewed from the outside. The court was less clear about why Sandoval had an objective expectation of privacy. Rather than laying out a principle that other courts could apply in the future, the court distinguished *Sandoval* from a case involving a trespasser who was found *not* to have a reasonable expectation of privacy in the home in which he was squatting. The court distinguished *Sandoval* on two grounds: First, because public lands are often unmarked, society would more readily recognize the privacy expectation of a camper on public land than those of a squatter in a private residence. Second, the squatter was told to vacate the premises on multiple occasions, whereas Sandoval was not asked to leave before his arrest.

To summarize, *Sandoval* establishes that a reasonable expectation of privacy in a shelter located on public land does not depend on whether the individual had permission to camp in the area, but on whether the individual was told to leave on a previous occasion. Unfortunately, *Sandoval* did not articulate a clear principle or standard for courts to follow. In fact, due to this lack of clarity, later cases have eroded *Sandoval's* main holding.

Several years after *Sandoval,* in *People v. Nishi,* a California Court of Appeal upheld the warrantless search of Nishi's makeshift shelter, located in a public nature reserve, because he did not have a camping permit to stay in the area.[716] Although the court considered several factors—including whether Nishi had a

---

713. *Sandoval,* 200 F.3d at 660.
714. Ibid., 661.
715. Ibid.
716. *People v. Nishi,* 207 Cal. App. 4th 954.

subjective expectation of privacy in the tarped area immediately surrounding his shelter and the fact that he had been told to vacate other campsites within the park—the "most significant, and ultimately controlling, factor... is that defendant was not lawfully or legitimately on the premises where the search was conducted."[717] Nishi "was not in a position to legitimately consider the campsite—or the belongings kept there—as a place society recognized as private to him. Nor did he have the right to exclude others from that place. He had no ownership, lawful possession, or lawful control of the premises searched."[718]

What *Sandoval* and its erosion in *Nishi* means moving forward in the context of warrantless searches on the tents, encampments, or belongings of unhoused people in public places is unclear. The extent to which the Fourth Amendment protects the right to privacy in makeshift dwellings in other jurisdictions is equally unclear. For example, the Colorado Supreme Court in *People v. Schafer* determined that "a person camping in Colorado on unimproved and apparently unused land that is not fenced or posted against trespassing, and in the absence of personal notice against trespass, has a reasonable expectation of privacy in a tent used for habitation and personal effects therein."[719] This reasoning is consistent with *Sandoval*.

In contrast, the Tenth Circuit Court of Appeals in *United States v. Ruckman*,[720] determined that Ruckman had no reasonable expectation of privacy in a cave located on BLM land that he had lived in for several months. In the court's view, Ruckman was a "trespasser... and subject to immediate ejectment," and, as such, his expectation of privacy was not reasonable.[721] The court also took issue with the fact that Ruckman's cave could not be considered a "house" for Fourth Amendment purposes.

The *Ruckman* dissent, which is frequently cited in defense of the Fourth Amendment rights of "trespassers," made several compelling arguments.[722] First, the dissent questioned the court's distinction between the privacy afforded to a temporary shelter, and that afforded to a house. In the dissent's view, the court "implicitly assumes that only homes and houses are accorded fourth amendment protection" and failed "to appreciate both the underlying, broader

---

717. Ibid., 961.
718. Ibid.
719. *People v. Schafer*, 946 P.2d 938 (Colo. 1997).
720. *Ruckman*, 806 F.2d at 1471.
721. *Ruckman*, 806 F.2d at 1472–73.
722. Ibid., 1475.

concerns of the fourth amendment and the ramifications its opinion will have in other contexts."[723] Second, the dissent argued that Ruckman's status as a trespasser should not be the deciding factor:[724]

> The court takes a giant step backward in fourth amendment analysis when it hinges its determination of whether Mr. Ruckman had a legitimate expectation of privacy in his dwelling on whether or not he was a "trespasser...."[725]
>
> Recognizing that, in our modern society, the fourth amendment protects people, not places... what a person seeks to preserve as private, even in an area accessible to the public, may be constitutionally protected....[726] In other words, failing to have a legal property right in the invaded place does not, ipso facto, mean that no legitimate expectation of privacy can attach to that place....[727]
>
> [Ruckman's] expectation of privacy in his wilderness home was both reasonable and legitimate. It was perfectly legitimate for him to expect to be free from a warrantless search of the dwelling in which he lived continuously for eight months....[728]
>
> This finding... means that the Government may not search his dwelling without a search warrant, as prescribed by the fourth amendment, or without sufficient justification excusing the warrant. The fact that Mr. Ruckman may have violated a federal law by living in this cave (a fact not established by this record) simply does not strip him of all his constitutional rights....[729]

The *Ruckman* dissent has been used since to defend the Fourth Amendment rights of unhoused people in their temporary homes, regardless of the legality of their presence in a particular location. Of course, this protection is not limitless—courts have made clear that society is unwilling to extend Fourth Amendment protections to individuals trespassing on private property, or at least not in private homes.[730]

---

723. Ibid., 1476.

724. Ibid.

725. Ibid., 1476–77.

726. Ibid., 1477.

727. Ibid.

728. Ibid., 1478.

729. Ibid.

730. *Sandoval*, 200 F.3d at 661, citing *Zimmerman v. Bishop Estate*, 25 F.3d 784, 787–88 (9th Cir. 1993).

5. Abandoned Property in the Context of Search

Courts have long recognized that an individual has no right to object to the warrantless search of property that has been deemed abandoned.[731] The test for abandonment of property is whether an individual has "voluntarily discarded, left behind, or otherwise relinquished his interest in the property" such that it would be unreasonable to have an expectation of privacy in the property at the time of the search.[732] Whether an individual has relinquished the expectation of privacy is "a question of intent" which can be inferred from the surrounding circumstances, including "words spoken, acts done, and other objective facts."[733]

In *State v. Mooney*, the Connecticut Supreme Court considered whether Mooney had a Fourth Amendment right to privacy in a cardboard box and duffel bag located in an area under a bridge abutment that Mooney considered to be his home. The state argued that Mooney had "abandoned any reasonable expectation of privacy in those goods by leaving them in a place accessible to the public, and that he could not reasonably expect that his possessions would remain shielded from the curiosity of passersby or from the scrutiny of the police."[734] Mooney made two Fourth Amendment arguments. First he argued that he had a legitimate expectation of privacy in the area, because although not a typical home in the sense that it had four walls and a roof, he treated the area as such, had exclusive possession in the area because he lived there alone, and "was no less entitled to privacy under the fourth amendment because he was homeless than are the more fortunate members of society."[735] In response to this, the state argued the following:

> The defendant had no reasonable expectation of privacy in the area...[because] the area in question was not protected by the fourth amendment because: (1) it was in effect an open field [open fields, even on private property, have been traditionally excluded from Fourth Amendment protection]; (2) the defendant was not legitimately residing there, but was an interloper on public land; and (3) it was an area

---

731. *Edwards*, 644 F.2d at 2.
732. Ibid., quoting *United States v. Colbert*, 474 F.2d 174, 176 (5th Cir. 1973).
733. *United States v. Kendall*, 655 F.2d 199, 201 (9th Cir. 1981).
734. *State v. Mooney*, 218 Conn. 85, 98 (Conn. 1991).
735. Ibid., at 93.

accessible to the public at large, and thus was by its nature incapable of sheltering a reasonable expectation of privacy.[736]

The court rejected Mooney's first argument based on the state's reasoning, which was consistent with other cases involving trespassers in general. However, the court accepted Mooney's second and much narrower argument, that he had a reasonable expectation of privacy in the contents of the duffel bag and cardboard box found in the area.[737] In the court's view, Mooney's argument presented a clear tension "between, on one hand, the deference ordinarily afforded to expectations of privacy in luggage and other appropriate closed containers and, on the other hand, the proposition that property left by persons in open fields or public places may not command fourth amendment protection."[738] The court settled on a narrow view of the issue, and limited its inquiry to the following:

> Whether the fourth amendment applies to the unique factual circumstances of this case, where the closed containers were found by the police in a secluded place that they knew the defendant regarded as his home, where the defendant's absence from that place at the time of the search was due to his arrest and custody by the police, and where the purpose of the search was to obtain evidence of the crimes for which he was in custody.[739]

The court's consideration of whether Mooney's expectation of privacy was reasonable was "a fact-specific inquiry," and, although the luggage was found on public land and Mooney was a trespasser, those facts were not dispositive.[740] The court reasoned that Mooney had a reasonable expectation of privacy in the duffel bag and the box because: First, the "place" searched was the interior of a closed duffel bag and box, areas traditionally afforded a high degree of deference to expectations of privacy. Second, the containers were in a place that Mooney regarded and maintained as his home. Third, because he was not present at the time the search occurred, he was unable to assert his Fourth

---

736. Ibid., 93–94.
737. Ibid.
738. Ibid., 99.
739. Ibid., 100–01.
740. Ibid., 110–11.

Amendment rights in the luggage. Fourth, the purpose of the search was to gather evidence of criminal activity.[741]

Mooney is useful to advocates for several reasons: first, it moves the inquiry of the search from the spatial notion of *place*, which in this case would be the public property of the abutment under the bridge, to the physical item searched, in this case the luggage. This view transfers the subject of the search to the interior of the luggage itself. This is meaningful when looking at trespass and abandonment cases, because it can mean that although the item searched is physically located in an area accessible to public (which might implicate an abandonment or an open field argument), or in a location on which the individual who owns the item is not authorized to be (in other words is a trespasser), the content of the item itself is still subject to Fourth Amendment protections.[742]

E. Fourteenth Amendment Due Process

The Due Process and Equal Protection Clauses of the Fourteenth Amendment provide that no state shall "deprive any person of life, liberty, or property, without due process of law; nor deny to any person within its jurisdiction the equal protection of the laws." Laws can violate due process when they fail to set forth clear legal standards so that "ordinary people can understand what conduct is prohibited and in a manner that does not encourage arbitrary and discriminatory enforcement."[743] This aspect of due process is known as the "void-for-vagueness" doctrine. [744]

Vagueness can be used to challenge a law for two independent reasons. First, if a law fails "to provide the kind of notice that will enable ordinary people to understand what conduct it prohibits," and second, if a law is ambiguous to the extent that it "may authorize and even encourage arbitrary and discrimi-

---

741. Ibid., 111.

742. Compare *Mooney* with *United States v. Wilson*, 984 F. Supp. 2d 676 (E.D. Ky. 2013), in which the court determined a homeless individual did not have a reasonable expectation of privacy in a suitcase found near an encampment located in the wooded area of a cemetery, because although he had a subjective expectation of privacy in the suitcase, it was not objectively reasonable because he had not locked the suitcase and had not completely hidden it from view.

743. *Kolender*, 461 U.S. at 357.

744. Ibid., 357–58.

natory enforcement."[745] Void-for-vagueness is meant to ensure that individuals know exactly what conduct the law prohibits and to ensure that discretionary enforcement cannot sweep a broad range of non-criminal activity within the scope of the law.

Equal protection requires that laws be applied equally to everyone, meaning that law enforcement cannot choose to enforce laws in a discriminatory manner. "Even when a law is nondiscriminatory on its face, equal protection is violated if the law is applied in a manner that discriminates against a particular group."[746] However, to establish that an ordinance violates equal protection, "it is not enough to show that the ordinance has a disproportionate impact upon the homeless…. A law neutral on its face yet having a disproportionate effect on the group will be deemed to violate the Equal Protection Clause only if a discriminatory purpose can be proven."[747]

The Fourteenth Amendment can be used to challenge any anti-homeless law that is considered vague or discriminatory but is most successful in challenging vagrancy laws. Laws prohibiting loitering, loafing, and vagrancy cover activities such as "standing idly," sitting or standing in one area for too long, "standing about aimlessly" and "hanging around."[748] Thirty-three percent of cities have city-wide bans on loitering in public, which means that the mere presence of unhoused people within the city is banned, unless they are in motion.[749] Cities commonly enforce these laws selectively against unhoused people and choose not to enforce them against the general public.[750] The cases below illustrate the different contexts in which the Fourteenth Amendment has been used to challenge anti-homeless ordinances.

1. Void-for-Vagueness

In *Kolender v. Lawson*,[751] the United States Supreme Court considered whether a criminal anti-vagrancy law requiring "persons who loiter or wander on the streets to provide a 'credible and reliable' identification and to account

---

745. *Desertrain v. City of L.A.*, 754 F.3d 1147, 1155 (9th Cir. 2014).

746. *Allen v. City of Sacramento*, 234 Cal. App. 4th 41, 62–63 (2015).

747. *Joel*, 232 F.3d at 1359, citing *Joyce v. City & County of San Francisco*, 846 F. Supp. 843, 858 (N.D. Cal. 1994).

748. *No Safe Place*, 21.

749. *No Safe Place*, 21.

750. Berkeley Law Policy Advocacy Clinic, *California's New Vagrancy Laws: The Growing Enactment and Enforcement of Anti-Homeless Laws in the Golden State*, February 2015.

751. *Kolender*, 461 U.S. at 357.

for their presence when requested by a peace officer"[752] was unconstitutionally vague within the meaning of the Due Process Clause of the Fourteenth Amendment. Lawson, who was detained or arrested under the law fifteen times between 1975 and 1977, mounted a facial challenge to the law on the basis that it failed to clarify what was meant by the requirement that an individual provide a "credible and reliable" identification.[753] The statutes required an individual stopped by law enforcement to provide "'credible and reliable' identification that carries a 'reasonable assurance' of its authenticity, and that provides 'means for later getting in touch with the person who has identified himself.'"[754] In addition, officers could also ask individuals to "account for their presence… to the extent it assists in producing credible and reliable identification."[755]

The law, which afforded full discretion to law enforcement in determining whether the identification provided was sufficient, provided "a convenient tool for harsh and discriminatory enforcement by local prosecuting officials, against particular groups deemed to merit their displeasure, and confer[ed] on police a virtually unrestrained power to arrest and charge persons with a violation."[756] Because the law failed to specify how an individual could satisfy the identification requirement, and therefore encouraged arbitrary enforcement, the court found the law unconstitutionally vague under the Fourteenth Amendment.[757]

In *Desertrain v. City of Los Angeles*, four plaintiffs challenged a Los Angeles law that prohibited the use of a vehicle on any public street "as living quarters either overnight, day-by-day, or otherwise."[758] Officers enforcing the law were given informal training and internal policy memorandums directing them to look for vehicles that contained possessions "normally found in a home, such as food, bedding, clothing, medicine, and basic necessities," and were instructed that individuals did not need to be found sleeping or ever to have slept in their vehicles to violate the law. Officers were directed to "issue a warning and to provide information concerning local shelters on the first instance of a violation, to issue a citation on the second instance, and to make an arrest on the third."[759]

---

752. Cal. Penal Code § 647(e) (1970).

753. *Kolender*, 461 U.S. at 353–54.

754. Ibid., at 359–60, citing *People v. Solomon*, 33 Cal. App. 3d 429, 438 (1973).

755. Ibid.

756. Ibid., at 360 (1983), quoting *Papachristou v. City of Jacksonville*, 405 U.S. 156, 170 (1972).

757. Ibid., at 361.

758. *Desertrain*, 754 F.3d at 1149, citing Los Angeles Municipal Code § 85.02.

759. Ibid.

The plaintiffs, Steve Jacobs-Elstein, Chris Taylor, Patricia Warivonchik, and William Cagle were each cited or arrested for engaging in different activities the arresting officer alleged had violated the law. Jacobs-Elstein was told on various occasions that his conduct, which included sitting in his car while waiting for a local church to open and sitting in his car while talking on his phone, violated the law.[760] Jacobs-Elstein was eventually arrested, as he was exiting his vehicle. Each time officers confronted him about the law, he had personal belongings stored in his car.[761]

At the time Taylor was arrested for violating the law, he was sitting in his car to get out of the rain. Although he had very few belongings in the vehicle and offered proof that he slept at a local shelter instead of in his car, officers arrested him anyway.[762] Warivonchik, who legally parked and slept in her RV at a local church parking lot, was pulled over for failing to use her turn signal, and was given a written warning for violating the vehicle-dwelling law and was told she "would be arrested if ever seen again in Venice with her RV."[763] Cagle, whose vehicle contained personal belongings at the time he was cited under the law, informed officers he had not been sleeping in his vehicle. Officers told him he did not need to sleep in the vehicle to violate the law and cited him anyway.[764]

The Ninth Circuit found that the law violated both prongs of the void-for-vagueness doctrine. Not only did the law fail to clearly state the precise conduct that the law prohibited, but it also allowed for arbitrary and discriminatory enforcement. Under the law,

> Plaintiffs [were] left guessing as to what behavior would subject them to citation and arrest by an officer. Is it impermissible to eat food in a vehicle? Is it illegal to keep a sleeping bag? Canned food? Books? What about speaking on a cell phone? Or staying in the car to get out of the rain? These are all actions Plaintiffs were taking when arrested for violation of the ordinance, all of which are otherwise perfectly legal. And despite Plaintiffs' repeated attempts to comply with [the law], there appears to be nothing they can do to avoid violating the statute short of discarding all of their possessions or their vehicles, or leaving

---

760. Ibid., at 1150.
761. Ibid., at 1151.
762. Ibid.
763. Ibid.
764. Ibid., at 1152.

Los Angeles entirely. All in all, this broad and cryptic statute criminalizes innocent behavior, making it impossible for citizens to know how to keep their conduct within the pale....[765]

[The law] is broad enough to cover any driver in Los Angeles who eats food or transports personal belongings in his or her vehicle. Yet it appears to be applied only to the homeless. The vagueness doctrine is designed specifically to prevent this type of selective enforcement, in which a "'net [can] be cast at large, to enable men to be caught who are vaguely undesirable in the eyes of the police and prosecution, although not chargeable in any particular offense.'"[766]

Desertrain is only one of many cases that have struck down anti-vagrancy statutes as vague. Courts have long recognized that vagrancy laws have historically been used to "roundup...so-called 'undesirables,' resulting in 'a regime in which the poor and the unpopular [we]re permitted to stand on a public sidewalk...only at the whim of any police officer.'"[767] In *Papachristou v. City of Jacksonville*, the U.S. Supreme Court struck down a Jacksonville vagrancy statute as vague, commenting that the motivation to prevent future criminality, "the common justification for the presence of vagrancy statutes," was incompatible with the U.S. Constitution.[768] The court in *Papachristou* wrote of the statute,

Those generally implicated by the imprecise terms of the ordinance—poor people, nonconformists, dissenters, idlers—may be required to comport themselves according to the lifestyle deemed appropriate by the Jacksonville police and the courts. Where, as here, there are no standards governing the exercise of the discretion granted by the ordinance, the scheme permits and encourages an arbitrary and discriminatory enforcement of the law. It furnishes a convenient tool for "harsh and discriminatory enforcement by local prosecuting officials, against particular groups deemed to merit their displeasure." It results in a regime in which the poor and the unpopular are permitted to "stand on a public sidewalk...only at the whim of any police officer."[769]

---

765. Ibid., at 1155–56.
766. Ibid., at 1156.
767. Ibid., at 1157, citing *Papachristou*, 405 U.S. at 170.
768. *Papachristou*, 405 U.S. at 169.
769. Ibid., at 170, quoting *Thornhill v. Alabama*, 310 U.S. 88, 97–98 (1940), and *Shuttlesworth v. Birmingham*, 382 U.S. 87 (1965).

A presumption that people who might walk or loaf or loiter or stroll or frequent houses where liquor is sold, or who are supported by their wives or who look suspicious to the police are to become future criminals is too precarious for a rule of law. The implicit presumption in these generalized vagrancy standards—that crime is being nipped in the bud—is too extravagant to deserve extended treatment. Of course, vagrancy statutes are useful to the police. Of course, they are nets making easy the roundup of so-called undesirables. But the rule of law implies equality and justice in its application. Vagrancy laws of the Jacksonville type teach that the scales of justice are so tipped that even-handed administration of the law is not possible. The rule of law, evenly applied to minorities as well as majorities, to the poor as well as the rich, is the great mucilage that holds society together.[770]

2. Equal Protection

The plaintiff in *Joel v. City of Orlando* challenged an anti-camping law under the Fourteenth Amendment's Equal Protection Clause on the basis that it encouraged "discriminatory, oppressive and arbitrary enforcement."[771] Although Joel presented evidence that at least 98 percent of those arrested under the ordinance were unhoused, the court rejected the equal protection challenge because Joel failed to prove that the law was enacted for the purpose of discriminating against the unhoused.[772]

Similarly, in *Davison v. City of Tucson*, a Federal District Court for the District of Arizona rejected plaintiffs' argument that an anti-camping law violated equal protection. Reaffirming that no court has recognized unhoused people as a suspect class, "the level of scrutiny to be applied to government action that discriminates on the basis of homelessness is rational review."[773] Finding compelling the city's stated purpose for enacting the law, which was out of "concerns for crime, sanitation, aesthetics, and unhoused people's use of fire," the court held that the law withstood rational basis review.

770. Ibid., at 170–71.
771. *Joel*, 232 F.3d at 1359.
772. Ibid.
773. *Davison v. City of Tucson*, 924 F. Supp. 989, 994 (D. Ariz. 1996).

3. Status

It is worth noting briefly that due process has also been used to challenge anti-vagrancy "disorderly persons" laws, on the basis that the effect of such laws was to make the *status* of poverty a crime. Two Nevada Supreme Court cases dealt with this issue. In *Reno v. Second Judicial Dist. Court*, the contested law prohibited "persons of evil reputation from consorting for an unlawful purpose."[774] In *Parker v. Municipal Judge of Las Vegas*, the challenged law made it a crime for an individual to be within the city limits with "the physical ability to work [but] no visible means of support."[775] In both cases, the court determined that the challenged law prohibited conduct that could not in itself be considered a crime, and therefore criminalized status.

PRACTITIONER NARRATIVE

Interview with Adele Nicholas, Chicago-based Civil Rights Attorney.[776]

Q: How did you get involved in the kind of civil rights work you did in Norton v. Springfield?[777]

My first job out of law school was doing Fourth Amendment cases, I worked at a small civil rights firm. In the course of the past nine or ten years I transitioned to working on more policy type cases—challenging things like government policies and local ordinances or state laws that implicate constitutional rights.

My co-counsel Mark Weinberg did a case a long time ago on behalf of a class of people who panhandle in Chicago on a couple of issues—one being that the city of Chicago was using an ordinance about obstruction of bridges to continually harass, ticket, and arrest people being peaceful. He had a lot of contacts in that community when we started working together, and so we had several cases that touched on those issues, one being Norton v. Springfield. We had two Norton cases actually, both against the city of Springfield and both

---

774. *Reno v. Second Judicial Dist. Court*, 83 Nev. 201, 202 (1967).

775. *Parker v. Mun. Judge of Las Vegas*, 83 Nev. 214, 215 (1967).

776. Nicholas, Adele, Interview with Sarah Taranto, July 24, 2020.

777. *Norton v. City of Springfield*, 806 F.3d 411, 612 F. App'x 386 (7th Cir. 2015).

were challenges to different iterations of Springfield's ordinances that sought to prohibit or criminalize panhandling in various ways.

We also had a case against the Cook County Sheriff's Department. *Pindak*[778] was about their prohibition of panhandling in Daily Plaza, which is a permanent public square in downtown Chicago outside the courthouse. It was a really fun case. We ended up trying the case, which was super interesting and really gratifying to work on.

Q: After litigating Norton and Pindak, did you continue doing homeless advocacy type work?

Mark and I worked for a long time on issues involving panhandling, and we did a lot of interesting stuff, and there was a flurry of activity. Then I think that around the time we got our positive Seventh Circuit decision in Norton, which was based on Reed,[779] a lot of communities realized that ordinances they had about panhandling or the ways they were treating panhandling raised serious constitutional issues. And so, for instance, the City of Chicago has now completely repealed its panhandling law, because I think they realized that if they didn't, it was very likely to be found unconstitutional, so they just repealed it.

Q: Do you think Chicago's repeal of its panhandling law was a direct result of *Norton*?

One hundred percent. Mark and I talked about suing the City about it but there were a few reasons we didn't. Then the ACLU wrote a letter to the city saying "hey, we think your ordinance is unconstitutional," and they repealed it about a week later.

Q: Have you seen any beneficial policies or programs that have been more effective in combating homelessness than criminalization?

So many of our clients are facing these unanswerable questions, about "how can I service under all these laws and what options are there?" I think about these questions every day—what are effective responses and how can we help?

I think we need more comprehensive case management solutions for people, especially for returning citizens coming out of prison,

---

778. *Pindak v. Dart*, 125 F. Supp. 3d 720 (N.D. Ill. 2015).
779. *Reed v. Town of Gilbert*, 576 U.S. 155 (2015).

because housing is one piece of the puzzle. But if someone gets out, and they don't have an ID, they don't know how to apply for SNAP or other government benefits they are entitled to, and they have such difficulty finding work because of their criminal history—there are all of these barriers, and housing is just part of it. Even if we find some charity or church or someone who is willing to take them in and give them a place to live, it doesn't really answer their long-term questions.

So, I don't have good answers to any of that, and I feel like we don't have an effective response to that, at least not here in Illinois. That's what I'm coming to learn. It's depressing. It's very, very challenging. It challenges our clients' faith. It's just been an education for me to see how many barriers they put in the way of people being able to do the most normal aspects of life.

There's a lot to be gained politically for local lawmakers to pass these types of anti-homeless laws because it sounds good. People confront poverty as something they don't want to look at or be aware of. So, people feel safer and people feel like the government is looking out for them when the government takes steps to banish those folks from the street, either by criminalizing their activities or just pushing them further and further to the margins.

It's an intractable problem. Legislators don't actually understand what they are doing and are not educated on the policy implications of the laws they make. I talk to people who work in law enforcement all the time, and they realize how dumb these laws are. People who actually have to enforce these laws and have to deal with the consequences of these laws realize that they are not functioning and not actually making society safer in any way. But, it's very difficult for a legislator to be the person who stands up to be the face of a controversial law.

Q: From the advocacy perspective you are coming from, do you see litigation as one of the more effective ways to get government officials to stop making these laws and find better solutions?

I do feel like sometimes litigation is the only way. When there is such political disincentive for lawmakers to do anything to actually help these populations, sometimes your only way forward is to sue.

PART II

Models & Solutions

This book aims to provide training that people of all personal and professional backgrounds can use to view their work through the lens of homeless advocacy and develop new strategies to improve the circumstances of unhoused people. The first chapter in Part II: Models & Solutions focuses on prevention (Chapter 5), while the following three (Chapters 6–8) review hurdles to housing along with emerging solutions. The line between (post hoc) solutions and preventive programs or services is blurred; for example, providing free legal services for eviction defense would be a preventive solution if implemented nationally and is already available in some jurisdictions. But for purposes of looking more closely into areas needing additional focus (prevention, Chapter 5) and broader implementation and refinement (addressing hurdles to housing, Chapters 6–8), this book section is divided into digestible topics in the hope of inspiring areas of work for advocates.

FIVE

Prevention as Housing Solution

This chapter presents a prevention-based framework to introduce models for homeless prevention advocacy. Central to implementing prevention-oriented advocacy solutions are advocates. The more advocates interested in working with the unhoused population, the more work could be done preventively instead of reacting to the stark worsening realities that unhoused people face.

Prevention as a housing solution therefore starts with advocates, people trained in working towards policy solutions for specific populations. This book focuses on solutions based broadly in the legal spaces—litigation, policy, or legislative change. However, advocates of many professional backgrounds can and do have positive and significant impact on the lives of unhoused people.

Looking broadly at access to resources as one area with supporting data, studies show that food access mostly importantly, and then access to employment to and public medical care, have significant impact on the location of where unhoused people live.[780] These findings offer opportunities for planners, developers, city officials, and others to assess the realities by, for example, locating shelters and essential services the government provides in areas within walking distance of people receiving these services. Professionals in all of these areas could work as homeless advocates if trained on the needs of unhoused people.

---

780. Abram Kaplan, Kim Diver, Karl Sandin, and Sarah Kafer Mill. "Homeless Interactions with the Built Environment: A Spatial Pattern Language of Abandoned Housing." *Urban Science* 3, no. 2 (2019): 65–79.

Looking at a specific program as an example, USC Master of Social Work students prepare for homeless advocacy by analyzing how different populations experience homelessness to address social inequalities and enable social change through their emerging policy advocacy practice.[781] When graduate students are taught how to use various advocacy tools and strategies to understand the pathways to homelessness, they may be able to generate advocacy strategies to address the gaps in both the policy landscape and the service delivery system.

The topical and social work examples given above are oriented towards prevention, since homelessness "solutions" are not realistic without preventive measures.

I. An Emergent Paradigm Shift Toward Prevention-Based Approaches to Homelessness

A well-functioning, efficient Homeless Prevention Program (HPP) is commonly understood as a necessary component of any strategy to end homelessness, particularly in a system where new entries into homelessness outpace housing placements. For people without a safety net of social and financial resources, a financial shock such as a medical expense that insurance does not cover can be the first step in a downward spiral toward homelessness.[782] Numerous studies have proven that the benefits of keeping someone housed and out of the homeless services system far exceed the estimated costs of an HPP.

The goal of Homeless Prevention is to assist people who are at imminent risk of homelessness retain their housing, accomplished by either (1) providing people with financial assistance and housing stabilization services necessary to maintain their current housing or (2) helping them find new affordable housing to avoid becoming unhoused and entering the emergency shelter system.

Generally, eligibility for an HPP is based on four criteria: (1) The client must be able to demonstrate self-sufficiency after they receive assistance; (2) the client must have an eligible financial crisis (e.g., job loss or medical emer-

781. Smith-Maddox, Renée, Lauren E Brown, Stacy Kratz, and Richard Newmyer. "Developing a Policy Advocacy Practice for Preventing and Ending Homelessness." *J. of Social Work Education* 56, no. sup1 (2020): S4–S15.

782. Rae, Matthew; Claxton, Gary; Amin, Krutika; Wager, Emma; Ortaliza, Jared; and Cox, Cynthia. 2022. "The Burden of Medical Debt in the United States." March 10, 2022. *Peterson-KFF Health System Tracker.* https://www.healthsystemtracker.org/brief/the-burden-of-medical-debt-in-the-united-states.

gency) that has led to the need for assistance; (3) the client must face imminent risk of homelessness;[783] and (4) the current crisis must be solvable by financial assistance.

At the outset of each HPP intake and assessment, a case worker determines whether to help keep the person housed in their current location (perhaps by paying rental arrears and other related expenses), or to move them to a new location that will be more affordable for them going forward. This determination is typically made based on whether the person can afford to maintain the housing going forward. For example, if the financial crisis that caused the person to fall behind on rent was a one-time emergency, often simply paying the person's rental arrears will suffice. If, however, the financial crisis is more ongoing or is perhaps caused by a rent burden based on the person's income and rental amount, the provider will partner with them to find more affordable housing.

The most common strategy case workers use to keep people housed is temporary financial assistance, such as rental assistance, rental arrears, utility payments and arrears, documentation fees, and fees relating to gaining employment. When necessary, case managers also provide landlord support. When the person needs to move, HPP case managers also provide housing navigation services.

Financial assistance is a crucial aspect of most HPPs because participants who receive financial assistance through the HPP in Los Angeles, for example, are four times more likely to remain housed after exiting the program. In Los Angeles and some other jurisdictions, people enrolled in Homeless Prevention also receive a referral to an attorney funded by Measure H, a sales tax Los Angeles voters imposed on themselves to help generate resources to address homelessness. These lawyers represent people with a wide variety of legal hurdles to maintaining their housing, including in negotiations with landlords and in eviction court proceedings.

A. The Need for Efficiency and Effectiveness in Successful Homelessness Prevention

Homeless Prevention Programs must be operated in a quick, timely, efficient, and equitable manner to achieve maximum success. Most individuals and families who seek assistance with homeless prevention are almost always

---

783. "Imminent risk of homelessness" is a term of art in homeless services but often is defined or interpreted as individuals who will lose their nighttime residence within fourteen days.

facing time-sensitive legal and other issues. Their requests for assistance must be prioritized to quickly screen them for eligibility. If they are eligible, they need to be enrolled quickly and referred to the appropriate parties who can immediately address the emergency they are facing that threatens their housing (often, this includes a referral to legal services).

Additionally, once a person is determined to be eligible for the HPP and is referred to legal services, time is of the essence to spot the legal issues involved in the case and to respond to the short-time turnaround that eviction cases require.

Finally, concurrently with a referral to legal services, case workers should decide quickly the level of financial assistance to which the person will be entitled, to help the attorneys assess the negotiation posture of each such case at the outset.

B. Background on Efficiency

Early homeless prevention frameworks[784] borrowed from public health paradigms by conceptualizing prevention at three levels—primary (targeting households before they experience some crisis that precipitates their loss of housing); secondary (assisting households that actually lost their housing); and tertiary (intervening early on behalf of households who, without assistance, would likely remain unhoused for an extended time period). However, these prevention levels are misleading on their own and may be better seen as a continuum on which points converge between keeping households at imminent risk of homelessness from becoming unhoused and moving newly unhoused households back into housing.[785] In other words, a homeless prevention framework is only efficient if service providers individualize resource allocation on a continuum instead of categorizing people into levels at which they might not fit neatly.

---

784. Culhane, Dennis P, Stephen Metraux, and Thomas Byrne. "A Prevention-Centered Approach to Homelessness Assistance: a Paradigm Shift?" *Housing Policy Debate* 21, no. 2 (2011): 295–315 (explaining that the continuum-of-care approach, which developed upon a 1994 federal pronouncement that funding would be distributed through local "continuums of care" to shape shelters and homeless services into regionally-based systems, has expanded since the mid-1990s but has become more insular and removed from community supports).

785. Ibid.

C. Background on Effectiveness

After homelessness service providers determine households to be suitable for prevention assistance, providers may assess effective practices by framing community-wide initiatives under two approaches to primary prevention: either 1) low-cost, time limited interventions suitable for most at-risk households (i.e., time-limited housing subsidies, emergency cash assistance, and mediation in housing courts); or 2) costlier, more extended interventions suitable for select households with more uncontrollable problems related to their housing instability (i.e., extended housing supports and ongoing support services via Housing First programs). Regardless of the chosen approach, agencies that operate HPPs need to market the program broadly because research suggests most households that become unhoused are only incidentally in contact with the homelessness system.[786]

D. The Need for a Prevention-Oriented Research Agenda

Research evaluating the efficiency and effectiveness of prevention initiatives is essential because current policy favoring prevention initiatives will only continue to do so if prevention programs show results. More information is needed to be able to examine the housing outcomes of several at-risk groups receiving prevention assistance of varying types, intensity, and durations within a singular context.[787]

II. The Move Toward a New Conceptual Framework (and Its Implications)

A. Breaking Away from Previous Policy Frameworks

Older models focused most of their resources on persons and families experiencing long-term homelessness and maintained a large *ad hoc* services system in parallel to existing service systems (e.g., the shelter system recreating community-based service systems inside the homelessness system). In contrast, a prevention-based model for homeless services shifts its focus away from shelters and related homeless services and more toward the com-

---

786. Ibid.
787. Ibid.

munity-based network of services better suited to help people attain and maintain stable housing. Otherwise stated, two focal points exemplify the new model: 1) attaining housing stability and 2) maintaining ties with networks of community-based social and health service delivery systems. Under the prevention-based model, the role of shelter changes from being the center of homeless services to being one resource among a broader set of supports, with shelter being accessed only when necessary.[788]

B. Implications of a New Conceptual Framework

Shifting to a prevention-based framework skips ahead of any clear policy agenda focused on homelessness prevention because much remains to be learned about how to organize an effective, efficient homelessness prevention and rapid re-housing system. Evidence suggests that best practices target resources to households facing an imminent risk of homelessness, but also that, despite their successes, the expense of Housing First and other long-term housing initiatives limits their availability to households with the greatest service needs. Still, this evidence from the research literature and policy experiments has the potential to guide this new conceptual framework.[789]

III. Homelessness Prevention Strategies and Interventions

A. Community-Wide Homelessness Prevention Strategies

In *A Prevention-Centered Approach to Homelessness Assistance* Culhane explains these categories of initiatives: "Primary prevention initiatives are those which prevent new cases; where efforts focus on reducing the risk for acquiring a particular condition. Secondary prevention identifies and addresses a condition at its earliest stages. Thus it does not reduce the number of new cases, but rather treats conditions close to their onset while they are presumably easier to counteract. Finally, tertiary prevention seeks to slow the progression or mitigate the effects of a particular condition once it has become established. Providing three distinct categories, however, is misleading. These prevention classifications should more be seen as ranges in a continuum, with boundaries between them being somewhat indeterminate." Ibid.

---

788. Ibid.
789. Ibid.

The following prevention activities may be implemented at all prevention levels (primary, secondary, and tertiary):[790]

- housing subsidies (with evidence indicating that, among several potential interventions, housing subsidies had the greatest effect in reducing homelessness);

- supportive services coupled with permanent housing (with evidence from Massachusetts indicating declining rates of homelessness among state psychiatric hospital admits over the ten years of expanding such services);

- mediation in housing courts (with evidence from housing courts showing the ability to preserve tenancy even after an eviction filing);

- cash assistance for rent or mortgage arrears (with evidence showing effectiveness for households still in housing but threatened with housing loss if such assistance is efficient and well-targeted); and

- rapid exit from shelter (with evidence showing this strategy reduces the average length of shelter stay by 50% and achieves high success in keeping formerly unhoused families from returning to shelter within 12 months).

Above all, evidence suggests that the approaches offering the most appropriate targeting and that achieve sufficient success rates include rapid exit from shelter (for both families and single adults with serious mental illness) and community support strategies involving housing and services for those adults exiting psychiatric and correctional facilities.[791]

---

790. In A Prevention-Centered Approach to Homelessness Assistance Culhane explains these categories of initiatives: "Primary prevention initiatives are those which prevent new cases; where efforts focus on reducing the risk for acquiring a particular condition. Secondary prevention identifies and addresses a condition at its earliest stages. Thus it does not reduce the number of new cases, but rather treats conditions close to their onset while they are presumably easier to counteract. Finally, tertiary prevention seeks to slow the progression or mitigate the effects of a particular condition once it has become established. Providing three distinct categories, however, is misleading. These prevention classifications should more be seen as ranges in a continuum, with boundaries between them being somewhat indeterminate." Ibid.

791. Burt, Martha R, Carol Pearson, and Ann Elizabeth Montgomery. "Community-Wide Strategies for Preventing Homelessness: Recent Evidence." *J. of Primary Prevention* 28, no. 3 (2007): 213–228.

B. Rapid Re-Housing

Rapid re-housing involves moving households rapidly from shelters directly into housing in the private market with their own names on the lease, within a matter of weeks when possible, and with partial rental assistance and limited services from the service provider for up to a year. Whether households are gradually transitioned or rapidly placed into housing does not seem to affect the likelihood of returning to shelter.[792]

C. Transitional Housing

Transitional housing involves either service providers maintaining apartment leases for households or those households residing in central facilities owned and operated by service providers themselves. The effect of transitional housing for households without children seems to depend highly on its implementation.[793]

As mentioned previously, some areas (like transitional housing) both need to be further developed as preventive programs as well as improved upon as currently implemented.

---

792. Rodriguez, Jason M, and Tessa A Eidelman. "Homelessness Interventions in Georgia: Rapid Re-Housing, Transitional Housing, and the Likelihood of Returning to Shelter." *Housing Policy Debate* 27, no. 6 (2017): 825–842.

793. Ibid.

SIX

Hurdles to Housing and Interim Solutions

Part I: Employment Barriers

I t is overly simplistic to categorize criminal records and lack of access to treatment of mental health conditions simply as barriers to employment.[794] But it is a reality that the stigmatization of people with mental health conditions and those with criminal records create real barriers to employment. And so those unhoused people with mental health conditions who have insufficient support or those with criminal records without means to expunge them have difficulty finding jobs even as they are eager to work.

Despite negative stereotypes to the contrary, unhoused people are willing and hoping to work. For example, in a 2019 survey of unhoused single adults (24 and older) in Los Angeles County, approximately half of the unemployed unhoused adults reported that they were actively looking for work.[795] Yet a large portion of the unhoused population struggle with finding employment. If it is not an unwillingness to work, what really is preventing unhoused people from finding a job?

This chapter aims to show some of the legal and non-legal struggles that unhoused populations must face in an effort to explain why the unemployment

---

794. Criminalization of unhoused people is treated in-depth in Chapter 4, and the intertwined nature of mental health and the state of being unhoused is well documented.

795. Ibid.

statistics are so high. From a lack of resources to employment discrimination, homelessness presents a plethora of hurdles that prevent unhoused people from obtaining a job. Specifically, this chapter examines logistical hurdles that unhoused people looking for work face, as well as two difficult cycles that can arise for unhoused people if they have either mental health/substance abuse conditions or criminal records.

I. Logistical Hurdles

Even if an unhoused person is qualified and fully capable of doing a job, there are several logistical hurdles that they must overcome to even be considered for a job. These logistical struggles are caused by a lack of resources that are often taken for granted. This section aims to explore the different ways in which the lack of a permanent address and access to technology can cause logistical difficulties that preemptively bar unhoused populations from obtaining employment.

A. Lack of Permanent Address

When applying for anything, virtually or physically, people are almost always expected to provide an address. Employment is no exception. Resumes, an essential part of the job application process, are expected to include the applicant's permanent address as part of their contact information. But what if the applicant does not have an address?

When an unhoused person fails to provide an address or uses their shelter address, it raises a red flag to many employers.[796] When there's an indication that the applicant is unhoused, many employers start having doubts about the applicant's motivation, dependability, and ability to assimilate into the workplace, as well as concerns about their poor appearance, attire, behaviors, and hygiene.[797] In a 2014 survey the National Coalition for the Homeless conducted, 70.4% of unhoused respondents felt that they were discriminated

---

796. Golabek-Goldman, Sarah. "Ban the Address: Combating Employment Discrimination Against the Homeless." *The Yale L.J.* 126, no. 6 (April 2017): 1790.

797. "Overcoming Employment Barriers." National Alliance to End Homelessness, October 25, 2016. https://endhomelessness.org/resource/overcoming-employment-barriers/.

against by employers because of their housing status.[798] Even if effort is put into actively finding a job, "when you don't have an address, it is impossible for [an employer] to call you back."[799]

Employers also set requirements for positions that prevent applicants without housing from qualifying or discourage them from applying in the first place. For example, some employers require a current address where the applicant has lived for a few years.[800] Employers that have adopted this requirement have even fired unhoused people due to a lack of residence.[801] This presents a challenge for unhoused people because, even if they tried to get around the lack of permanent housing by writing down a family member's or friend's address, it would be hard for them to show that they were living at that address for a long period of time. Furthermore, many employers require an address for background checks. Although there are some disputes about whether an address is required, some of the leading background screening companies require an address to conduct an accurate check.[802] This has given employers more reasons to require an address during the application process.

With the advancement of technology, this discrimination is exacerbated by screening methods, like Artificial Intelligence (A.I.), hiring software, and website structures, that prevent many unhoused applicants' resumes from even being reviewed by an employer.[803] For example, many online applications and websites are set up so that you cannot get past the page or submit the application if you do not enter a valid address.[804] Even if someone could submit the application, there are now A.I. or software programs that can screen specific elements of an application or resume, meaning that an application without

---

798. "Discrimination and Economic Profiling among the Homeless of Washington, DC," National Coalition for the Homeless, April 2014. https://nationalhomeless.org/publication/view/discrimination-economic-profiling-2014/.

799. Golabek-Goldman, 1790.

800. Golabek-Goldman, 1807.

801. HuffPost. "Eunice Jasica Claims KFC Franchise Reneged Job Offer Because She Is Homeless." *HuffPost*, March 28, 2013. https://www.huffpost.com/entry/eunice-jasica-kfc-homeless_n_2974067.

802. Golabek-Goldman, 1830.

803. Weber, Lauren. 2012. "Your Résumé vs. Oblivion," *Wall Street Journal*. January 24, 2012. https://www.wsj.com/articles/SB10001424052970204624204577178941034941330.

804. Golabek-Goldman, 1805.

an address could be filtered out completely or flagged for missing an address before it ever reaches the employers for review.[805]

All of this begs the question: is this discrimination legal? By reading laws like Title VII at face value, it does not seem to necessarily be illegal; while there is clear language prohibiting employment discrimination based on factors like race, sex, and religion, there is no language prohibiting discrimination based on housing status.[806] While there are some ideas about how to apply Title VII to unhoused people, and certain states have created new legislation to specifically target discrimination against unhoused people (further discussed in the Solutions section below), employment discrimination against unhoused populations still goes unchecked for the most part.[807] In 2013, Eunice Jasica got a job at KFC to do "prep work" but was fired on the first day; the reason the franchise owner cited in a letter was "concerns of lack of residence and transportation."[808] In 2015, a Pizza Hut employee said that they had to provide the addresses that they lived at for the past five years during their interview because they needed "to be at the same address for a few years."[809] Employers are not hiding the fact that they have housing status requirements or that they have concerns about lack of housing, yet many of these instances of discrimination remain uncurbed because there is a strong perception that discrimination based on housing status is legal.[810]

Discrimination is not the only challenge that the lack of a permanent address can create. When an employer chooses to correspond via mail, the lack of address can be a huge roadblock for unhoused people. Options such as getting a post office box or using a shelter's address do exist, but many unhoused people do not have access to those resources. Furthermore, the lack

805. Weber, Lauren. 2012. "Your Résumé vs. Oblivion," *Wall Street Journal.* January 24, 2012. https://www.wsj.com/articles/SB10001424052970204624204577178941034941330.

806. Civil Rights Act of 1964 § 7.

807. House the Homeless, "KFC Says, Get a Job—LOL!" House the Homeless, April 9, 2013. https://housethehomeless.org/2013/04/kfc-says-get-a-job-lol/.

808. HuffPost, "Eunice Jasica Claims KFC Franchise Reneged Job Offer Because She Is Homeless," *HuffPost*, March 28, 2013. https://www.huffpost.com/entry/eunice-jasica-kfc-homeless_n_2974067.

809. Guterman, Amy. "3 High-Impact Ways Technology Can Help Combat Homelessness," *Salesforce,* Salesforce.org LLC, August 25, 2020. https://www.salesforce.org/blog/3-ways-tech-can-combat-homelessness/.

810. House the Homeless. "KFC Says, Get a Job—LOL!"

of a permanent address also complicates obtaining an ID, which many employers require.[811]

While some may find an address to be a basic requirement, unhoused people must strategize and carefully plan how to meet residence requirements, and even then, it is often not enough to give them a chance at employment even if they are qualified for the position. Reform will be needed to either make discrimination illegal by establishing housing status as a protected class or to give unhoused people the resources they need to circumvent the address requirements and the hurdles of not having a permanent address.

B. Lack of Access to Technology

As mentioned before, many employers are turning towards a digital or electronic way of hiring. While this can create a more efficient process for both the employer and the applicants, it also creates a barrier to unhoused people who may not have regular access to the technology needed to participate in this way of hiring.

Navigating the job search process can be extraordinarily difficult without consistent access to technology and the internet. Many employers have (exclusively) digital advertisements for job positions and even the application process, and "everything has to be online now. If you don't have access to the Internet, you're at even more of a disadvantage."[812] Unfortunately, many unhoused people have very limited access to technology to access these opportunities; many do not own a personal computer or have access to a computer in general.[813] The lack of technology also prevents unhoused people from keeping in contact with employers, especially in an age where emails are used so frequently; this can be detrimental to the job search if an employer needs the applicant to do something within a set amount of time.[814]

Some free resources and programs have led to misconceptions on how much access unhoused people have to these online opportunities. For exam-

---

811. Wiltz, Teresa, "Without ID, Homeless Trapped in Vicious Cycle," The Pew Charitable Trusts, May 15, 2017. https://www.pewtrusts.org/en/research-and-analysis/blogs/stateline/2017/05/15/without-id-homeless-trapped-in-vicious-cycle.

812. "Limited Access to Technology Keeps Homeless Families Down," Housing Families First, January 22, 2018. https://housingfamiliesfirst.org/2018/01/22/limited-access-technology-keeps-homeless-families/.

813. Ibid.

814. Ibid.

ple, the Lifeline Program designed to provide smartphones to unhoused and low-income families has increased smartphone usage amongst unhoused populations, which has fueled the perception that unhoused people do have the technology necessary to search for jobs.[815] The problem is that it is challenging to use a smartphone for typing resumes and applications; moreover, there are inconsistencies and limitations to programs like the Lifeline Program.[816] Data plans needed to access the internet are extremely limited, and based on a survey done in 2017, 3-month turnover in phones was at 56% and phone numbers at 55% of unhoused people who had smartphones.[817] This sort of inconsistency could prevent unhoused people from effectively communicating with employers. Another thing that people often overestimate is the effectiveness of libraries. While libraries can be a great resource to unhoused people, they cannot provide the consistency and privacy of having a personal computer and internet access at home. Libraries often have limited time slots that the user can use the computer, meaning that some unhoused people may not have access to the computer when they need it, or they may run out of time after an unfruitful search.[818] This can be a huge risk to the job search if an employer needs the applicant to do something by a specific time. Consistent access to the internet is also crucial for keeping up with job position updates and listings, especially if eligibility requirements change.[819] Additionally, job applications often require individuals to save files, like resumes, onto the computer and require people to enter sensitive information; a public computer at the library would not give the applicant the privacy needed to do all of those tasks.

Even with certain programs and resources that have made technology more available to unhoused people, there is not enough consistency or privacy in these resources. Without these key components, unhoused people are competing at a huge disadvantage in an already competitive job market.

---

815. Rhoades, Harmony, Suzanne L. Wenzel, Eric Rice, Hailey Winetrobe, and Benjamin Henwood. "No Digital Divide? Technology Use among Homeless Adults." *J. of Social Distress and the Homeless* 26, no. 1 (2017): 73–77. https://doi.org/10.1080/10530789.2017.1305140.

816. "Limited Access to Technology Keeps Homeless Families Down."

817. Rhoades, Wenzel, Rice, Winetrobe, and Henwood. "No Digital Divide? Technology Use among Homeless Adults." *J. of Social Distress and the Homeless* 26, no. 1 (2017): 73–77. https://doi.org/10.1080/10530789.2017.1305140.

818. "Limited Access to Technology Keeps Homeless Families Down."

819. Guterman, Amy. "3 High-Impact Ways Technology Can Help Combat Homelessness." Salesforce.org LLC, August 25, 2020. https://www.salesforce.org/blog/3-ways-tech-can-combat-homelessness/.

C. Solutions

As discussed previously, most of the current discrimination laws do not include either homelessness or housing status as a "protected" class, and this affects employment opportunities for unhoused people. However, new laws and propositions are emerging to specifically protect unhoused people from employment discrimination.

For example, "Ban the Address" campaigns push for law reform to ban the address requirement on job applications and resumes.[820] Rhode Island has proposed a state "Homeless Bill of Rights" (HBOR) in reaction to these sentiments. Unlike other discrimination laws, which do not specifically mention homelessness, it states: "A person experiencing homelessness…[h]as the right not to face discrimination while seeking or maintaining employment due to his or her lack of permanent mailing address, or his or her mailing address being that of a shelter or social service provider."[821] Although these types of cases will still need to be pursed through the courts like any other discrimination case,[822] laws like Rhode Island's HBOR add specific protections against discrimination for unhoused people, which should theoretically make it easier for unhoused people to win cases regarding a lack of address. More work is needed, however, in developing a more streamlined claims process for unhoused people who are not familiar with the system and have little to no legal aid. And, of course, jurisdictions should create and fund more legal aid resources for more unhoused people.

II. Mental Health and Substance Abuse Conditions

According to a 2015 U.S. Department of Housing and Urban Development assessment, 25% of unhoused people in the U.S. had serious mental illness, and 45% of unhoused people in the U.S. had at least one mental illness.[823] This is

---

820. Golabek-Goldman, Sarah. "Ban the Address: Combating Employment Discrimination Against the Homeless." *Yale L.J.* 126, no. 6 (April 2017): 1788–1869.

821. Drywa, Michael F. "Rhode Island's Homeless Bill of Rights: How Can the New Law Provide Shelter from Employment Discrimination?" *Roger Williams Univ. L. Rev.* 19, no. 3 (2014): 723.

822. Ibid.

823. Tarr, Peter. "Homelessness and Mental Illness: A Challenge to Our Society." Brain & Behavior Research Foundation, November 19, 2018. https://www.bbrfoundation.org /blog/homelessness-and-mental-illness-challenge-our-society.

a stark contrast to a study done in 2016 that found that 4.2% of U.S. adults in general have been diagnosed with serious mental illness.[824]

The statistics for substance abuse are also high for unhoused populations. In 2017, it was estimated that 38% of unhoused people are alcohol dependent, and 26% are dependent on other harmful chemicals.[825] As discussed in previous sections, there are certain stigmas that are tied to unhoused people, which is why many employers are hesitant to hire someone without a permanent address. Because of the high statistics of mental illness and substance abuse, these topics have become a point of concern for employers when employing unhoused people, and the ways in which these concerns affect employment amongst unhoused people needs further examination.

A. Mental Illness

Mental illness and the perceptions surrounding the topic amongst unhoused populations present challenges from the very beginning of the employment process. Unhoused people suffering from serious mental illness can have trouble even starting the job search, because they can find it difficult to be consistently available and highly functioning for work.[826] Because flexible work schedules are often not available for jobs, unhoused people who cannot stay consistently available due to their mental illness have a much harder time even finding a position to which they can apply. Furthermore, due to trauma, some unhoused people suffering from mental illness have trouble persuading themselves to apply to positions because they fear that "their anxieties associated with their trauma would resurface on the job."[827] For some unhoused people with mental illnesses, the first step of even finding and applying to a job becomes exponentially complicated due to individual barriers.

Mental illness also plays a large role during the application process. Employers, even the ones who are supportive of employing people with mental

---

824. Ibid.

825. Murray, Krystina. "Homelessness and Addiction." Addiction Center, June 15, 2021. https://www.addictioncenter.com/addiction/homelessness/#:~:text=The%20end%20result%20of%20homelessness,is%20a%20result%20of%20homelessness.

826. Harris, Lynne M., Lynda R. Matthews, Jonine Penrose-Wall, Ashraful Alam, and Alison Jaworski. "Perspectives on Barriers to Employment for Job Seekers with Mental Illness and Additional Substance-Use Problems," *Health & Social Care in the Community* 22, no. 1 (2013): 67–72.

827. Gabriel, Ian, Elly Schoen, Victoria Ciudad-Real, and Allan Broslawsky. "Homelessness and Employment." Homelessness Policy Research Institute, August 24, 2020: 3.

illness, often have concerns about productivity.[828] With this in the back of many employers' minds, unhoused people often face passive discrimination and start the employment process with a disadvantage. Even worse, unhoused applicants are aware of how the employers and the community perceive them; unhoused people know that "[employers] think mental health problems, schizophrenic, that person's an axe murderer."[829] This pressure, coupled with symptoms of mental illness like extreme anxiety—which creates problems with communication skills—can lead to poor interview results and poor communication in general with employers.[830]

Even if an unhoused person with mental illness can jump these hurdles, they still face challenges when they start to work. While there are laws that require reasonable accommodations and prevent discrimination based on mental illness, unhoused people often are afraid to ask for accommodations due to the stigmas surrounding mental illness.[831] As one man pointed out in a 2020 study on formerly unhoused adults:

> [W]hat if I'm working somewhere and someone finds out that I have a mental illness? That scares me because people outside of the mental health community, you know, when they think of mental illness, they think of really dangerous people, like serial killers for example. You know people who are evil and dangerous, and out to hurt them. And will I be like I don't know, some kind of a pariah or something?[832]

Again, the pressures arising from the perception that people have about unhoused people with mental illnesses may prevent unhoused people from applying to jobs, and it can also prevent unhoused people from asking for the help they need once they start working, which jeopardizes their job stability.[833]

---

828. Harris, Matthews, Penrose-Wall, Alam, and Jaworski, "Perspectives on Barriers to Employment," 72.

829. Ibid.

830. Ibid.

831. Tiderington, Emmy, Benjamin F. Henwood, Deborah K. Padgett, and Bikki Tran Smith. "Employment Experiences of Formerly Homeless Adults with Serious Mental Illness in Housing First versus Treatment First Supportive Housing Programs." *Psychiatric Rehab. J.* 43, no. 3 (2020).

832. Ibid.

833. Harris, Matthews, Penrose-Wall, Alam, and Jaworski, "Perspectives on Barriers to Employment," 72.

B. Substance Abuse

Substance abuse is often linked to mental illness and can also have negative impacts on an unhoused person's employment. Substance abuse prevents some unhoused people from getting a job, and it can also prevent them from maintaining a job even if they are able to secure one.

Although it is true that substance abuse can have negative effects on housed people's employment, substance abuse seems to negatively affect employment options for the unhoused population more than their "housed" counterparts.[834] Many unhoused people have shared that substance abuse increases or can bring back mental illness symptoms and complications, which in turn interfered with their ability to conduct interviews or perform well during employment.[835] This was especially true for people who lived in shelters with zero-tolerance policies regarding substance abuse; the potential mental illness complications combined with the stresses of losing their limited options in shelter impacted job performance greatly.[836] The combined effect of substance abuse and mental illness complications contributed to a lower rate of unhoused people in higher level positions as well as inconsistencies in work retention.[837]

Additionally, as the next section will discuss, criminal records arising from substance use and possession can have negative impacts on an unhoused person's ability to obtain employment. When the employment process also requires a drug test or screening, this can be exacerbated.

C. Solutions

There are two types of solutions commonly proposed to mitigate the negative effects of mental illness and substance abuse. One type focuses on changes to the unhoused people themselves and the other focuses on changes for the employers.

---

834. Gabriel, Ian, Elly Schoen, Victoria Ciudad-Real, and Allan Broslawsky. "Homelessness and Employment." Homelessness Policy Research Institute, August 24, 2020: 3.

835. Poremski, Daniel, Rob Whitley, and Eric Latimer. "Barriers to Obtaining Employment for People with Severe Mental Illness Experiencing Homelessness." *J. of Mental Health* 23, no. 4 (2014): 182.

836. Ibid.

837. Zuvekas, Samuel H., and Steven C. Hill. "Income and Employment among Homeless People: The Role of Mental Health, Health and Substance Abuse." *J. of Mental Health Pol'y and Econ.* 3, no. 3 (2000): 160.

An example of the first type is the "First Step" job training program that was introduced in New York City. Unlike the usual job training or employment assistance programs that primarily focus on reinforcing job skills and soft skills, the First Step program takes a more holistic approach and tries to train more physically and mentally healthy individuals.[838] The program focuses on creating more self-esteem and self-confidence while also providing hobbies like Zumba and yoga to help with physical and mental health to give unhoused people a way of relieving stress without the use of substances.[839]

An example of the other type is the initiative proposed by the Heartland Alliance. The initiative pushes employers to reach out to more local human service providers and workforce development programs, to increase the number of unhoused people being considered for jobs and also so that the employers can understand and get help with creating reasonable accommodations for the unhoused employee.[840] By communicating with these programs more, the employer can better understand the needs of the unhoused person, especially those with mental health or substance abuse issues, and they can also be connected with the proper government or workforce development agencies to get advice on reasonable accommodations as needed.[841] Having local human service providers or workforce development programs work closely with the employer would also remind employers of their responsibility to provide reasonable accommodations under discrimination laws like Title VII and may also provide the unhoused person with the aid needed to request these accommodations. For this to work, however, unhoused people's access to these agencies would need to be streamlined and there would need to be safeguards to prevent employers from using the agencies' information to discriminate even further.

---

838. "First Step Employment Program Helps Women." SAMHSA, April 19, 2016. https://www.samhsa.gov/homelessness-programs-resources/hpr-resources/first-step -employment-program.

839. Ibid.

840. Young, Melissa. "Creating Economic Opportunity for Homeless Jobseekers: The Role of Employers and Community-Based Organizations." *Heartland Alliance National Initiatives*, April 18, 2017: 5, 8.

841. Ibid.

III. Criminal Record

As discussed in previous sections and Chapter 4, there are several ways in which the criminal justice system in the United States criminalizes homelessness and continually builds the criminal record of unhoused people. In addition to all of the barriers to employment discussed so far, these criminal records add another hurdle that unhoused people must surmount if they want to obtain employment.

A. Active and Passive Crimes

Actively committing a crime is one of the more obvious ways of getting a criminal record. For unhoused populations, a commonly targeted form of active crime is substance use. Many states have or are looking to implement laws that criminalize the use of substances, which has a large impact on unhoused communities due to the relatively high rate of substance use amongst unhoused people.[842]

There are also passive crimes, as discussed in detail in Chapter 4; these crimes do not require the individual to do anything and are usually about the individual just existing or being somewhere. For example, there was a large uptick of criminalization laws between 2006 to 2019 regarding things like city-wide and area-specific sleeping, camping, and panhandling.[843] For many unhoused people, this criminalizes their existence, because many of them do not have anywhere that they can carry out these essential activities. To make matters worse, this initial criminalization starts a cycle of criminalization because citations for breaking such laws usually come with a fee that most unhoused people cannot afford, leading to warrants for arrest and even jail.[844]

---

842. Flory, Jen. "Arresting People Who Are Homeless Will Make a Bad Problem Worse." CalMatters, February 12, 2020. https://calmatters.org/commentary/2020/02/arresting-homeless-people-will-make-a-bad-problem-worse/. Also see Uprety, Aastha. "How Criminal Background Checks Can Prevent People with Disabilities from Finding Stable Housing." Equal Rights Center, September 19, 2019. https://equalrightscenter.org/criminal-record-disability-housing/.

843. National Law Center on Homelessness & Poverty, *Housing Not Handcuffs: Ending the Criminalization of Homelessness in US Cities* (December 2019), 37–38.

844. Stuart; Coalition on Homelessness, *Punishing the Poorest: How the Criminalization of Homelessness Perpetuates Poverty in San Francisco,* (2015): 33–34.

B. Impact of a Criminal Record

With the criminalization of substance abuse as well as the criminalization of essential, every day activities needed for survival, it is no surprise that many unhoused people have a criminal history. For example, based on a 2018 study, 70% of the unhoused population in California had a history of incarceration.[845]

Many employers choose to screen job applicants for a criminal record in the first phase of the application process, regardless of the nature of the job.[846] As expected, this tends to screen out many unhoused people, barring unhoused people from many jobs for which they are otherwise fully qualified.[847] Studies have shown that over 75% of employers were negatively influenced by a felony conviction or arrest, which led to applicants with criminal histories to not be considered for the job or to a reduction in pay of up to 40%.[848] This is especially problematic, because most of these screening processes or companies do not delve deeply into what kind of criminal history the applicant has, meaning that even harmless offenses, like being arrested for not paying a fine for sleeping on a public bench, can bar the unhoused person from being considered for the job.[849] While most employers will justify these practices by saying that they are removing "risky" applicants from consideration, there is little evidence that having a criminal record predicts future workplace crime; on the contrary, research demonstrates that workers with a criminal record are productive and loyal employees.[850] By using criminal record screening, employers have created a systematic way of keeping many unhoused people, even the ones who are qualified, from even being considered for job opportunities.

---

845. California Health Policy Strategies, L.L.C. *Criminal Justice System Involvement and Mental Illness among Unsheltered Homeless in California*, 2018.

846. Young, Melissa. "Creating Economic Opportunity for Homeless Jobseekers: The Role of Employers and Community-Based Organizations." *Heartland Alliance National Initiatives*, April 18, 2017: 6.

847. Ibid.

848. Homeless Initiative Policy Summit. *Discharges Into Homelessness*, 2015.

849. Young, Melissa. "Creating Economic Opportunity for Homeless Jobseekers: The Role of Employers and Community-Based Organizations." *Heartland Alliance National Initiatives*, April 18, 2017: 6.

850. Ibid.

C. Solutions

In trying to alleviate this type of employment discrimination, there are initiatives to bring about changes from the perspectives of both the employers as well as the unhoused applicants. Groups like the Heartland Alliance call for employers to stop these types of blanket screening practices and instead "assess the legality, need for, and assumptions behind each application or interview question" by only having screenings when really necessary and by focusing more on the qualifications of the applicant rather than ways of screening out applicants.[851] Like the "Ban the Address" campaign, this could give unhoused people an actual shot at interviewing for or even obtaining employment by getting them through the initial hurdles of the job application process and giving them the opportunity to show their qualifications.

On the unhoused applicants' end, there are movements to clear criminal records by connecting unhoused jobseekers to legal advocates who can help modify or expunge their records. Initiatives like the Los Angeles County Criminal Record Clearing Project (LACCRCP) were proposed that try to gather legal advocates in county departments, nonprofit legal service centers, and community-based organizations that have experience with both the law and issues that unhoused people face.[852] By using Proposition 47 and the legal infrastructure available in California in conjunction with the various groups' expertise, the program sought to clear criminal records and help unhoused people with reentry into the job market.[853] Although some may think that this is complicated, many of these issues can be sorted out by asking the judge to clear the criminal record in the interests of justice or by filing modification or expungement motions.[854]

Unhoused people face unique hurdles to employment. Even with enough qualifications, logical issues coupled with mental health instability and criminal history often get in the way of employment for unhoused people. As mentioned in the introduction, people often think of unemployment as the reason for homelessness, but the reverse is true as well. Both statuses can contribute to each other in a cycle that will continue unless help is offered to either alleviate some of the problems that unhoused people regularly confront or until a shift in perception and legal framework happens.

---

851. Ibid.
852. Homeless Initiative Policy Summit. *Discharges Into Homelessness*, 2015: 30.
853. Ibid., 31.
854. Ibid.

PRACTITIONER NARRATIVE

Interview with Deborah Diamant, New York City-based Housing Attorney and Director of Government Relations and Legal Affairs at Coalition for the Homeless, Inc.[855]

Q: How did you become interested in housing work?

After I moved to New York City to work on my master's in art history, more and more of my friends were facing legal issues in terms of the heavy-handed policing of certain communities, especially people who cycle in the city and who were part of activist groups during the late 1990s to early 2000s Green Scare. At the time, I had been working for a women's health nonprofit for eight years when a couple of people there convinced me to go to law school at the age of 30.

Once I got to law school, I thought I'd use my experience on some health-related legal issues. A natural fit for my first summer was working in a legal aid program that assisted individuals with government benefits, called Project FAIR, which would provide information and resources to individuals at the Fair Hearing office in the city so that they could continue their benefits or get them back. At Project FAIR, I was able to shadow a few of the housing attorneys and just loved it, especially being in a city like New York where landlord-tenant issues are so common. I am indebted to the legal services attorneys that supervised me and acted as mentors because it was very hard to get a legal services job when I graduated in 2010, so the only housing experience that I had was from my internships. I worked for two-and-a-half years for a firm that mainly focused on police misconduct-related Section 1983 civil rights litigation until I finally found a position in a housing defense unit. I worked there for a year-and-a-half, but I always wanted to work at the Brooklyn housing court, the court that I got to see as an intern, so I took a job at the Legal Aid Society of NYC in Brooklyn, and I was there until I came to the coalition.

---

855. Diamant, Deborah. Interview with Tammi Matsukiyo. March 15, 2021.

Q: How have legal housing services in NYC changed since you began your career?

I finished law school before New York City passed a bill[856] for universal access to counsel for tenants facing evictions, which many people colloquially call a right to counsel for tenants. It's not quite a right to counsel—it's a phased-in process that was supposed to take place over five years by targeting zip codes with the highest numbers of evictions. This expands access to housing attorneys exponentially, meaning that programs need many more lawyers. There's still an income cap for legal services generally in New York City and for full representation at 200% of the federal poverty level. But with the 2017 universal access to counsel legislation, individuals above that income line can get free legal advice as well.

Because of the pandemic,[857] I think a lot of people across the country realized that in order to be prepared for the next one, people need to be in safe spaces where they can quarantine. In response to the pandemic, New York has had this patchwork of eviction moratoria[858] in place, which reduces the numbers of evictions while the numbers of tenant attorneys are rising in housing courts.[859] New York City has responded by trying to connect pretty much everyone to an attorney, regardless of zip codes. Really, the city just wants to make sure that people facing eviction are at least talking to a lawyer—so if you call 311 here in New York City, you'll be connected to a helpline that routes calls to legal services providers. Pretty much all civil legal services providers that receive funding from the city are answering questions

---

856. The right to counsel law, Local Law 136 of 2017, was an amendment to the New York City Administrative Code § 26-1301 et seq. that requires New York City to provide access to legal services for individuals in housing court in phases.

857. This interview was conducted on March 15, 2021, during the COVID-19 pandemic.

858. City of New York, New York, "Eviction Moratoria and Courthouse Operations: Know the Facts." Accessed April 17, 2021. https://perma.cc/V68A-EHQW. New York City (1) suspended eviction cases pending as of December 28, 2020 until February 26, 2021; (2) allowed tenants to file a "Hardship Declaration" to extend the suspension until at least May 1, 2021; and (3) suspended eviction cases filed starting December 29, 2020 for at least 60 days.

859. The Centers for Disease Control also issued a residential eviction moratorium in September 2020, which was extended through June 30, 2021. Temporary Halt in Residential Evictions to Prevent the Further Spread of COVID-19, 86 Fed. Reg. 16,731 (March 31, 2021).

and responding to these individuals, which is vastly different from how things were when I got started. As more and more cities are adopting a right to counsel, you're going to see more and more tenants who are represented, and the numbers show that evictions go down when people have attorneys.

Q: **Do you have any advice for advocates or students who are interested in this career path?**

For students, absolutely take clinics and courses on landlord-tenant law if your school has them. If it doesn't, I'd highly recommend interning as much as possible if this is something you know you want to do. Internships can be competitive—you just have to make yourself available and go to those optional things, like the tenant association meeting on a weeknight if you have time. In the end, you shouldn't spend your entire time at law school learning black and white law that you're going to learn before the bar and as an attorney again—you need to get practical experience.

[...]

Luckily, when I was a new housing attorney, I had a bit of work experience behind me. I was a few years into my 30s and had already had a career prior to law school, so I had the self-confidence to represent people who have been oppressed by multiple systems—racism, sexism, etc.—and who didn't have anybody to help them stand up to their landlords. It did feel lonely sometimes, but you end up bonding very quickly with other tenant attorneys because it's very hard. You're dealing with vicarious trauma because your clients are going through the worst possible situations. It's a high-volume practice, and it requires a lot of expertise. The people in housing court tend to be low-income people that have been dealing with oppressive systems for their entire lives, so there is a lot that you have to navigate while also trying to win. And winning here is keeping your client and their family housed or getting necessary repairs to their apartment.

I was also quite unprepared for what percentage of my practice was actually law versus serving as a counselor in a social work sense. I've learned a lot from my social worker colleagues about addressing difficult client communications and setting boundaries, which is hard because you feel responsible for keeping your client housed and you want to be there for them. Ultimately the more you do the work, the better you understand how to identify and manage those situations before they get out of hand.

I think having strong, involved supervision is key not just for the law but for serving our clients as well. And part of serving our clients as best as we can is to make sure that we're also taking care of ourselves. Even just knowing how to put a bad day behind you and start again the next day is something I wish there was more training and discussion for. You've got to have support networks, even if it's just another staff attorney sitting across the desk from you because if you don't talk about it, you'll burn out.

Q: The Coalition helped fight for the right to shelter in New York City. How effective do you think it has been, and what is the Coalition working on now?

I look at press from twenty, thirty years ago about the homelessness crisis and it's as if it was written today. So we have various administrations come into office in the city, and they think that they're going to be able to solve modern mass homelessness, but they can't. Then, to steal something my colleague said, they throw the police at it. But I don't think that the problem is with the right to shelter. Here in New York City, we have an upcoming election, so a lot of people are saying, "we need to dismantle the shelter system," but you can't do that, because we need a place for people to sleep. New York City doesn't have the high levels of unsheltered street homelessness like you see in other parts of the country because of the shelter system. Having a legal right to shelter is key—and there should be a legal right to shelter everywhere—but the shelter system should be a short-term stop, a safety net before you move to the logical next step, the right to permanent housing. The right to housing looks like a lot of different things: rent subsidies, section 8 entitlements, having a right to counsel, supportive housing, and affordable housing—truly affordable housing, not for a middle-income individual but affordable to someone who's at 30%.

[...]

The Coalition was recently a part of a grassroots campaign to ensure that all housing developments with over 40 units that are receiving any form of city funding would actually need to set aside 15%

of all of those units for unhoused people and families. It culminated in a bill[860] that passed in December 2019, became law in January 2020, and went into effect in July 2020. So we're really working on monitoring the shelter system and creating a path forward from shelters to permanent housing.

We're also very concerned with the details of how people qualify for permanent housing. For example, how burdensome is the application process, and how do we keep people from having to return to the NYC welfare office, or the Human Resources Administration, job centers. Being poor is really a full-time job because you're making all these appointments and trying to find or maintain a job and get your kids to school. What is the practicality of all these different hoops that we expect people to jump through to gain one benefit? These are the types of holes that can be filled by making phone calls or program changes. Sometimes you do have to send a demand letter and then litigate it—hopefully you can settle, but sometimes you do have to go to court. It's just a series of escalations until the government makes the change that you need.

---

860. Local Law 19 of 2020 added Chapter 28, § 28-2801 et seq., to the New York City Administrative Code, which requires most new housing developments that receive financial assistance from New York City to set aside at least 15 percent of apartments for unhoused people and families.

SEVEN

Hurdles to Housing and
Interim Solutions

Part II: Affordable Housing and Shelter

I. Affordable Housing

This section focuses on the small "a" affordable housing, which includes United States government Affordable Housing projects but extends beyond them. Capital "A" Affordable Housing refers only to government subsidized housing. The affordable housing shortage affects not only those living unhoused and taking home the lowest income, but also those at imminent risk of becoming unhoused due to rising housing costs.[861] A sustainable solution requires that housing remain affordable so that lower income renters do not get pushed out of their housing and take housing intended for even lower income renters.

---

861. This definition distinction is arguably critical to the success of affordable housing, because, for example, "[p]olitically, affordable housing as something just for the poor just won't be built." Aimee Custis. "What is affordable housing? Is it different from housing affordability? Should we care?" *Greater Washington*, Aug. 13, 2015. https://ggwash.org/view/38889/what-is-affordable-housing-is-it-different-from-housing-affordability-should-we-care.

A. Defining "Affordable Housing": Affordable for Who?

Housing created under the affordable housing model is scarcely affordable for the average low-income renter. Thresholds of "affordable" rent are determined by a U.S. Department of Housing and Urban Development (HUD) calculation of Area Median Income (AMI)—meaning that rents are determined by the wealth of an entire county, rather than neighborhoods where housing is located.

In Los Angeles, a person making up to $63,100 a year, 80% of the AMI, will qualify as "low income."[862] Comparatively, in Atlanta, housing is defined as "affordable" "if it is priced for people who make under 60% to 80% of the area's annual median income."[863] To directly compare to Los Angeles, in the Atlanta-Sandy Springs-Roswell metro area, the 80% income limit for a single person is $48,300.[864] Not surprisingly, AMI varies widely across the nation, likely depending on factors such as desirability of location and population density; accordingly, affordable housing plans within different states also target different AMI percent groups.[865]

HUD defines housing as affordable if its cost is less than or equal to 30% of a household's income. This ratio criterion is reflected in the common renter's income requirement of making three times the rent amount. The renter's monthly income requirement is often satisfied with a renter's gross income, rather than net; HUD's definition of 30% is intended to be calculated after

862. *L.A. Alliance for Human Rights v. City of Los Angeles*, Case 2:20-cv-02291-DOC -KES, Document 277 at 23.

863. Capelouto, J.D. 2021. "Atlanta to Use City-Owned Land to Build Affordable Housing," *Atlanta Journal-Constitution*, April 29, 2021. The City of Atlanta also has an interactive Housing Affordability Tracker available online at https://www.atlantaga.gov. Atlanta's Tracker details what housing projects have been built, the public agency funds used, number of total units, the number of affordable units, and, most significantly, the average median income (AMI) of each "affordable" unit.

864. FY 2021 Income Limits Documentation System, U.S. Housing Department of Housing and Urban Development. https://www.huduser.gov/portal/datasets/il/il2021 /2021summary.odn. This HUD resource is interactive and is updated yearly. Selecting different states and counties can provide insight on the varying cost of living and income levels nationally, which invariably affects how "affordable housing" is defined within different municipalities.

865. For example, a new plan to build affordable homes over five years targets Maui County residents below 120% AMI. This higher AMI percent threshold, however, may make sense in light of the average cost of a single-family home being over $1 million as of July 2021. JD Pells. "Rally Touts Affordable Housing Plan Amid 'Housing Crisis,'" *Maui Now*, July 21, 2021, 7:51 AM. https://mauinow.com/2021/07/21/rally-touts-affordable-housing -plan-amid-housing-crisis/.

taxes, however.[866] Thus, many American households are cost-burdened or shelter poor, spending approximately 50% of their take-home wages on their housing bills, which includes rent and utilities, and leaving too little for other non-housing necessities such as food, medical care, clothing, and transportation.[867] Judge David O. Carter's observation in L.A. Alliance for Human Rights v. City of Los Angeles that "[h]ousing created under the affordable housing model is scarcely affordable for the average low-income renter" aptly describes the current challenge of creating affordable housing for all.[868]

Additionally, it is worth mentioning that the COVID-19 pandemic highlights the consequences of the lack of affordable housing. As HUD Secretary Marcia Fudge surmised:

Even before the pandemic, our nation had a shortage of 7 million affordable and available homes for renters with the lowest incomes. As a result, 70% of these households routinely spent more than half of their incomes on rent. They have little ability to save—and one emergency or unexpected expense could send them into homelessness.[869]

1. Challenges

Every year, HUD receives data from the U.S. Census Bureau—known as the Comprehensive Housing Affordability Strategy (CHAS) data—illustrating "the extent of housing problems and housing needs" for low income house-

---

866. U.S. Department of Housing and Urban Development, "Glossary of Terms to Affordable Housing," Aug. 18, 2011. https://archives.hud.gov/local/nv/goodstories /2006-04-06glos.cfm ("Affordable housing is generally defined as housing on which the occupant is paying no more than 30 percent of gross income for housing costs, including utilities.").

867. Albert P.C. Chan, Michael Atafo Adabre, "Bridging the Gap Between Sustainable Housing and Affordable Housing: The Required Critical Success Criteria (CSC)," *Building and Environment* 151 (2019) 112, at 114; Xiaolong Gan, et al., "How affordable housing becomes more sustainable? A stakeholder study," *J. of Cleaner Production* 162 (2017) 427, 428–29.

868. In fact, many proponents argue that housing "[a]ffordability must involve whether a household has enough income left over for other needs of life after paying housing bills" and must take "into account the full amount required for housing and other basic needs." Albert P.C. Chan, Michael Atafo Adabre, "Bridging the Gap Between Sustainable Housing and Affordable Housing: The Required Critical Success Criteria (CSC)," *Building and Environment* 151 (2019) 112, at 114.

869. Secretary Fudge, Preface, "Out of Reach: The High Cost of Housing," National Low Income Housing Coalition, 2021. https://nlihc.org/sites/default/files/oor/2021/Out-of -Reach_2021.pdf.

holds.[870] Local governments use the CHAS data when spending HUD funds.[871] Notably, according to the CHAS data, there are more homeowners than renters, but more than half of all renters in America are at or below 80% AMI,[872] and more than half of households at or below 80% AMI are renters rather than owners.[873] This disparity reveals the segregation of the housing market, which disproportionately affects households of color.[874]

Rather than a lack of awareness or knowledge of the need for affordable housing, however, the challenges that impede regulatory proposal and project success are less obvious. For example, there may be local opposition to major changes in a neighborhood or against the people who are thought to live in affordable housing.[875] Or lower income renters may be squeezed out of desirable markets, due to phenomena outside of their control such as gentrification, which are often locations where jobs are located. Or perhaps it is the most obvious challenge that is the most difficult to overcome—that the cost of building more housing, including labor costs and the cost of securing loans, is simply expensive.[876]

In addition to overcoming the fiscal and social challenges facing the creation and success of affordable housing projects, a sustainable solution will require many other factors to be considered, including employment opportuni-

---

870. Office of Policy Development and Research, Consolidated Planning/CHAS Data, Aug. 25, 2020. https://www.huduser.gov/portal/datasets/cp.html.

871. Ibid.

872. AMI may also be called HUD Area Median Family Income or HAMFI.

873. Office of Policy Development and Research, Consolidated Planning/CHAS Data, Aug. 25, 2020. https://www.huduser.gov/portal/datasets/cp.html.

874. "While 82 percent of all renters earning less than $25,000 were cost burdened in 2019, the shares for Hispanic (86 percent), Black (83 percent) and Asian (84 percent) households all exceeded the share for white households (80 percent). In addition, some 69 percent of low-income homeowners were cost burdened, but the shares of Hispanic (72 percent), Black (74 percent), and Asian (81 percent) households were also higher than for white households (68 percent)." Joint Center for Housing Studies of Harvard University, "The State of the Nation's Housing 2021" at 32.

875. Commonly dubbed NIMBY ("not in my backyard"), NIMBYism is a discriminatory opposition that is rooted in racist, classist, and sexist beliefs; NIMBYists will justify their opposition on the fiscal basis that "These households will cost more to serve than they will pay in taxes." Matthew Palm & Deb Niemeier, "Achieving Regional Housing Planning Objectives: Directing Affordable Housing to Jobs-Rich Neighborhoods in the San Francisco Bay Area," *J. Am. Planning Ass'n*, 83:4 (2017) 377, 378. DOI: 10.1080/01944363.2017.1368410.

876. The cost of building incentives the building of luxury units over affordable units, simply from a cost-benefit analysis. "What is Affordable Housing Anyways?," *CoEverything*, Mar. 12, 2020. http://coeverything.co/blog/2020/3/12/what-is-affordable-housing-anyway.

ties, access to health care and public benefits, and the availability of short- and long-term shelters.

B. Finding a Sustainable Solution—Successes, Failures, and Ongoing Initiatives

"The story of American public housing is one of the quiet successes drowned out by loud failures."[877] Although affordable housing headlines often criticize government failures in providing housing to all, there are smaller, successful projects. This section provides a brief overview of some popular affordable housing regulations and projects and of some lesser-known proposals that may be worth investigating further on a larger scale.

1. Legislation & Voting—Regulation of the Housing Market

Our democracy enables us to vote and elect public officials who support funding affordable housing projects and exploring innovative solutions to eliminate the affordable housing shortage. Through education and awareness, legislation has and will enable great social change, including making affordable housing for all possible. Advocacy can bring legislation to the table and voting can help to elect the public officials who are prepared to support such legislation for their communities.

For example, the City of Seattle passed legislation[878] that will allow affordable housing projects on religious properties to rise one to six stories higher than allowed by normal zoning rules of the city. The legislation will require these projects' average household income across all units in the project to be no greater than 60% of the median annual income and no one household can have an income greater than 80% of the median income.[879] Under this law, the

---

877. Semuels, Alana. 2015. "The Power of Public Housing," *The Atlantic*, Sept. 22, 2015, quoting Ed Goetz in his book, *New Deal Ruins: Race, Economic Justice and Public Housing Policy.*

878. Council Bill No. CB 120081, Ordinance No. 126384 was approved unanimously, 8–0, on June 28, 2021.

879. Ketil Freeman, Amendment 1 the Council Bill 120081, June 22, 2021. Translated to dollars: "At 60% of AMI, a qualifying one-person and four-person household would have an income no greater than $46,500 annually and $66,400 annually, respectively. Affordable rents for a studio and 3-bedroom at 60% of AMI is $1,162 monthly and $1,726 monthly, respectively." Ibid.

city would be required to provide a density bonus for affordable housing on religious organization properties.[880]

One challenge in passing such legislation in other regions, however, may be the dubbed "home voter" hypothesis. The strong version asserts that "voters work to suppress housing supply as a way to protect higher housing values"; the weaker version, however, claims "that home owning voters are not strongly motivated to add supply because housing unaffordability does not directly hurt them, so other factors like the desire to avoid traffic or the desire to protect the character of their neighborhoods outweigh the appeal of seeking to reduce housing costs for other people."[881] Whichever may be the case, this lack of support may severely hinder legislative efforts in areas with higher wealth concentrations, leading to the continued segregation of neighborhoods that Affordable Housing and other past initiatives have caused.

2. Capital "A" Affordable Housing—Government-Owned Housing, Vouchers, and Privately-Owned Subsidized Housing[882]

In 2015, there were "1.2 million Americans living in housing managed by some 3,300 public-housing authorities, many of which . . . received scores of 98 or higher out of 100 in HUD's public-housing assessment system."[883] Affordable Housing undoubtedly has provided affordable opportunities to many lower income residents. However, common belief holds that public housing is a "failed policy" due to the record of the 1970s to1990s, at which time dysfunctional public housing complexes were torn down.[884] Government-owned housing projects made policy makers acutely aware of the harmful impacts of the overconcentration of poor residents, including how such segregated neighborhoods resulted in a lack of contacts and social networks for securing jobs.[885]

---

880. Nick Welch, Summary and Fiscal Note, OPCD Affordable Housing on Religious Organization Property SUM, June 28, 2021.

881. Gabriel Metcalf. "Sand Castles Before the Tide? Affordable Housing in Expensive Cities." *Journal of Economic Perspectives*, Vol. 32, No. 1, Winter 2018, pp. 59–80, p. 71.

882. Please see section on *Models and Solutions* later in this chapter for a more in-depth exploration of Section 8 vouchers and reforms.

883. Semuels, Alana. 2015. "The Power of Public Housing," *The Atlantic*, Sept. 22, 2015.

884. Ibid. By the 1970s, public housing was poorly-run, under-financed, and facing urban decline, crime, and gangs. In 1992, HOPE VI statutorily oversaw the demolition of public housing complexes. Ibid.

885. Matthew Palm & Deb Niemeier, "Achieving Regional Housing Planning Objectives: Directing Affordable Housing to Jobs-Rich Neighborhoods in the San Fran-

As a result, there are no efforts to build public housing, although there remain some successful projects in smaller regions.[886]

Housing vouchers have similarly revealed a gap in expectation and reality. For example, while rental vouchers have enabled millions of Americans to secure housing in the private market, many landlords are not willing to rent to voucher holders because voucher dollar amounts—determined yearly for each city by HUD—are often insufficient in expensive housing markets, resulting in pervasive discrimination against voucher holders.[887] Further, while programs such as "Section 8"—which allows households to pay 30% of their income in rent and have the remainder covered by the local Housing Authority—exist, success is limited. In fact, only about one in four people who need or qualify for a voucher receives federal assistance.[888] If a person ultimately receives assistance, the average wait time is about two and a half years, although the longest wait time, among the fifty largest housing agencies, is up to eight years.[889]

Lastly, privately-owned subsidized housing is a short-term solution at best because the process of rehousing is challenging for lower income renters who are often priced out of their former neighborhoods due to a lack of reinstated affordable housing opportunities.[890] For example, the most widely used subsidy program for the creation of privately-owned subsidized Affordable Housing is the Low Income Housing Tax Credit (LIHTC). Introduced in the 1986 Tax Reform Act, this tax credit lowers the taxes paid by developers over ten (10) years in exchange for keeping the rents low—typically 60% AMI or lower—but for only 15 years, or 30 years total if the extended compliance

cisco Bay Area," *J. of the American Planning Association*, 83:4 (2017) 377, 378. DOI: 10.1080/01944363.2017.1368410.

886. Semuels, Alana. 2015. "The Power of Public Housing," *The Atlantic*, Sept. 22, 2015 (discussing successful public housing complexes in Austin, Texas; Cambridge, Massachusetts; Portland, Oregon; and St. Paul, Minnesota).

887. Metcalf, 64–65.

888. Ibid., 64 (citing Center on Budget and Policy Priorities 2017).

889. Sonya Acosta & Erik Gartland, "Families Wait Years for Housing Vouchers Due to Inadequate Funding: Expanding Program Would Reduce Hardship, Improve Equity," Center on Budget and Policy Priorities, July 22, 2021. https://www.cbpp.org/research/housing/families-wait-years-for-housing-vouchers-due-to-inadequate-funding. Only two of the fifty largest agencies have an average wait time under a year for families who have made it off the waiting list. Ibid.

890. Aditi Mehta et al. "Affordable Housing, Disasters, and Social Equity," *J. of the American Planning Association*. Vol. 86, No. 1, 75.

period is imposed.[891] Nevertheless, "[a]s the federal government's primary tool for financing affordable housing, LIHTC currently produces an estimated 100,000 units per year," and the Biden-Harris Administration proposed to invest an additional $55 billion in tax credits under the American Jobs Plan.[892]

3. Raising the Minimum Wage

So why not shift the responsibility to the higher level of government by advocating for a higher minimum wage? Federalism aside, this may seem like an obvious solution, especially when considering how raising the federal minimum wage could ensure that the lowest income households are spending less on housing.[893] This solution alone, however, could not ensure that there is enough affordable housing for the long-term, as it would likely result in an increase in housing prices. As mentioned previously, the cost of building is expensive, and as the AMI increases, so too will the thresholds of what defines affordable housing. While raising the minimum wage could provide short (and long) term relief, it would need to be supplemented with another approach—such as regulation of the housing market—to be a sustainable solution.

Further, the local government is better equipped to serve its community. Because the social challenges that face each community differ, the public officials elected locally should be more sensitive to such challenges within their community and should be better able to consider what approaches and legislative efforts may be more successful there.

As may be obvious, different states and cities have implemented different solutions and continue to explore different solutions dependent on available resources, existing infrastructure, and community support. Thus, different states experience varying results when implementing the same program. For

---

891. Tax Policy Center, "Briefing Book: What is the Low-Income Housing Tax Credit and How Does It Work?," Urban Institute & Brookings Institution, 2021. https://www.taxpolicycenter.org/briefing-book/what-low-income-housing-tax-credit-and-how-does-it-work.

892. The White House, Statements and Releases, "Fact Sheet: The American Job Plan Will Produce, Preserve, and Retrofit More than 2 Million Affordable Housing Units and Create Good-Paying Jobs," May 26, 2021. https://www.whitehouse.gov/briefing-room/statements-releases/2021/05/26/fact-sheet-the-american-jobs-plan-will-produce-preserve-and-retrofit-more-than-2-million-affordable-housing-units-and-create-good-paying-jobs/.

893. The 2021 *Out of Reach* report from the National Low Income Housing Coalition estimates that "a full-time worker must earn at least $20.40 per hour to rent a modest one-bedroom home, or $24.90 per hour to rent a modest two-bedroom home." Secretary Fudge, Preface, "Out of Reach: The High Cost of Housing," National Low Income Housing Coalition, 2021. https://nlihc.org/sites/default/files/oor/2021/Out-of-Reach_2021.pdf.

example, a 2020 study in the Northeast compared five states and analyzed why Massachusetts alone was able to statistically improve housing outcomes through their State Affordable Housing Appeals System (SAHAS).[894] Such observations reveal how the solution to create affordable housing for all is like the "cure for cancer" misnomer—there is no one cure because every cancer is a different disease, just as every state or county has unique challenges in creating and maintaining affordable housing.

4. Increase Spending on Social Housing: Government vs. Developers

Given the stagnation of government Affordable Housing due to the chronic lack of sufficient funding, any expectation of increased government spending may be misplaced. Nonetheless, it may be worth exploring innovative opportunities with independent developers to develop a concerted effort vertically across all levels of government and horizontally across the public and private sectors.

In fact, some development organizations have taken it upon themselves to discover feasible long-term affordable housing solutions. For example, the Workforce Housing Group (WFHG), an affordable housing organization in New York City, partnered with Morgan Stanley, NY Green Bank, and Flume, Inc. to use solar power to subsidize internet costs across twenty-two buildings in Brooklyn by 2022.[895] Despite the hefty upfront cost, the expected utility bill savings through solar technology is expected to contribute towards a sustainable and cost-effective solution towards digital equity. As John A. Crotty, principal of WFHG advocates: "This is a revolutionary model that can be sustainably replicated across the city and eventually on a national level. Solar Powered Community Wi-Fi should become a new de facto standard for affordable housing."[896] Although the success of this project is yet to be evaluated, such innovative solutions may be what is necessary to help lower housing bills and the number of cost burdened households nationwide.

---

894. Nicholas J. Marantz and Huizin Zheng, "State Affordable Housing Appeals Systems and Access to Opportunity: Evidence from the Northeastern United States," (2020) *Housing Policy Debate*, Vol 30, No. 2, 370, 388.

895. Learn more about the Workforce Housing Group and their projects on their website: http://www.workforcehousinggroup.com.

896. "How solar funded Wi-Fi could be the new normal for affordable housing," *Real Estate Weekly*, June 14, 2021. https://rew-online.com/how-solar-funded-wi-fi-could-be-the-new-normal-for-affordable-housing/.

a. Other Opportunities

Advocates who support affordable housing for all suggest endless ideas and opportunities. The most comprehensive ideas include a refundable renter's tax credit offered through the tax code at the annual cost of $24.1 billion to reduce the poverty rate by 12.4 percentage points and the deep poverty rate by 8.8 percentage points;[897] mandatory affordable housing agreements to ensure that all relevant parties are invested and consequent negotiations result in mutual gains for all stakeholders;[898] increasing inclusionary housing;[899] and integrating thoughtful design to allow for affordable multifamily housing.[900]

Other scarcely discussed opportunities are worth considering, such as whether manufactured housing (i.e., mobile homes or trailers) or tiny houses[901] could be a potential solution. Manufactured homes, for example, house approximately 18 million residents and are the largest source of unsubsidized affordable housing in the United States, although largely ignored by scholarship and policymakers.[902] Various advocates have also proposed other solutions such as creating land community trusts and community land cooperatives, building more cities, and pooling taxes. There are many opportunities to explore on a larger scale and, given the recent efforts of policymakers and developers, the future of affordable housing has promising models to explore.

897. Kimberlin, Sara, Laura Tach, and Christopher Wimer. 2018. "A Renter's Tax Credit to Curtail the Affordable Housing Crisis," *Russell Sage Foundation J. of the Social Sciences* 4(2): 131–60. DOI: 10.7758/RSF.2018.4.2.07.

898. Katrina Raynor, Matthew Palm & Georgia Warren-Myers, "Ambiguous, Confusing, and Not Delivering Enough Housing," *J. Am. Planning Ass'n* (2021) 1–15. DOI: 10.1080/01944363.2021.1875870.

899. Emily Thaden and Ruoniu Want, "Inclusionary Housing in the United States: Prevalence, Impact, and Practices," Lincoln Institute of Land Policy, Working Paper WP17ET1 (2017).

900. Hannah Hoyt and Jenny Schuetz, "Thoughtful design can create high-quality affordable multifamily housing," *Brookings Report*, June 17, 2020. https://www.brookings.edu/research/affordable-housing-doesnt-have-to-look-cheap-inside-or-out/.

901. Emily Keable, "Building on the Tiny House Movement: A Viable Solution to Meet Affordable Housing Needs," 11 *U. St. Thomas J.L. & Pub. Pol'y* 111 (2017).

902. Noah J. Durst & Esther Sullivan (2019) "The Contribution of Manufactured Housing to Affordable Housing in the United States: Assessing Variation Among Manufactured Housing Tenures and Community Types," *Housing Policy Debate*, 29:6, 880, 880. DOI: 10.1080/10511482.2019.1605534.

5. Conclusion

The Housing Act of 1949[903] promises the "realization as soon as feasible of the goal of a decent home and suitable living environment for every American family." Some argue that this is an explicit contract that remains unfulfilled.[904] Studies, however, have found that strong comprehensive affordable housing plans are linked to a decline in the number of cost-burdened households.[905] Further, many more residents today are housed as a direct result of Affordable Housing and other housing initiatives. So while scholarship and news outlets suggest a sustainable, long-term solution to the affordable housing shortage, it may require a greater coordination of efforts[906] or more leaders willing to invest in innovative opportunities. The small victories for affordable housing are worth recognizing. The small victories for affordable housing are worth recognizing; they provide ideas to replicate and lend hope to achieving affordable housing for all.

II. Shelter: Short- and Long-Term

This section shifts its focus from affordable housing to short and long-term shelter by looking at and commenting on the shelter model in detail, then discussing the shelter model's impact on shelter populations, as well as other models that might work. This section will compare short-term emergency shelters with long-term transitional shelters. In its commentary on the shelter model, this section will focus on unhoused youth. But first, here is an excerpt of Judge Carter's order in which he points out the importance of shelter as an intermediary measure in housing unhoused city residents:

---

903. 42 USC §§ 1441–1490r (1994).

904. Lance Freeman, "America's Affordable Housing Crisis: A Contract Unfulfilled," *Am. J. Public Health*. 2002 May; 92(5): 709–712. DOI: 10.2105/ajph.92.5.709.

905. Matthew Palm & Deb Niemeier, "Achieving Regional Housing Planning Objectives: Directing Affordable Housing to Jobs-Rich Neighborhoods in the San Francisco Bay Area," *J. Am. Planning Ass'n*, 83:4 (2017) 377, 381. DOI: 10.1080/01944363.2017.1368410 (discussing a 2014 and 2017 study in Florida and Georgia, respectively).

906. Hoffman suggests that "housing advocates should try to protect government funding to preserve and renovate viable public and subsidized housing developments and to maintain the number of rental vouchers and certificates . . . [and] should work to preserve tax credits to assist nonprofit community-based low-income housing efforts." Alexander von Hoffman, "High Ambitions: The Past and Future of American Low-Income Housing Policy," *Housing Policy Debate* (1996) Vol. 7, Issue 3, 423, 442.

Even if this Court ignored the entire history of conscious decisions by the government that led to the creation of Skid Row and the rampant depravity before us today, there is still incontrovertible evidence that the danger of living on the streets—which led to 1,383 deaths last year alone—is state-made. The strongest evidence for a state-made danger is the deliberate, political choice to pursue the development of long-term supportive housing at the expense of interim shelters to get people off the streets in the near-term. **As Plaintiffs pointed out in their brief, Proposition HHH—the $1.2 billion ballot initiative to create 10,000 housing units for the homeless—provided funding that could be used either for long-term supportive housing or for temporary shelters.... Nevertheless, the City and County "unilaterally" decided to focus on housing at the expense of shelter, even knowing that massive development delays were likely while people died in the streets. Over the four years since HHH's passage, a mere 489 housing units have been built, while over 5,000 people lost their lives in the streets due to a lack of shelter.** The vast majority of those deaths were preventable. Defendants argue that "Plaintiffs have not established that any City official affirmatively placed Plaintiffs in danger they would otherwise not have been in," but pursuing housing at the expense of shelter, suspending HHH deadlines (and thereby evading accountability), and ramping down Project Roomkey despite the availability of federal funds to support it were all political choices that created this crisis. Without these choices, the death rate among L.A.'s homeless population would not be growing exponentially.[907]

A. A Detailed Look at the Shelter Model

1. Status of Shelters in the United States

Shelters are often categorized as either emergency (providing housing for only short periods of time in typically no more than large rooms with cots) or transitional (providing longer-term housing while occupants transition to the housing market). While residents of more home-like, transitional shelters receive protection from sex and familial discrimination under the Fair Housing Act (FHA), residents of emergency shelters receive a lower level of protection

---

907. *L.A. All. for Human Rights v. City of Los Angeles*, 2021 U.S. Dist. LEXIS 76053, 2021 WL 1546235 (C.D. Cal. 2021).

from sex and familial discrimination but still have constitutional and statutory protections against other forms of discrimination.[908]

2. Potential Effect of Prohibiting Discrimination on Short- and Long-Term Shelters

Although facially discriminatory admissions policies in shelters are widespread and tolerated, strong arguments in favor of giving FHA protections to at least a portion if not all of those housed in shelters involve either a stratified regime (the status quo under which longer-term transitional shelters receive FHA protections and shorter-term emergency shelters receive on non-FHA protections) or a categorical regime (an alternative under which all shelters received FHA protections). If shelters react to a ruling under a stratified regime by switching from transitional to emergency shelters to avoid providing FHA protections, then the goal of the U.S. Department of Housing and Urban Development (HUD) to promote transitional housing may be set back; if shelters react to a decision under a categorical regime by draining resources in an attempt to comply by creating all mixed-use shelters (which do not have policies that restrict based on sex or familial status), they may not be able to serve as many individuals and may ultimately hurt the unhoused population (or possibly close in response to such a decision).[909]

B. Movement Toward and Beyond Shelters

1. Shelter Users

Beginning in the 1990s, researchers began to categorize three groups of shelter users: transitionally unhoused people (staying in the shelter system for a short period and unlikely to return), episodically unhoused people (using the shelter system on multiple occasions and having low-level support needs), and chronically unhoused people (only ten percent of total shelter residents but using half of available beds annually because of their long and repeated shelter stays). Studies have found that the small group of chronically unhoused people

---

908. Cheyne, Greg C. "Facially Discriminatory Admissions Policies in Homeless Shelters and the Fair Housing Act." *The University of Chicago Legal Forum* (2009): 459–501 (alluding that both short and long-term shelter residents share constitutional protections under the Equal Protection Clause and the Establishment Clause as well as statutory protections under Section 1982 of the Civil Rights Act of 1866, Title II of the Civil Rights Act of 1964, Title VI of the Civil Rights Act of 1964, and the Americans with Disabilities Act).

909. Ibid.

are also the heavy users of public services like emergency services and acute hospital care.[910] Given that chronically unhoused people are often targeted and ensnared with the criminal justice system, they also remain heavily on the receiving end of policing and, thereafter, the system itself.[911]

2. Beyond Shelter and Toward Housing

In discussing shelter, one should also consider the concept of "Housing First" (see Chapter 2 for in-depth discussion of this principle of homeless advocacy), which places people, particularly those people suffering severe mental illnesses, who have experienced long-term homelessness, into permanent rental housing as quickly as possible with ongoing, flexible and individual but voluntary support as long as needed. Given that Housing First focuses on chronic homelessness, seeing shelters as a steppingstone to housing also remains important because it is conceivable that focusing on chronic homelessness may provide cover for politicians to disinvest in services like shelters, which remain essential to the much larger population of transitionally or episodically unhoused people who may be less visible.[912]

C. Impact of Shelter Model

1. Focus on the Youth Population: Evaluating Chronic Homelessness

In a study of Los Angeles County unhoused youth who were monitored for two years, three trajectories of unhoused youth remaining sheltered or returning to shelter were identified: "consistently sheltered," "inconsistently sheltered, short-term," and "inconsistently sheltered, long-term."[913] In evaluating whether a sheltered youth falls into chronic homelessness,[914] the ability of an unhoused youth to return to their prior home (due to factors of disaffiliation from family

---

910. Baker, Tom, and Joshua Evans. "'Housing First' and the Changing Terrains of Homeless Governance." *Geography Compass* 10, no. 1 (2016): 25–41.

911. Ibid.

912. Ibid. (mentioning Pathways to Housing, a New York City organization considered to have invented the "housing first" model in the 1990s, and Beyond Shelter, a Los Angeles organization that practiced a housing-led approach around the same time).

913. Tevendale, Heather D., W. Scott Comulada, and Marguerita A. Lightfoot. "Finding Shelter: Two-Year Housing Trajectories Among Homeless Youth." *J. of Adolescent Health* 49, no. 6 (2011): 615–620.

914. Compare Tevendale et al. (2011) (using the descriptors "consistently sheltered," "inconsistently sheltered, short-term," and "inconsistently sheltered, long-term") with Baker

like a lack of instrumental support from parents, not having a home to return to, and having been made to leave home) is more determinative of their outcome than their degree of individual impairment (e.g., substance use or mental health problems).[915]

2. Suggestions of Los Angeles County Reported Findings

Results from the Los Angeles County study suggest not only potential value in working with the families of unhoused youth to help them return home safely whenever possible, but also that youth indicating they chose to leave home may need targeted intervention that enhances motivation to leave life on the street behind. Additionally, some results suggest that youth who are consistently sheltered are likely to continue to be sheltered even if they indicated that they did not have their own home, which further suggests the importance of preventing unhoused youth from beginning to spend their nights in unsheltered locations.[916]

D. What Models Might Work

1. "Life Course" Approach to Shelter Residents

Based on interview information from a sample of Texas short-term and long-term shelter residents, researchers recommend that efforts geared toward remediating, alleviating, or preventing homelessness be driven by one's life course, which essentially means that the sheltered population should be met with compassion and empathy rather than criminalization and stigmatization. For instance, chronically unhoused people, unlike temporarily unhoused people, must rely on a combination of short-term arrangements, emergency services, shelters, or even jails and prisons periodically for survival because of their life course.[917]

---

and Evans (2016) (using the descriptors "transitionally homeless," "episodically homeless," and "chronically homeless").

915. Tevendale et al. (2011).

916. Ibid.

917. Paat, Yok-Fong, Jessica Morales, Ray Tullius, Eva M Moya, and Ruben Alcantara. "A Life Course Approach to Understanding Homelessness of Shelter Residents." *J. of Social Distress and the Homeless* 28, no. 2 (2019): 176–185. Noting that there is a life course does not imply that homelessness is a choice, only that advocates should attempt to understand the course the unhoused person is on (due to circumstances, etc.).

2. Compassionate and Empathetic Approaches

Various types of resources can be allocated to individuals depending upon varied stages of homelessness so that supportive services can bridge the gap for those in transition from a transitional living arrangement to permanent housing. Setting realistic goals with shelter residents is imperative because those residents navigating social and health care services beyond what are offered at the shelter may also face structural issues such as lack of affordable housing, limited access to quality mental health services and health care, high unemployment rates, discriminatory hiring, and social forces like family breakdown or substance addiction.[918]

3. Service Model for Women with Children

Professions need to understand how the experience of being unhoused affects all aspects of unhoused people's lives. For example, nursing, a helping profession, involves encounters with unhoused people in daily practices of inner-city hospitals, public health clinics, and communities. Therefore, nurses may be more aware of the unique problems inherent in being unhoused by being more understanding of the issues surrounding unhoused women with preschool children living in temporary shelters. For example, nurses may design innovative interventions which include formulating realistic client care plans (especially regarding discharge planning), planning programs to assist unhoused clients to resolve their homelessness, and providing policymakers with important information necessary to the understanding of and potential solutions to the homelessness problem.[919]

4. Transitional Services for Shelter Residents: Breaking the Cycle of "Shelternization"

New York City (and other cities) may equip its unhoused population with the means necessary to sustain an independent living by, first, prioritizing short-term goals such as ensuring that shelters provide transitional services, which need to be readily accessible so that city officials can take the necessary steps in preventing unhoused population growth and breaking the cycle of "shelternization." Thereafter, New York City (and other cities) must prioritize interagency collaboration to successfully achieve a seamless and effective social services system for unhoused people.[920]

---

918. Ibid.

919. Ibid.

920. Kim, Salley. "Preventing Shelternization: Alleviating the Struggles of Unhoused People and Families in New York City." *The Fordham Urb. L.J.* 42, no. 4 (2015): 1019–1061.

5. Beyond the Solution of Shelter

Emergency shelters remain a prohibitively expensive short-term solution in response to populations in imminent crisis. Taxes finance these facilities. In Los Angeles, placing four chronically unhoused people into permanent housing saves the city more than $80,000 per year. Generally, emergency shelters designed for families are equally if not more expensive than transitional and permanent housing. In addition to short-term shelter, cities may offer long-term solutions like tenant education, guaranteeing legal representation, and reforming strict eviction policies to allow for more flexibility. More than being less expensive, supportive housing programs have demonstrated that access to transitional services can improve housing retention. Thus, implementing transitional services narrowly tailored to support the unhoused population, improve their practical skills, and counsel them will also better situate them in their efforts not only to obtain but also to keep permanent housing.[921]

LIVED EXPERIENCE NARRATIVE

Robert is a former client of the Chicago Coalition for the Homeless and is now a grassroots leader and active community advocate for those experiencing homelessness. After experiencing homelessness for over 45 years, Robert has been living in a rental apartment for approximately five years.[922]

On Living Unsheltered[923]

What caused me to get into that situation was that at that particular time I was much younger. I made a lot of bad decisions. So, my homelessness at that particular time was basically a self-inflicted wound. I was hanging around the wrong people.

After a while I wound up getting addicted to drugs and that's what caused my spiral and made it impossible for me to get an apartment. After the years went on, I got tired of living that particular way and made up my mind to really truly start looking for an apartment.

---

921. Ibid.

922. Henderson, Robert. Interview with Angela Hwang. March 22, 2021.

923. Mr. Henderson's narrative has been reorganized into thematic sections and does not necessarily follow the structure of the interview. The "[. . .]" indicates that the separated paragraphs are taken from different moments of the interview. Furthermore, some grammatical edits have been made to clarify and contextualize his statements.

You can't make no career out of being homeless. Those streets are unforgiving. Out there, I was sleeping in the streets, sleeping on the buses, sleeping in the park, sleeping in O'Hare and Midway,[924] any-where. Riding the bus all night or riding the train all night—that was my life. That's what I did. And then there were a couple of times where I experienced where young people tried to take advantage of me and I wound up going to the hospital because I got a concussion from getting hit in the head by a two by four.

On Services for Unhoused People

There are a lot of organizations, even churches—places where you can go and lounge around and work on the computers and get your resume together, get clothes, take a shower.... There are organizations out here that try to help you get your life together. Then you have these shelters.... I never did like shelters.

But at the same time, in the wintertime, what I used to do as well; by me having a medical card, I used to go to a hospital in Cook County, and I would tell them I am homeless and I wanted to go to a nursing home. And the social workers there at the hospital, they would find a nursing home that would accept you. And I would get placed in a nursing home. But the thing of it is, is that I would only do it during the wintertime and I could only stay no longer than sixty days. If I stayed there longer than sixty days, then they would take my disability check. So, I stayed less than sixty days then stayed on the street for a week or two and then go back to the same hospital and they would find me another nursing home. That was my routine in the wintertime. That was one of the ways when it was too cold; that was one of my ways to get off the streets in the wintertime.

But there are groups—a lot of groups out here—if you want the help. If it's mental, if it's clothing ... they can help you get housing, help you fill out a resume, help you get yourself together. They can even help you get your birth certificate or ID. If you don't have that, they'll help you get that. You can't get a job without an ID. If you try to get some type of benefit, you need an ID. Social Security card. You need something with your signature on it. They will help you try to obtain that information.

---

924. These are airports located in Chicago.

The services that they have here in Chicago are good. But some services are on one particular side of town. Say for instance, if I'm living on the West side, and I need a particular service, I have to go to the North side. And if I don't have the funds or the transportation to get there, then that service is useless to me. I can't get to that particular service.

A lot of times there are groups that can help you get a bus pass, or something like that. But it's for a week or a couple days just to get to the place you are trying to get to—transportation there and back. At the same time, they'll only give it to you if you only come once a month or once every other month. There's a limit.

On His Experience with the Law and Legal Services

When I was homeless…I think I was living up in Oakley under the metro there then, and people knew us. People would come and feed us every Monday, Wednesday, and Friday. And what happened was, this particular time, the city of Chicago came. I got up in the morning to go find me some palettes—to grab stuff for the scrap yard to get some money—so I went out there in the morning and when I came back, my property—the stuff that I had, the stuff that I needed—my medications and a lot of other things were thrown in the city garbage can. I mean—I couldn't—there was no sense in cussing them out. I politely walked over to a lady in a pick-up truck who was the supervisor. I asked her some questions and she gave me some answers and I asked her for her card and she gave me her card. Then I went over to some other ladies—they were Department of Human Services—and they asked me "Where do you want us to take you?" and I replied, "I am where I want to be."

So, what had happened was that the lady who come to feed us every Monday, Wednesday, and Friday, she was so torn up about what the city had done. It just so happened that she had a flyer for the Chicago Coalition for the Homeless. She said, "Call the people here and they may be able to help you." And that's what I did.

Diane[925] came out to where I was living at that particular time and I gave her everything I collected, like the contact information for the two ladies at the Department of Human Services. She was able to get the rest of the information that she needed and put together a lawsuit. And it just so happened that I had the right case because there was a

---

925. Diane O'Connell, Community Lawyer for the Chicago Coalition for the Homeless.

law that was just passed about the homeless people. That even though they may be on the street, they have rights. So, you know, I had the perfect case to test that new law.

BILL OF RIGHTS FOR THE HOMELESS ACT[926]

(a)   No person's rights, privileges, or access to public services may be denied or abridged solely because he or she is homeless. Such a person shall be granted the same rights and privileges as any other citizen of this State. A person experiencing homelessness has the following rights:

1. the right to use and move freely in public spaces, including but not limited to public sidewalks, public parks, public transportation, and public buildings, in the same manner as any other person and without discrimination on the basis of his or her housing status;

2. the right to equal treatment by all State and municipal agencies, without discrimination on the basis of housing status;

3. the right not to face discrimination while maintaining employment due to his or her lack of permanent mailing address, or his or her mailing address being that of a shelter or social service provider;

4. the right to emergency medical care free from discrimination based on his or her housing status;

5. the right to vote, register to vote, and receive documentation necessary to prove identity for voting without discrimination due to his or her housing status;

6. the right to protection from disclosure of his or her records and information provided to homeless shelters and service providers to State, municipal, and private entities without appropriate legal authority; and the right to confidentiality of personal records and information in accordance with all limitations on disclosure established by the federal Homeless Management Information Systems, the federal Health Insurance Portability and Accountability Act [215 ILCS 97/1 et seq.], and the federal Violence Against Women Act; and

7. the right to a reasonable expectation of privacy in his or her personal property to the same extent as personal property in a permanent residence.

(b)   As used in this Act, "housing status" means the status of having or not having a fixed or regular residence, including the status of living on the streets, in a shelter, or in a temporary residence.

---

926. 775 Ill. Comp. Stat. 45/10 (2013).

So, after she put that [lawsuit] together, we constantly stayed in communication throughout the whole ordeal. There were a couple times they tried to get the case thrown out, and the judge would say, "no," that I got a good case. As time went on, after I took the deposition and others took their depositions, Diane called and said that the final offer was $27,000, today. So that was the arrangement. And they had sixty days—and they took advantage of that too—but on the sixtieth day I got $27,000 from the City of Chicago.[927]

---

927. Settlement amount is publicly available on the City of Chicago, Department of Law—Judgment/Verdict & Settlement Report (2018).

EIGHT

Hurdles to Housing and Interim Solutions

Part III: Legal Representation and Models

Robert, who shared his experience in Chapter 7, was part of an impact litigation case. But there are other more direct forms of legal assistance that, along with debt advice, are promising interventions that seem to be effective in decreasing the risk of being evicted. Legal support improves a tenant's chances of avoiding eviction in court, while debt advice helps to prevent evictions by decreasing rent arrears.[928] In addition to direct legal services, there are other legal models that, if expanded (e.g., housing courts, medical-legal partnerships) or explored (e.g., role of judiciary) could help unhoused people. This chapter explores some of these forms of legal representation and models.

---

928. Holl, Marieke, Linda van den Dries, and Judith R.L.M Wolf. "Interventions to Prevent Tenant Evictions: A Systematic Review." *Health & Social Care in the Community* 24, no. 5 (2016): 532–546.

I. Lifting Restrictions to Representation in the Housing Context

A. The Civil Right to Counsel: How a Civil Gideon Addresses Concentrated Poverty

Gideon v. Wainwright held that the Sixth Amendment guarantees a right to counsel to those accused of a crime, including in state court by way of the Fourteenth Amendment.[929] In order to prevent people from becoming unhoused or sinking into deeper poverty, there is a similar need for a right to counsel for eviction proceedings and other civil needs. Civil needs (e.g., food insecurity; neglected rental housing with mold, lack of heat, vermin infestation, and landlords who refuse to repair those conditions; inadequate safety net benefits with strict work rules; failing schools with excessively large classrooms and not enough teachers; too few jobs that pay a living wage) increase surveillance of marginalized communities by law enforcement and drive these communities into criminal court. In turn, their criminal justice involvement has civil ramifications that can be severe and burdensome (such as eviction proceedings), yet no equivalent to *Gideon* exists in the civil sphere.[930]

1. Home Ownership

Legal representation can play an important role in helping homeowners retain their housing or avoid homelessness as a result of foreclosure because, if the government provided poor people with meaningful access to lawyers, then they might adopt many of the strategies proposed for addressing concentrated poverty in the nation's cities such as: "channel[ing] federally-assisted housing expenditures to lessen racial concentration"; "requir[ing] fair-share affordable housing obligations"; "encourag[ing] balanced distribution of... housing"; "promot[ing] racially mixed neighborhoods"; "help[ing] families that are receiving place-based services and supports remain in place, if they want to

---

929. *Gideon v. Wainwright*, 372 U.S. 335 (1963).

930. Rajagopal, Runa. "Diary of a Civil Public Defender: Critical Lessons for Achieving Transformative Change on Behalf of Communities," *The Fordham Urb. L.J.* 46, no. 4 (2019): 876–901.

stay"; "help[ing] families recognize and address housing discrimination"; and "promot[ing] housing choice and relocation for those who want it."[931]

2. Building a Right to Counsel in Evictions

Since 2017 when New York City became the first jurisdiction in the United States to pass legislation guaranteeing a right to counsel in eviction cases, San Francisco and Newark, New Jersey also passed laws guaranteeing such a right. In New York City, a steep drop in evictions could be indicating that landlords are choosing not to bring frivolous suits because they know their tenant will have an attorney (although the law may be too new to fully analyze this outcome); however, the city saw a twenty-four percent decline in evictions when it increased its budget for legal services to low-income tenants before the legislation was signed into law. Currently, the city's "Universal Access to Counsel Program" not only guarantees representation to income-eligible tenants in eviction proceedings in the city's housing court but also provides for either representation or advice to tenants in New York City Housing Authority administrative proceedings to terminate tenancy, which is required to seek an eviction order in the housing court.[932]

3. Strengthening and Expanding the Right to Counsel in Evictions

In most jurisdictions where the right to counsel in evictions exists, the right attaches at the time of an administrative housing assistance termination hearing under current laws (except in San Francisco, where the right attaches thirty days after receiving a notice from the landlord indicating an intent to evict), but advocates argue the right should attach upon receipt of a notice terminating tenancy to meaningfully protect many tenants.[933] The right to counsel in eviction proceedings has expanded across several cities and at the state level in Washington, which became the first to give its indigent tenants a right to counsel.[934]

---

931. Ortiz, Pamela Cardullo. "How a Civil Right to Counsel Can Help Dismantle Concentrated Poverty in America's Inner Cities." *Stan. L. & Pol'y Rev.* 25, no. 1 (2014): 163–191.

932. Petersen, Ericka. "Building a House for *Gideon*: The Right to Counsel in Evictions." *Stan. J. of C.R. & C.L.* 16, no. 1 (2020): 63–112.

933. Ibid.

934. Cassens Weiss, Debra. "Washington Is First State to GIVE Right-to-Counsel Protections to These Litigants." *ABA J.* Accessed July 28, 2021. https://www.abajournal.com/

II. Other Restrictions to Representation

While the federal government provides neither a civil right to legal nor full counsel, the Legal Services Corporation (LSC) uses congressionally appropriated funds to issue grants to regional legal services providers who then assist those who qualify financially. However, LSC funding prohibits representing people in evictions from public housing if they have been convicted with drug crimes that are alleged to threaten the health or safety of public housing residents or employees. As a result, many legal services providers decline LSC funding and, consequently, struggle to sustain themselves without federal help.[935]

III. Homeless Advocacy in the Courtroom

A. Homeless Courts: Establishment of Specialized Housing Courts and Programs

Beginning in the early 1970s, New York City and a number of other large cities created specialized housing courts to enforce state and local laws regulating housing conditions and also to adjudicate landlord-tenant disputes, which involved a range of issues, the most common being landlords suing to evict tenants for nonpayment of rent. In New York's housing court, most landlords have lawyers, while the vast majority of tenants represent themselves in court.[936] Nationwide, ninety percent of landlords are represented by legal counsel in evictions, but fewer than ten percent of tenants have representation.[937]

---

news/article/washington-is-first-state-to-give-right-to-counsel-protections-to-these-litigants (giving a right to counsel to tenants who receive public assistance or earn no higher than 200% of the federal poverty level, which amounts to $25,760 per year for individuals and $53,000 per year for a four-person household).

935. Zarnow, Zachary H. "Obligation Ignored: Why International Law Requires the United States to Provide Adequate Civil Legal Aid, What the United States Is Doing Instead, and How Legal Empowerment Can Help," *Am. U.J. of Gender, Social Policy & the L.* 20, no. 1 (2011): : 273–308.

936. Seron, Carroll, Gregg Van Ryzin, Martin Frankel, and Jean Kovath. "The Impact of Legal Counsel on Outcomes for Poor Tenants in New York City's Housing Court: Results of a Randomized Experiment." *Law & Soc'y Rev.* 35, no. 2 (2001): 419–434.

937. Park, Sandra, and John Pollock. "Tenants' Right to Counsel Is Critical to Fight Mass Evictions and Advance Race Equity During the Pandemic and Beyond." American Civil Liberties Union. Accessed July 28, 2021. https://www.aclu.org/news/racial-justice/tenants

In its first randomized experimental evaluation of a legal assistance program for low-income tenants, New York City's Housing Court demonstrated that providing legal counsel produces large differences in outcomes for low-income tenants. Additionally, the results suggest that a legal assistance program for low-income tenants would not significantly increase the number of appearances in court (although it would increase the number of days to final judgment).[938]

B. Supply-Side Reform

Supply-side reform relates to the belief among poverty lawyers, scholars, courts, and the organized bar that supplying more lawyers will best address the problems of the unrepresented poor. Access to justice through the supply-side approach is based on the vigorous pursuit of full representation with other resources spread across any remaining unrepresented litigants. But civil *Gideon* rights have been regularly rejected by courts and legislatures and resulted in unbundled legal services as the leading alternative for responding to representation issues. While unbundled legal services help individuals prepare pleadings and can foster a better mindset among unrepresented litigants, it is not a fully comprehensive access to justice model because of its limits in assisting with more complex litigation and improving substantive case results.[939]

C. Demand-Side Reform

Demand-side reform is defined as "an overhaul of the processes and rules that govern litigation so that they best serve the interests of the overwhelming majority of customers in the lower state courts—the unrepresented."[940] Access to justice through demand-side reform means revising both procedural and evidentiary rules of the court and requiring judges to elicit as much legally relevant information as possible from litigants. While reform of court processes would not be as effective as providing full representation in every case, it could offer otherwise unrepresented litigants a functional substitute for attor-

---

-right-to-counsel-is-critical-to-fight-mass-evictions-and-advance-race-equity-during-the-pandemic-and-beyond/.

938. Seron et al. (2001).

939. Steinberg, Jessica K. "Demand Side Reform in the Poor People's Court." *Conn. L. Rev.* 47, no. 3 (2015): 741–807.

940. Ibid.

ney assistance in a move that the U.S. Supreme Court endorsed in 2011 via *Turner v. Rogers*.[941]

D. Engaging in a Demosprudence of Poverty

Judges may engage in a demosprudence of poverty, which is "a democracy-enhancing jurisprudence" that actively seeks to learn from poor people themselves and movements for economic justice.[942] When judges intervene on behalf of poor litigants to ensure that legal claims, especially landlord-tenant disputes, are expressed in the courtroom, judges better meet their ethical obligations as well as protect the fundamental interests of equal and equitable justice under law.[943]

IV. Appropriate Oversight by Government Actors

A. Defining the Role of the U.S. Department of Housing and Urban Development (HUD)

Section 8 reform consumed former rental assistance policies to create an overarching, comprehensive rental assistance program handing out payments to property owners of new or "substantially rehabilitated" rental units in exchange for them leasing these units to low-income families paying income-based rents. When this model grew unsustainable, HUD began reserving contracts for existing properties only with the tenant-based system, making state and local public housing agencies responsible for issuing Section 8 vouchers.[944]

While Section 8 vouchers cover market rent through a federally-backed guarantee, landlords can and often do refuse to accept them. Today, people remain on waitlists for years, if they can get on the waitlist at all, because the system cannot keep up with demand.[945]

---

941. Ibid. (discussing *Turner v. Rogers*, 131 S. Ct. 2507 (2011)).

942. Bell, Monica, Stephanie Garlock, and Alexander Nabavi-Noori. "Toward a Demosprudence of Poverty." *Duke L.J.* 69, no. 7 (2020): 1473–1528. See Cal. Rules of Court, Canon 3 (California Code of Judicial Ethics); N.Y. C.L.S. Rules Comm on Jud Conduct § 7000.9 (New York Code of Judicial Conduct).

943. Ibid.

944. Smucker, K. Heidi. "No Place Like Home: Defining HUD's Role in the Affordable Housing Crisis." *Admin. L. Rev.* 71, no. 3 (2019): 633–662.

945. Ibid.

The Affirmatively Furthering Fair Housing (AFFH) rule,[946] which the Obama administration promulgated to clarify existing fair housing obligations under the Fair Housing Act, has faced calls for an overhaul that provides HUD grantees with localized data so they could analyze their fair housing landscape and work toward complying with those obligations and that wields the rule as an enforcement mechanism. Reviving the structure of the AFFH rule means making targeted adjustments to measure and quantify success within the affordable housing context, which, in turn, enables HUD to address the nationwide homelessness crisis while leaving the responsibility of creating and maintaining affordable housing with state and local governments.[947]

PRACTITIONER NARRATIVE

Interview with Janet Kelly, Honolulu-based Legal Aid attorney.[948] Janet Kelly has been involved in homeless advocacy and outreach work for 20 years. Among other efforts, she developed the homeless outreach and medical legal partnership programs at the Legal Aid Society of Hawaii (LASH).

Q: What were the biggest challenges in establishing the homeless outreach program at LASH?

When LASH first got money in this program in 2000,[949] they did what they always do: establish an intake hotline and wait for the calls to

---

946. "What Is AFFH?" Affirmatively Furthering Fair Housing | HUD.gov / U.S. Department of Housing and Urban Development (HUD). Accessed July 28, 2021. https://www.hud.gov/program_offices/fair_housing_equal_opp/affh.

947. Smucker (2019).

948. Kelly, Janet. Interview with Angela Hwang. February 16, 2021.

949. In 2000, LASH received a joint grant from the U.S. Department of Housing and Urban Development (HUD) under the Fair Housing Initiatives Program (FHIP) for establishing a new organization to provide fair housing education and enforcement services throughout the state (U.S. Department of Housing and Urban Development. 2000. "Hawaii Received Over $9 Million in HUD Grants." Honolulu Field Office Newsletter 3:1. Content archived December 19, 2011. https://archives.hud.gov/local/hi/newsletters/nlwin2000.cfm.). LASH previously received small grants for providing housing counseling in previous years (*see, e.g.*, U.S. Department of Housing and Urban Development. 1999. "1999 Housing Counseling Grants: Hawaii." Content archived January 20, 2009. https://archives.hud.gov/funding/1999/hacg/hacghi.html.). In 2002, LASH received a HUD grant specifically for outreach efforts (U.S. Department of Housing and Urban Development. 2002. "HUD

come in. The problem was the people weren't coming in. And why is that? When you are dealing with those who are unsheltered or some distance from you, they either: A) Don't have the money to travel to you, or B) Don't want to leave their camp because the minute they walk away, what little they do have is going to get stolen from them. And that fear—losing what they do have—keeps them from addressing what they need to address.

Ultimately, you have to get into the mindset of someone who is living on the street: "What is my immediate need?" My immediate need to get a vital document or replacement ID isn't that high on the priority list if I am starving or if I'm thirsty, right? They just want food or to stay warm, a blanket. And it's circular: you're never going to get permanent housing unless you have all your stuff in order—your documentation, your ID—but it kind of puts them farther behind if they don't have a stable living circumstance.

So, I think that those are the two biggest lessons. #1: You need to go to them, and, the other thing has nothing to do with the law, but #2: You have to spend a lot of time trying to build trust with a client. Just like you do with anybody else. You can't just assume that you're going to walk up to somebody and say, "Hey, I'm going to help you get your birth certificate" and that they are then going to trust you and want to work with you. In fact, most of the time it's even harder because they have some type of mental condition that keeps them from wanting to trust anybody at all.

To illustrate the second point: there was one woman who we would see around since the program was established, who I knew would probably qualify for disability from the little background I gathered from the health center. I'd ask her every time I saw her if she wanted to do a Social Security disability application. But it wasn't until one day, maybe eight years after I first spoke to her, that she came to me and asked, "Hey, can you help me do this application." And that's how long it took for her. So that's the other thing too—to be respectful of the other person. They have their own right to self-determination and

Awards $14,542,753 to Hawaii in New Grants." Honolulu Field Office Newsletter 5:1. Content archived December 19, 2011. https://archives.hud.gov/local/hi/newsletters/nlwin2002 .cfm.).

so even if I need numbers to prove my grant, if that person is not ready to do it, you're not going to be successful.

Another way to build trust if you are doing a new program is to strap onto another program that is already developed and already doing outreach who can then introduce you to the folks living on the street. For example, one of the areas that were really bad when I started doing this was Waianae. There were tents on the street from the power plant all the way out to Yokohama. To be able to access that population, I partnered with the health center—the Waianae Coast Comprehensive Center—because they had a homeless outreach team. I asked them, "Hey, can I ride along with you in your van?"

I received a really interesting question from the administrator then: "Well, how long are you going to be here?" Because her experience had been that folks would come out and want to help the population out there but they would only be able to help for 3 months, 6 months, or one year. So, I think she was really concerned about the longevity of the program, and I was just honest and I told her, "Look, I have funding for three years and I'll be here at least that long—as long as I have funding, I'll be here." And we are still there; it's twenty years later and we're still providing services to that population. That's what they are looking for: commitment. You can't build trust if you all of a sudden disappear one day.

Q: **What are some effective advocacy techniques for working with this community?**

One thing you do have to think of is your safety—you can't be going to some of these encampments by yourself. My safety has never been threatened as long as I've done this work; there's been maybe three times when I was a little bit uncomfortable with people but that was probably because they were a little bit unstable or having a mental health crisis. But for the most part, you do have to think about your safety, so it's always good to go with those who are established.

There are several established service providers that I would recommend you contact if you're first starting out. #1: Community health centers. Most unsheltered folks go to community health centers to get their health care so if you can partner with a community health center, that's really great. For our program, we do provide outreach services at every single community health center on Oahu except one, and that's because they're just so remote. #2: Shelters, whether they are emergency or transitional. And #3: Homeless drop-in centers, which have been really helpful for us. Under the current administration, they developed the Punawai Rest Stop where there are showers, laundry facilities, and case management all on site. This drop-in center, because of the pandemic, is now open 24-hours a day. We are there one full day, usually Mondays, and we see anyone who walks in or who is referred by the case management team. It's a really effective way to access and build trust with clients. All in all, you got go where they go.

Q: What are medical legal partnerships (MLPs) and what motivated you to start that program?

The traditional MLP model is for an attorney to be embedded into a medical clinic. So, your office would be next door to the doctors and the doctors would refer patients. Some health centers screen for social determinants of health, like their environment and their income, and you can look at that screening tool to then go to that person and introduce yourself. When an attorney goes and introduces themselves to patients, it's so that they can build that trust factor and introduce the program. At that time, you can also do a legal check-up with them and you can screen for a legal issue that they don't even know actually is a legal issue.

Although providers usually know what is going on beyond a patient's medical symptoms, they don't realize that some of those issues can be resolved legally. There is a lot of educating of the providers that needs to happen. Especially if the attorney does not have the benefit of being able to sit in a room with the medical providers to discuss patients together. You are either relying on the patient telling you or on your legal check-up to pull out the information that you need in order to help them. From that perspective, issue spotting is a really great skill. If you're not really good at issue spotting, you're going to have a hard time.

Thus, MLPs are usually a very good partnership between a legal services corporation and a community health center. There are also MLPs where the onsite attorney does all the work. But for me, I think that limits the number of patients that you can assist. The logistics of what MLP model is best just depends on the size of the program and what you are trying to do. For example, some MLPs are focused on very certain things, like only helping kids or seniors, or only on providing support for one specific legal issue. There is a national MLP foundation, and if you want to learn more about that you can go to their website.

LASH's MLP program kind of bootstrapped off the outreach work that we were already doing. In some ways we were already doing MLP before it became a hot topic because we had already partnered with health centers to provide services. But the MLP has been super effective for Social Security cases because you can talk to the provider and ask, "Can this person go back to work? How severe is this?" For Social Security cases it's awesome.

Q: Working with a number of different providers, such as case workers, social workers, nurses, and doctors, do you have any insight or tips about how to make working with these different service providers better?

Case managers are your best friends. Ultimately, they are going to handle a lot of the stuff that you can't handle as a legal services provider. And they can help you get what you need, like documentation or copies of ID. Case managers can also be very helpful in referring cases to you and in getting some of the background story. Within the MLP, MAs (medical assistants) are your best friends because they are the ones who ensure you have an opportunity to meet the patient and introduce the program.

There is some goal to what a case manager is trying to do, so trying to find out what the goal is for a particular client can better enable you to work together to make that goal move ahead. For example, the case manager's objective might be to increase the person's income. If increasing that person's income means applying them for Social Security, then that is something a legal services provider can do. So, we can work in partnership. This takes something off their [the case manager's] plate, but I might need help getting medical records or getting them established with a medical provider. So, there is a lot of back-and-forth communication that happens.

Doctors are so busy, but I think that you help them better understand what you are trying to do. For example, for Social Security cases, a lot of doctors will just write diagnoses. I spent the very beginning of our MLP program educating all the providers on how to document their patients' illnesses in their medical records for Social Security applications. Rather than just writing a diagnosis, I told them how I and the Social Security Administration (SSA) needs to know how the patient is functioning with a particular diagnosis. Showing them SSA's bluebook online that shows what the level of functioning needs to be at to be a successful Social Security disability applicant can make the process more efficient and patients more successful.

Q: **What keeps you committed and excited about the type of outreach work you do? What changes do you hope to see in the future?**

The biggest thing that keeps me going is that I want to understand why. How did this happen to them? What got them in this position and how are we going to get them out of it? That's a puzzle that is individual for every single person that you encounter. There is no one blanket answer to ending homelessness. There are many factors that lead to why someone is homeless. So, you have to unpack those issues and get those issues addressed so that they can be successful and maintain their housing in the long run. Every solution to a homeless person's problem is individualized.

Q: **What are your thoughts about how a community, an agency, or the government could do better in supporting this vulnerable population? Have you seen successful programs?**

Some of the models now, like the Housing First model, is that you provide support as needed for the client and then as they become more stable you step those supportive services down a little bit. And I think that's the right way to do it. Housing needs to be coupled with supportive services and case management to ensure they are continuing to see their doctors and are taking the medications they are supposed to.

We should also look at new programs. There are new and innovative programs that are coming up and should be given the chance to be successful. There are always new things that we can try, and we have to be open to those things. People get very engrained in wanting to protect their jobs and their agencies in wanting to get funding and they are not supportive of those new programs. But I think that is how we move forward—we have to stop duplicating services, we have to work collaboratively together to end homelessness (because that is the only way that is going to happen), and we have to build a hell of a lot more housing.

People also don't realize that it is more expensive to keep somebody unsheltered or allow them to live unsheltered on the street than to actually house them. For maybe $800/month you could probably place them into a studio apartment and provide them the case management and supportive services that they need to maintain that housing. Whereas if you allow them to stay on the street, they're going to end up using city services. For example, they are going to have a lot of run-ins with the police, they are probably going to call the ambulance more often because their health is in a lot more critical state when they are unsheltered, they are going to go to the hospital through the emergency room a lot more.... Those costs are way more expensive than just paying for their rent and case management and keeping them stable. And ultimately then, they improve because their health improves and maybe they can go back to being a contributing member of society. They can go back to work or whatever the case may be. But this idea that they should fend for themselves isn't really efficient for any community to allow that to continue. Just from a financial perspective alone. Of course, it's the right thing to do—to allow people to have housing and to not allow them to sleep on the sidewalk—but beyond what is morally right, from a financial perspective, it's the right thing to do as well.

It's a very complex problem. Unfortunately, given our economy ... I would love it if I worked myself out of the job, but it's a huge problem and quite frankly, this pandemic is threatening to make a huge rain cloud of homelessness. Once that eviction moratorium lifts, there's going to be a huge number of folks who can't afford to rent, and then if they get an eviction on their record, they're going to even have a harder time finding a place to live. It's really scary that this pandemic could create a huge wave of homelessness. And I think we have already started to see those effects, that the homeless numbers are going up.

Conclusion

The most powerful part of learning comes after reading, after absorbing and questioning. It comes during the transformation of knowledge into meaningful change. *Homeless Advocacy* is a guide to legal and policy issues affecting unhoused people, and suggestions of what models could be used and improved upon by advocates. The hope is that readers will use the history, context, and current state of homelessness in the United States to develop themselves as advocates and innovate ways to disrupt and rebuild systems that serve the diverse populations of unhoused people appropriately.

Yes, In My Backyard

Building ADUs to Address Homelessness

Accessory dwelling units, or ADUs, could play a key part of the solution for homelessness by providing affordable housing for unhoused individuals and families or those experiencing housing insecurity. This appendix is a thorough report on what ADUs are, including examples of existing programs that facilitate ADU construction and rental across the United States, and what considerations to take into account when developing zoning regulations and implementing logistics. It is included in this book in order to show how complex even a partial solution for homelessness can be—needing private and public sector partners, individual and governmental cooperation—and also to break down how advocates can lead innovative programs to create meaningful change.

In reading this appendix, consider what zoning regulations, intra-agency collaboration, and other factors are necessary in order to implement accessory dwellings in a way that could provide housing to unhoused people or those at risk of losing housing. Consider the barriers to implementation, and what other innovative programs might complement this solution to homelessness.

YES, IN MY BACKYARD

Building ADUs to Address Homelessness

TRAN DINH
DAVID BREWSTER
ANNA FULLERTON
GREGORY HUCKABY
MAMIE PARKS

(May 2018). *Homeless Rights Advocacy Project*. 12.
(Sara K. Rankin, Nantiya Ruan, and Elie Zwiebel, eds.)
https://digitalcommons.law.seattleu.edu/hrap/12

TABLE OF CONTENTS

ACKNOWLEDGMENTS

This report was authored by Tran Dinh from Seattle University School of Law's Homeless Rights Advocacy Project and David Brewster, Anna Fullerton, Gregory Huckaby, and Mamie Parks from the University of Denver Sturm College of Law's Homeless Advocacy Policy Seminar. Professor Sara Rankin of the Seattle University School of Law and Professor Nantiya Ruan and Research Fellow Elie Zwiebel of the University of Denver Sturm College of Law supervised the preparation, drafting, and publishing of the report. Each of the authors are deeply grateful to these individuals for their time and contributions to this report:

- Aliza Allen, Allen Law Group, PLLC
- Jay Free, Montgomery Purdue Blankinship & Austin PLLC
- Madeline Harnois, Federal Civil Rights Clinic
- Rex Hohlbein, Facing Homelessness
- Javier Ortiz, Snohomish County Superior Court
- Mary Li, Multnomah Idea Lab
- Dan McGrady, Mary's Place
- Ayala Scott, Los Angeles County Department of Regional Planning
- John Infranca, Suffolk University Law School
- Suzanne Skinner, Esq.
- Sara Vander Zanden, Facing Homelessness
- Renee Martinez-Stone, West Denver Renaissance Collaborative
- Christopher Whitenhill, West Denver Renaissance Collaborative
- Terese Howard, Denver Homeless Outloud
- David J. Miller, Barton Institute for Philanthropy and Social Enterprise
- Rebecca Arno, Barton Institute for Philanthropy and Social Enterprise

The authors are especially grateful to Professors Sara Rankin and Nantiya Ruan and Research Fellow Elie Zwiebel for their patience, guidance, and dedication to advocating for the vulnerable and overlooked homeless populations in their communities. Your commitment to serving others continually inspires.

The University of Denver authors are also extremely grateful for the financial support of the Barton Institute for Philanthropy and Social Enterprise. Thank you!

EXECUTIVE SUMMARY

This report examines how cities and organizations use Accessory Dwelling Units ("ADUs") as a tool to house individuals experiencing homelessness. ADUs are self-contained living structures located on the property of a single-family home. Several U.S. cities are creating and implementing ADU programs to address affordable housing shortages. Currently, a few forward-looking municipalities and organizations within those municipalities are exploring the use of ADUs to address homelessness. For cities and organizations wishing to implement ADU programs to house individuals experiencing homelessness, this report provides guidance on logistical, legal, and messaging considerations to help make the programs successful.

First, this report highlights innovative programs in four case study cities: The BLOCK Project in Seattle, Washington; A Place for You in Multnomah County, Oregon; the Second Dwelling Unit Pilot Program in Los Angeles County, California; and the West Denver Renaissance Collaborative's Single Family Plus Initiative in Denver, Colorado. By reviewing the individual structure, funding, matching, and zoning regulations relevant to each project, prospective ADU project managers and homeowners wishing to implement new ADU programs should gain a better understanding of how to create an ADU program that houses individuals experiencing homelessness in their local community.

Next, the report analyzes logistical considerations that ADU project managers must weigh prior to implementing and developing their projects. Primarily, ADU project managers must determine how to fund and staff the project, how they plan on engaging with community members and entities to lower costs and build support for the project, and how to determine eligibility requirements and matchmaking strategies to create a cohesive fit between the homeowner and the resident.

Additionally, this report addresses legal frameworks and relationships implicated in ADU projects. Before an ADU project begins, project managers and interested homeowners must research and understand relevant local zoning regulations to determine whether the municipality permits ADUs on the target property. If local zoning laws do not permit an ADU on the target property, project managers and participants will likely need to contact a local city planner or land use attorney. Further, interested homeowners should understand the financial implications associated with ADUs, most notably, development permitting fees and potential increases in market value and property taxes. Throughout the life of an ADU program, project managers and participants should also recognize and understand the various contractual relationships that form, as well as the rights, responsibilities, and liabilities associated with those contractual relationships. If interested homeowners have outstanding questions about tax and market value implications, or about the contractual relationships that form, they should contact an attorney for accurate and detailed information.

ADUs are gaining national attention as tools to address the national affordable housing crisis. Local governments and public interest organizations are beginning to recognize ADUs as an innovative tool to provide consistent and integrative housing options for individuals experiencing homelessness. Although there are challenges associated with developing and implementing this type of ADU program, this report acts as a springboard of useful guidance to promote success for these programs.

INTRODUCTION

Cities around the United States are facing affordable housing shortages. Statistics paint a grim picture for the future of affordable housing and an even bleaker picture for individuals on the brink of, or already experiencing, homelessness.

In response to affordable housing shortages, many local governments and organizations are implementing programs that encourage and incentivize construction of ADUs on private property. Some of those programs specifically focus on building ADUs to house individuals experiencing homelessness. In many of those programs, community members can opt-in or apply to have an ADU constructed in their backyard, at little or no cost, in exchange for housing an individual experiencing homelessness.

Admittedly, ADU programs targeting homelessness are not a comprehensive solution to end homelessness, nor do they replace the overwhelming need for increased low-income housing options. However, those programs take an integrative approach in welcoming individuals experiencing homelessness back into communities rather than segregating them from society, and work to eliminate negative stigmas that create barriers between housed and unhoused individuals. Once individuals experiencing homelessness find secure housing within pre-existing community structures, they form relationships with members of the community and gain easier access to other services like addiction counseling and mental health treatment. For these reasons, homeless advocates and local governments across the country are formulating programs that take advantage of the integrative housing alternative that ADUs bring to the fight against homelessness.

This report highlights some of those innovative programs and offers guidance for advocates interested in using ADUs as part of a larger strategy to combat homelessness. It examines some challenges and opportunities associated with ADU projects as witnessed by four ADU project case studies: Seattle's BLOCK Project, Multnomah County's A Place for You, Los Angeles County's Second Dwelling Unit Pilot Program, and Denver's West Denver Renaissance Collaborative Single Family Plus Initiative. This report provides a general background on ADUs before analyzing the structure, eligibility and matching, funding, and zoning components of each case study. Then, it explores some practical questions and logistical considerations generally that should be considered in the beginning stages of an ADU project, such as the matching processes for residents and homeowners, project staffing and funding, and inter-agency cooperation and engagement. Next, the report focuses on three primary legal issues relevant to ADU projects: zoning laws, tax implications and property values, and contractual relationships. Finally, this report explores public messaging considerations that can help maximize support for using ADUs as a tool to address homelessness. By no means exhaustive, this report serves as a general blueprint for cities, local municipalities, and community partners around the country looking for creative alternatives to house individuals experiencing homelessness.

I. Background on Accessory Dwelling Units

ADUs are independent living quarters either attached or detached from the primary single-family home and are legally part of the same property as the primary single-family home.[1] This section first highlights a basic overview of

---

1. Martin John Brown, *Accessory dwelling units: what they are and why people build them*, AccessoryDwelling.org   https://accessorydwellings.org/what-adus-are-and-why-people -build-them/ (last visited Apr. 29, 2018).

traditional ADU formats. Next, it provides background on why an increasing number of local governments are instituting regulations to encourage ADU development. Finally, this section provides background on the growing housing and homelessness crises in urban centers with the specific goal of showing that ADUs are a useful and beneficial tool to address these concerns.

As independent living quarters, ADUs typically contain full amenities with living space, kitchens, and bathroom facilities.[2] Modern city planners and land use laws may call ADUs "in-law units, laneway houses, secondary dwelling units," or similar terms.[3] No matter how a locality refers to ADUs, they consistently appear in the same three general formats: internal, attached, or detached units. These unique classifications are characterized by the ADU's relationship to the primary structure on the single-family lot:

Internal ADUs are integrated within an existing structure; examples include converted attics and basements.

Attached ADUs, also known as mother-in-law apartments or accessory apartments, are built as additions to the primary dwelling.

Detached ADUs are structurally independent from the primary residence but are on the same lot. Backyard cottages or garage conversions are popular forms of detached ADUs.[4] Detached ADUs are the most common variation, and each of the case study programs highlighted in this report utilize or advocate for construction of detached ADUs.[5]

Although city planning practices have recognized the concept of ADUs in these three forms for many years, growing urban populations and accompanying affordable housing issues have increased interest in utilizing ADUs as a tool to create new affordable housing alternatives.

---

2. *Id.*

3. *Id.*

4. Municipal Research and Services Center, *Accessory Dwelling Units: Issues & Options* (1995), http://mrsc.org/getmedia/54c058a5-4d57-4192-a214-15f2fa5ac123/ADU30.pdf.aspx?ext=.pdf.

5. Although none of the case studies highlighted in this report build attached ADUs to house individuals experiencing homelessness, attached ADUs are generally less expensive to construct and maintain than detached ADUs, and therefore, attached ADUs should be considered as a viable alternative.

II. Case Studies

This section details four unique and innovative programs promoting and implementing ADU projects. First, Seattle's "BLOCK Project" is exclusively committed to providing permanent housing alternatives for individuals experiencing homelessness by building ADUs in single-family backyards. In contrast to the BLOCK Project, which focuses on housing single adults, Multnomah County's "A Place for You" aims to use ADUs to house families facing homelessness. Next, Los Angeles County created the "Second Dwelling Unit Pilot Program" with the explicit goal of promoting ADU development as a tool to house individuals experiencing homelessness. Finally, Denver's West Denver Renaissance Collaborative Single Family Plus Initiative does not target homelessness, but rather, aims to revitalize the neighborhoods of West Denver by promoting ADU development on single-family lots owned by low-income homeowners. By reviewing the structure, funding, eligibility and matching, and zoning regulations relevant to each project, prospective ADU project managers and homeowners wishing to implement new ADU programs should gain a better understanding of how to create an ADU program that houses individuals experiencing homelessness in their local community.

A. Seattle—BLOCK Project

The BLOCK Project is a community-driven program that calls on Seattle's community leaders and neighbors to end homelessness by building ADUs to shelter unhoused individuals.[6] Among the case studies highlighted in this report, the BLOCK Project is the most developed and demonstrably effective, having housed its first resident in September 2017.

Seattle declared a state of emergency because of the city's homelessness crisis in November 2015.[7] Between 2011–2016, homelessness in Seattle rose

---

6. Facing Homelessness, *Programs*, http://www.facinghomelessness.org/programs (last visited Apr. 5, 2018).

7. Lydia O'Connor, *Seattle Declares State Of Emergency On Homeless Crisis*, Huffington Post, Mar. 11, 2015, https://www.huffingtonpost.com/entry/seattle-homeless-emergency_us_56392c7fe4b0411d306eb2eb; By declaring a state of emergency, public officials "can suspend payments on certain government services in order to devote money to the declared emergency and pull additional staff in to address the problem...act faster in connecting people with behavioral health services and placing them in shelters...[and] raise public awareness about homelessness." J.B. Wogan, *Why Governments Declare a Home-*

by over 20 percent.[8] According to Seattle/King County's 2017 point-in-time count, at least 11,643 people were experiencing homelessness, with 47 percent of those individuals unsheltered.[9]

The BLOCK Project's mission is to address Seattle's community crisis of homelessness and "put a face on homelessness" using ADUs. Rex Hohlbein, an architect and homeless advocate, created the Project in 2016.[10] Two organizations collaborated to form the foundation of The BLOCK Project: Facing Homelessness, a non-profit aimed at building community connections and compassion for a grassroots movement towards ending homelessness; and BLOCK Architects, an architecture firm. Facing Homelessness' mission is to humanize and give homelessness "a face," using photographs, videos, and internet interaction.[11] The BLOCK Project builds on this mission by giving individuals experiencing homelessness a place in the community and reflecting their value as neighbors and community members.

The first BLOCK resident, who moved in on September 18, 2017, is still living in the ADU and has given tours to media, potential hosts, and the Mayor of Seattle. As of February 2018, roughly 100 homeowners expressed an interest in serving as BLOCK hosts. Recently, the BLOCK project employed a project manager and plans to build twenty ADUs by 2019.

Structure. To achieve its goals, the BLOCK Project places pre-fabricated ADUs on single-family residential lots. The prefabricated units have full amenities including a sleeping area, kitchen, bathroom, and storage. Further, the BLOCK Project designed the units to operate "off-grid" as a financially and environmentally friendly tool to provide housing for unhoused individuals. The BLOCK Project maintains ownership of the ADU after construction in the host's backyard.

The legal structure was designed to create clear legal relationships so the personal relationship between the host family and the resident could develop. Facing Homelessness enters a ground lease with the host family that permits

---

less State of Emergency, Governing.com, Nov. 10, 2015, http://www.governing.com/topics /health-human-services/gov-when-cities-declare-a-homeless-state-of-emergency.html.

8. Joint Center for Housing Studies of Harvard University, *supra* note 12, at 34.

9. All Home, *Seattle/King County Point-In-Time Count Of Persons Experiencing Homelessness: 2017*, 8 (2017), http://allhomekc.org/wp-content/uploads/2016/11/2017-Count -Us-In-PIT-Comprehensive-Report.pdf.

10. FACING HOMELESSNESS, *History*, http://www.facinghomelessness.org/about (last visited Apr. 5, 2018).

11. FACING HOMELESSNESS, *supra* note 25.

it to use a designated portion of the host family's back yard to install, maintain, and lease a detached ADU together with right to access the unit from the public right of way. The host family has an obligation to disclose existing easements, underground storage tanks, or other issues that may affect successful use of the site, but

The Block Project At-A-Glance

Management: Nonprofit organization

Funding: Crowdfunding

Target Population: Single residents

First resident move-in: October 2017

Duration of residency: Lifetime

Goal: 550 units by 2022

otherwise has few ongoing obligations under the lease. Both Facing Homelessness and the host family are required to carry insurance with the non-profit policy primary for losses related to the ADU. Defaults under the lease are resolved through a mediated process although each party may terminate the relationship with 60-days' notice if a satisfactory resolution is not achieved. As the owner of the detached ADU, Facing Homelessness bears any tax liability related to the unit.

Under the ground lease, Facing Homelessness retains title to the detached ADU and enters a lease with the resident approved by the host family. The lease includes a set of agreed rules, which the host family and resident customize to fit their situation (*e.g.*, smoking, quiet hours, etc.). Additionally, the lease allows occupancy for a one-year term (with renewal at the election of Facing Homelessness). Currently no rent is due under the tenant lease—just an agreement to adhere to the lease terms, the terms of use negotiated with the host family, and their agreement with the social service agency.

Individual residents are referred to the BLOCK Project by social service agencies that have an ongoing relationship with the residents and an agreement with Facing Homelessness to coordinate any needed social services to the resident. While the BLOCK Project does not interfere with the relationship between the caseworker and the resident, it asks the resident's social worker to meet regularly with the resident and assist if any conflict arises between the resident, the host family, and Facing Homelessness. For the first home, the homeowner, resident and social service agency all retained independent legal counsel to advise on their rights and responsibilities under the legal documents. Facing Homelessness is working on developing a network of attorneys to offer pro-bono representation for future host families, residents and affili-ated social service agencies.

Outside of the core relationships between the resident, the host, the BLOCK Project, and the case management agency, the BLOCK Project also partners with construction management professionals, mechanical engineers, landscape architects, and digital marketing firms.[12] Further, in the spirit of community building, the BLOCK Project enjoys a dedicated group of volun-teers who advocate for the project by spreading the word or by assisting in ADU construction.

Funding. The BLOCK Project funds its work through crowdfunding. "Team leaders" are asked to raise $35,000 in initial funding, which consists of $30,000 for building and placing the ADU and $5,000 to help cover Facing Homelessness' operating expenses.[13] In addition, Facing Homelessness is plan-ning to apply for public and private grants. Even with possible grants, Facing Homelessness views crowdfunding as a crucial ongoing method of fundraising for the organization.[14]

The BLOCK Project received a generous gift from Turner Construction, a large construction company, in the form of donated materials and general contracting services for the construction of the first four BLOCK units. Mul-tiple subcontractors also donated supplies and labor. Importantly, based on experience from building the first BLOCK unit, project managers reconsid-ered the involvement of non-professional labor for the construction process in the interest of time, safety, and efficiency.[15] As a result, certain materials are pre-fabricated because traditional construction is time consuming and requires substantial training for non-professional workers.[16]

Eligibility & Matching. Homeowners must meet the BLOCK Project's eligibility criteria, including ownership of a single-family home, three char-acter references, and a commitment to contact neighbors about the BLOCK

---

12. FACING HOMELESSNESS, *The BLOCK Project*, www.the-block-project.com /homelessness/ (last visited Apr. 29, 2018).

13. Interview with Sara Vander Zanden, Facing Homelessness Managing Director (Feb. 23, 2018).

14. *Id.*

15. *Id.*

16. Interview with Sara Vander Zanden, Facing Homelessness Managing Director (Sep. 29, 2017).

Project.[17] Character references are helpful in determining a prospective host's fitness for inclusion in the BLOCK Project and whether the host is invested in staying in Seattle permanently. While the ground lease commits the hosts for a five-year period, the BLOCK Project asks for an informal lifetime commitment. As the BLOCK project is primarily about building community and supporting all its stakeholders, Facing Homelessness will work with the needs of individual host families as they arise during the lease term. However, if the homeowner chooses to sell their residence or terminate participation in the program, the BLOCK project will relocate the ADU.

Currently, the BLOCK Project focuses on housing single adults. Before moving into a BLOCK Project home, the potential resident goes through a screening and matchmaking process with the BLOCK Project homeowner. In the initial matchmaking stages, the Project partners with local social service agencies to select potential residents.[18] To ensure compatibility, all potential BLOCK Project residents and hosts fill out questionnaires about their interests and comfort level regarding issues such as alcohol use.[19] Parties then review each other's profiles and decide if it is a good fit. While the BLOCK Project is only accepting single residents, there may be variations for families at later stages.[20]

Understanding that conflicts may arise, the BLOCK Project chose a people-first, de-escalation approach. This people-first approach means that the Project directs its messaging towards tackling fears about inviting a stranger into single-family backyards and addressing neighbors' concerns up front. Early on, the BLOCK Project created positive messaging by having its first host family, Kim and Dan, speak with potential hosts about their success and the benefits of hosting.[21] Moreover, during the site-selection process, the BLOCK Project requires that homeowners discuss BLOCK Project involvement with their neighbors and invite all neighbors to discuss the proposal with Project representatives. If one neighbor objects to the homeowner involvement, the ADU is not built in that particular neighborhood; in other words, the BLOCK Project requires complete consensus and buy-in from the hosting block. Facing

---

17. FACING HOMELESSNESS, *BLOCK Community*, www.the-block-project.com /community/ (last visited Apr. 29, 2018).

18. *Id.*

19. Other triggers may include things like airplane noises for people who suffer from post-traumatic stress disorders for example.

20. Interview with Sara Vander Zanden, *supra* note 36.

21. Interview with Sara Vander Zanden, *supra* note 33.

Homelessness is also working on building a network of professional mediators and health professionals to help listen to and resolve potential concerns and conflicts. This professional support also reflects the people-based approach to building relationships and support networks for residents, homeowners, and the community at large.[22]

Zoning. As with each case study, local zoning laws influence the BLOCK Project unit sizes and potential locations. For ADUs, Seattle's zoning laws establish, among other requirements, a minimum lot size of 4,000 square feet; minimum lot width of 25 feet; a limit to maximum combined back yard coverage of 40 percent; minimum separation from the primary structure of 5 feet, and maximum height limits.[23] Further, Seattle's Building and Construction Codes establish minimum habitable space requirements for bedrooms of "not less than 70 square feet of floor area size."[24] Besides these physical requirements, Seattle's Code requires an individual who owns at least a fifty percent interest in the property to occupy either the primary residence or the ADU for six or more months of each calendar year as their permanent residence,[25] and "if unrelated persons occupy either unit, the total number of persons occupying both units may not altogether exceed eight."[26]

B. Multnomah County—A Place for You

Multnomah County's A Place for You ("APFY") initiative is unique in its focus on embedding ADUs into existing social service programs. County officials created APFY to test the effectiveness of housing individuals experiencing homelessness in ADUs in concert with previously established systems of care. In contrast to ADU projects in other cities, APFY concentrates on providing long-term housing for families experiencing homelessness and to counteract the negative impact of housing instability on children.

Portland is the most populated city in Multnomah County.[27] In October 2015, the Portland City Council declared a state of emergency due to Portland's

---

22. Interview with Sara Vander Zanden, *supra* note 36.
23. Seattle, Wash., Mun. Code 23.44.041 Table B.
24. *Id.* at 22.206.020(C).
25. *Id.* at 23.44.041(C)(1).
26. *Id.* at 23.44.041(A)(3).
27. Hastie, Parish, Heck & White, Memorandum RE: Multnomah County Community Demographic Profile, Multnomah County, Oct. 1, 2014, https://multco.us/file/36649/download.

affordable housing crisis.[28] That state of emergency was extended by Portland's City Council in 2017, and is now in its third year.[29] A report by Portland State University's Population Research Center found that the leading causes of the ongoing housing crisis are increases in rental and housing costs, a lack of affordable housing, and stagnant incomes.[30] In 2016, Portland had the highest rental rate increase in the country. While rental rates have increased by 63 percent, incomes have only increased by 39 percent.[31] The average worker in Portland making minimum wage[32] would have to work at least 70 hours a week to afford a two-bedroom apartment.[33]

The County's 2017 point-in-time count reported 4,177 individuals experiencing homelessness on any given night, a nearly 10 percent increase from the 2015 count.[34] This number includes the over 300 families who primarily reside in motels and shelters. Portland's record-high housing shortage prompted the City of Portland and Multnomah County to allocate $61 million to increase affordable housing in the County.[35]

APFY is a test project spearheaded by the Multnomah Idea Lab (MIL), housed within the Multnomah County Department of Human Services. Enhabit, a local non-profit, is tasked with managing program implementation, overseeing unit design and installation, selecting sites, and communicating with homeowners.[36] Following significant media attention in April 2017, the

28. Associated Press, *Portland declares housing emergency*, The Seattle Times, Oct. 8, 2015, https://www.seattletimes.com/seattle-news/portland-declares-housing-emergency/.

29. Erica Cruz Guevarra, *Portland City Council Extends Housing Emergency, Relocation Assistance*, OPB, Oct. 4, 2017, https://www.opb.org/news/article/portland-oregon-housing-emergency-homelessness/.

30. Portland State University, 2017 Point-in-time Count of Homelessness in Portland/Gresham/Multnomah County, Oregon, 12 (Oct. 2017), https://pdxscholar.library.pdx.edu/cgi/viewcontent.cgi?article=1040&context=prc_pub.

31. Rebecca Hamilton, *You are here: A snapshot of Portland-area housing costs*, Metro News, (Oct. 25, 2016), https://www.oregonmetro.gov/news/you-are-here-snapshot-portland-area-housing-costs.

32. Oregon Minimum Wage Rate Summary, Oregon.gov, http://www.oregon.gov/boli/whd/omw/pages/minimum-wage-rate-summary.aspx (last visited Apr. 7, 2018) (As of July 1, 2017, the minimum wage in Portland, OR was $10.25/ hr.).

33. *Id.*

34. Portland State University, *supra* note 50.

35. Multnomah County Department of County Human Services, A Place for You, https://multco.us/dchs/a-place-for-you (last visited Apr. 8, 2018).

36. *Id.*; Multnomah County, *Everything there is to know now about the A Place for You granny flats project*, Mar. 28, 2017, https://multco.us/multnomah-county/news/everything

county was forced to close the application page after receiving over 1,100 homeowner applications.[37]

Structure. APFY's goal is to explore building ADUs on under-utilized space as an alternative strategy to fight homelessness. The program seeks to support families with stable housing and connect them with social services already in place. During the initial phase, four homeowners will be selected to have ADUs built in their backyards to house a family experiencing homelessness. Those families will be required to participate in the program for up to five-years. Once a family is referred to the program they are connected with social services provided by A Home for Everyone, an initiative implemented in Portland to help address the city's homelessness crisis, with services including job placement, assistance paying unexpected bills, skills training, and mitigation for potential disputes

---

A Place for You At-A-Glance

Management: Government/nonprofit hybrid

Funding: $500K from local government and private philanthropic organizations

Target Population: Family residents

First resident move-in: June 20 2018

Duration of residency: Up to 5 years

Goal: 4 units during initial test phase

---

with homeowners.[38] Further, homeowners receive tax abatements for the years they are enrolled in the program and have the opportunity to purchase the ADU for its fair market value after five-years.[39]

Program participants will receive one of two pre-fabricated units designed either by Washington-based Wolf Industries (pictured below left) or Portland-based SQFT Studios (pictured below right). Depending on which unit

---

-there-know-now-about-place-you-granny-flats-project.

37. Molly Harbarger, *Multnomah County idea to get homeowners to host homeless families hits delays*, THE OREGONIAN, Nov. 21, 2017, http://www.oregonlive.com/portland/index.ssf/2017/11/multnomah_county_idea_to_get_h.html.

38. MULTNOMAH COUNTY, *supra* note 56.

39. ENHABIT, *Multnomah County and Enhabit Launch Pilot Project 'A Place For You'*, https://enhabit.org/adu/ (last visited Apr. 29, 2018); MULTNOMAH COUNTY, *supra* note 55.

the homeowner receives, construction will take between two and six weeks to have the roughly 300-square-foot ADU move-in ready.[40]

Funding. APFY received $500,000 from the Joint Office of Homeless Services and philanthropic organizations, such as the Meyer Memorial Trust.[41] This initial grant, managed by Enhabit, covers all associated costs including design, installation, and program implementation. The pre-fabricated ADUs will cost roughly $75,000 per unit. Families who reside in the units are expected to contribute 30 percent of their income towards rent, which will go to help pay for maintenance and upkeep costs.[42]

Eligibility & Matching. In contrast to Seattle's BLOCK Project, which targets single adults, the APFY project aims to provide long-term housing for families experiencing homelessness. Potential unit occupants are referred by A Home for Everyone's Homeless Families' Coordinated Access system.[43] Homeowners will be selected based on factors including proximity to services, day care, shopping, transit, and public schools and any prior experience as a landlord.[44] Homeowners will also complete a questionnaire about the property's zoning and building codes, including locations of sewer lines and pipes.

Zoning. Portland's Zoning Code allows for developing ADUs in all R (Residential), C (Commercial), and EX (Central Employment) zone districts, and is one of the most ADU friendly zoning codes.[45] Physical guidelines for ADUs include that: 1) only one entrance may be on the front of the ADU; 2) no additional parking is required for the ADU; 3) the size of the ADU may not be more than 75 percent of the living area of the primary dwelling unit or 800 square feet of living area, whichever is less; and 4) the ADU must be set back 40 feet from the lot line, or located behind the rear wall of the primary house.[46] For use restrictions, Portland's Code requires that "[t]he total number of individuals that reside in both units may not exceed the number that is allowed for a household."[47]

---

40. Molly Harbarger, *supra* note 57.
41. MULTNOMAH COUNTY, *supra* note 56.
42. Molly Harbarger, *supra* note 57.
43. MULTNOMAH COUNTY, *supra* note 56.
44. *Id.*
45. PORTLAND ZON. CODE 33.205.020.
46. *Id.* at 33.205.040(C)(1)-(4).
47. *Id.* at 33.205.030(A) (Portland's Code defines a household as "One or more persons related by blood, marriage, legal adoption or guardianship, plus not more than 5 additional persons, who live together in one dwelling unit; one or more handicapped persons as

C. Los Angeles County—Second Dwelling Unit Pilot Program

Like the highlighted programs in Seattle and Multnomah County, Los Angeles County's Second Dwelling Unit Pilot Program involves building ADUs to house people experiencing homelessness.[48] L.A. County's Community Development Commission created the pilot program, which was then approved by the County Board of Supervisors with directives to: (1) develop and produce a Second Dwelling Unit Pilot Program that utilizes ADUs on single-family lots in unincorporated areas of the county; (2) technically assist homeowners implementing the plan; and (3) encourage the County to provide homeowners with incentives for new construction and for preserving existing units, in exchange for long-term affordability covenants or acceptance of Section 8 vouchers.[49]

Los Angeles declared its homelessness crisis a state of emergency in June 2016.[50] Strikingly, the county's homelessness rates rose by 23 percent between 2016 and 2017,[51] with approximately 57,794 individuals experiencing homelessness in 2017.[52] To address the crisis, the Board of Supervisors approved an action plan of interlocking strategies, including the Second Dwelling Unit Pilot Program aimed at combatting homelessness.[53]

---

defined in the Fair Housing Amendments Act of 1988, plus not more than 5 additional persons, who live together in one dwelling unit.").

48. Los Angeles County Homeless Initiative, *Approved Strategies to Combat Homelessness*, 116–120 (Feb. 2016), http://homeless.lacounty.gov/wp-content/uploads/2017/01/HI-Report-Approved2.pdf.

49. *Id.*

50. Abby Sewell, *L.A. County supervisors call for a state emergency declaration on homelessness*, L.A. Times, Jun. 14, 2016, http://www.latimes.com/local/lanow/la-me-ln-homeless-emergency-20160614-snap-story.html.

51. Susan Abram, *What If LA County Paid Residents to House the Homeless? Leaders Are Exploring the Idea*, Los Angeles Daily News, Sep. 5, 2017, https://www.dailynews.com/2017/08/14/what-if-la-county-paid-residents-to-house-the-homeless-leaders-are-exploring-the-idea/.

52. Los Angeles Homeless Services Authority, 2017 Greater Los Angeles Homeless Count - Data Summary - Total Point-In-Time Homeless Population by Geographic Areas, May 30, 2017, https://www.lahsa.org/documents?id=1354-2017-homeless-count-total-point-in-time-homeless-population-by-geographic-areas.pdf.

53. Los Angeles County, The Action Plan, http://homeless.lacounty.gov/the-action-plan/ (last visited Apr. 29, 2018).

Structure. The pilot program is fast-tracked: The Board of Supervisors approved the plan on August 15th, 2017, with directives to implement the program within eighteen months.[54] The plan does not specify whether homeowners will be allowed to choose the design of those new ADUs. In addition, the Los Angeles County Arts Commission is organizing an architectural design competition to encourage cost-efficient innovation and "generate momentum

> ## Second Dwelling Unit Pilot Program At-A-Glance
>
> **Management:** Government
>
> **Funding:** $550K one time pilot fund from the county
>
> **Target Population:** Family or Single residents
>
> **First resident move-in:** Unknown
>
> **Duration of residency:** Unknown
>
> **Goal:** Construct 2–3 new units and convert 2–3 existing units in 18 months

and interest for ADUs through engagement events and technical workshops."[55] The architectural competition will award $10,000 to each of the top three design entries.[56] Winners were scheduled to be announced on April 27, 2018.[57]

Funding. The project received a $550,000 one-time pilot fund from the County.[58] From that fund, L.A. County budgeted $225,000 to provide maximum subsidies of $75,000 per unit for construction of two to three new ADUs.[59] Those subsidies will be a forgivable loan tied to a commitment to rent the ADU to an unhoused family, unhoused individual, or individuals at risk of

---

54. LOS ANGELES DEPARTMENT OF REGIONAL PLANNING, Recommendation to Approve Secondary Dwelling Unit Pilot Project Under Homeless Initiative Strategy F4: Second Dwelling Units Pilot Program, (Aug. 15, 2017), http://file.lacounty.gov/SDSInter/bos/supdocs/116059.pdf.

55. *Id.*

56. *Id.*

57. LOS ANGELES COUNTY ARTS COMMISSION, Yes to ADU: Award Event and Exhibition, https://www.lacountyarts.org/calendar/yes-adu-awards-event-and-exhibition (last visited Apr. 29, 2018).

58. LOS ANGELES DEPARTMENT OF REGIONAL PLANNING, *supra* note 74.

59. *Id.*

becoming homeless as participants in the housing choice voucher program.[60] The County also budgeted $145,000 in subsidies for existing unpermitted ADUs, specifying that it will provide a maximum subsidy of $50,000 per unit for two to three owners of non-complying units to bring those units up to residential code and use it for the same purposes.[61] Subsidies for permitting and bringing non-complying ADUs up to code will be grants.[62]

Eligibility & Matching. Officials are screening applicants interested in this pilot project. Only homeowners in unincorporated parts of the county can qualify for the subsidies.[63]

Zoning. L.A. County is currently updating its ADU ordinances as mandated by recent state laws.[64] Provisions in L.A. County's proposed ADU ordinance include: that ADUs are limited to one per lot; that "[b]oth attached and detached ADUs cannot exceed 1,200 square feet."[65] For use restrictions, California's state law requires that ADUs are allowed in zones that allow residential uses with an existing or proposed single-family residence, and that one parking space is required per ADU.[66]

---

60. Los Angeles Department of Regional Planning, Second Dwelling Unit (Accessory Dwelling Unit) Pilot Program, http://planning.lacounty.gov/secondunitpilot (last visited Apr. 29, 2018).

61. Los Angeles County Homeless Initiative, *supra* note 68.

62. *Id.*

63. Marc Cota-Robles, *LA County Plan Offers Homeowners Money to Help the Homeless*, ABC7 Los Angeles, Aug. 16, 2017, http://abc7.com/society/la-county-plan-offers -homeowners-money-to-help-the-homeless/2315929/.

64. Los Angeles Department of Regional Planning, Accessory Dwelling Units, http://planning.lacounty.gov/adu/ordinance (last visited Apr. 29, 2018). The most recent update from Los Angeles County's Department of Regional Planning indicates that the proposed ordinance was still under consideration as of January 11, 2018. Los Angeles Department of Regional Planning, Accessory Dwelling Unit Ordinance (Jan. 11, 2018), http://planning.lacounty.gov/assets/upl/case/2017-004091_staff-report-20180124 .pdf.

65. Los Angeles County, California, Proposed Ordinance Amending Title 22 (Planning and Zoning) of the Los Angeles County Code related to accessory dwelling units (Jan. 24, 2018), http://planning.lacounty.gov/assets/upl/case/2017-004091_attachmentC -20180124.pdf.

66. One parking spot per ADU is required unless: "It is located within one-half mile of public transit...[i]t is located within an historically significant historic district...[i]t is part of the existing primary residence or an existing accessory structure...[or] [w]hen there is a car share vehicle located within one block...." Kevin J. Keller & Ara Sargsyan, *Interdepartmental Correspondence*, Dec. 30, 2016, https://planning.lacity.org/documents /Citywide/MemoAB2299.pdf.

D. Denver—West Denver Renaissance Collaborative Single Family Plus Initiative

The mission of the West Denver Renaissance Collaborative ("WDRC") is to facilitate the equitable revitalization of West Denver by improving the livelihood of existing residents and preserving the rich multicultural character of Denver's neighborhoods. WDRC's revitalization efforts include launching a housing program called the Single Family Plus initiative, which encourages homeowner stability by educating homeowners and promoting ADU development. Unlike the other case study cities, this project is not specifically targeted to house individuals experiencing homelessness. Further, the project is still in the planning and fundraising stages, and WDRC has not built any ADUs at this time. Even so, the Single Family Plus initiative's cost-efficient model, public outreach strategy, homeowner education, and community partnership strategy can serve as a model for future projects in Denver that wish to build ADUs for individuals experiencing homelessness.

Colorado is one of the least affordable places to live in the country.[67] In March 2018, the average price of a single-family home in Denver rose above $500,000 for the first time.[68] For those that cannot afford to buy, the median rent for a one-bedroom apartment is roughly $1,380.[69] Rental vacancy rates in Denver were only 6.8 percent in the third quarter of 2017, leaving roughly 93.2 percent of the rental market occupied.[70] Meanwhile, local incomes are not keeping pace with these increasing rates.[71] As a result, individuals in Denver who are already experiencing the impacts of poverty are at an increased risk of

---

67. Lydia DePillis, *How Colorado became one of the least affordable places to live in the U.S.*, CNN, Nov. 1, 2017, http://money.cnn.com/2017/11/01/news/economy/colorado-housing-prices/index.html.

68. Lance Hernandez, *Average Denver area home prices break half-million mark for first time*, Mar. 5, 2018, https://www.thedenverchannel.com/news/local-news/average-denver-area-home-prices-break-half-million-mark-for-first-time.

69. Michael Roberts, *Denver Rent: Highest Priced Neighborhoods in April*, Westword, Apr. 5, 2017, http://www.westword.com/news/denver-rent-highest-priced-neighborhoods-in-april-2017-8939069.

70. Apartment Association Metro Denver, *Denver Metro Apartment Vacancy and Rent (2017)*, https://drive.google.com/file/d/0B-vz6H4k4SESZDRESm9aR2ZHYVU/view.

71. Michael Roberts, *Why So Many Denver Workers Are Hurting Despite Economic Boom*, Westword, Jun. 28, 2017, http://www.westword.com/news/denver-workers-hurt-by-high-rent-stagnant-wages-9197536.

becoming homeless, remaining homeless, or suffering from chronic homelessness.

According to Metropolitan Denver Homeless Initiative's 2017 Point-in Time Report for the seven-county Denver metropolitan area, of the 5,116 total individuals experiencing homelessness metro-wide, 3,336 individuals experiencing homelessness resided in Denver County.[72] Most concerning, of those 5,116 individuals experiencing homelessness, 924 individuals were unsheltered and forced to survive the harsh conditions of Colorado's winter without shelter.[73]

Structure. Based on extensive research of other ADU projects, WDRC created a catalog of five pre-fabricated ADUs. These pre-fabricated units will be designed to conform to zoning regulations in WDRC's target neighborhoods

WDRC Single Family Plus Initiative

Management: Collective impact organization

Funding: Selected lenders will provide guaranteed financing at reduced interest rates for constructioin of ADUs, and WDRC is seeking grant funding to launch the program until operations are covered by development fees.

Target Population: Mid & Low-income residents in West Denver

First resident move-in: No residents at this time

Duration of residency: Unknown

Goal: 250 units over the next five years with 1–5 built in 2018

and will be pre-approved by Denver's Planning Office. [74] Pre-fabrication and pre-approval will limit administrative costs and time, and as a result, WDRC plans to build 250 ADUs over the next five years in eligible neighborhoods.[75]

---

72. METRO DENVER HOMELESS INITIATIVE, 2017 Point-In Time Report Seven-County Denver Metro Region, p. 4 (2017), https://d3n8a8pro7vhmx.cloudfront.net/mdhi/pages/12/attachments/original/1498599733/2017_Metro_Denver_PIT_Final.pdf?1498599733.

73. *Id.*

74. Telephone Interview with Renee Martinez-Stone, Director of the West Denver Renaissance Collaborative, Mar. 22, 2018.

75. *Id.*

Funding. Due largely to costs and zoning restrictions associated with ADU development, only 139 ADUs were built in Denver between 2010 and 2017.[76] WDRC is collaborating with Habitat for Humanity Metro Denver and other non-profit partners to reduce the costs associated with building ADUs. Further, WDRC receives funding for its programs from the City and County of Denver, the Denver Housing Authority, Enterprise Community Partners, and the Denver Foundation.

Eligibility & Matching. WDRC focuses on preserving homeownership and autonomy for middle and low-income residents while providing low-cost housing.[77] Initial homeowners in the program must be below 120 percent of the Area Median Income.[78] In contrast to the other programs highlighted in this report, homeowners enrolled in the Single Family Plus Initiative oversee both the resident selection process and landlord/tenant relationship.[79] Importantly, WDRC will provide comprehensive education programs and resources to support and prepare homeowners, including: homeowner education forums, connections to trusted refinance and rehabilitation providers, and an ADU education and development program for qualifying homeowners.[80]

Community leaders and program partners in West Denver are currently reviewing the WDRC Single Family Plus initiative. The proposed services and resources, including the ADU pilot program, will roll out as funding becomes available.[81]

Zoning. Denver's Zoning Code has only recognized ADUs as a permissible use in certain neighborhoods since 2010.[82] The Code establishes ADU regulations on a district-by-district basis identifiable by zone lot naming con-

76. Erica Meltzer, *Carriage houses and casitas could help fight gentrification on Denver's West Side*, Denverite, Nov. 14, 2017, https://www.denverite.com/denver-gentrification-carriage-houses-45585/?src=parsely.

77. *Id.*

78. Telephone Interview with Renee Martinez-Stone, *supra* note 94. The Area Median Income is a statistic that is calculated and used to determine various affordable housing metrics. According to the City of Denver, "Anyone you know who earns less than the [AMI] is very likely to be adversely affected by housing costs here." OFFICE OF ECONOMIC DEVELOPMENT, About Affordable Housing, CITY & COUNTY OF DENVER, https://www.denvergov.org/content/denvergov/en/denver-office-of-economic-development/housing-neighborhoods/about-affordable-housing.html (last visited Apr. 29, 2018).

79. *Id.*

80. *Id.*

81. *Id.*

82. Meltzer, *supra* note 96.

ventions. [83] Using the U-SU-C1 (Urban, single-unit, minimum zone lot area of 5,500 sq. ft.) zoning district as an example, Denver's Code establishes that ADUs are permitted on all lots in that zone district, and must have height limits of 1.5 stories or 24 feet, bulk requirements, set-back requirements to the rear 35 percent of the zone lot and specific footprint and habitable space requirements based on the total square footage of the whole zone lot.[84] For use restrictions, Denver's Code establishes basic requirements for ADUs in all zone districts including, but not limited to, prohibiting "[m]obile homes, recreational vehicles, [or] travel trailers," and must comply with the Denver Building and Fire Code.[85]

III. Logistical Considerations

ADU project managers and prospective participants must recognize and address logistical considerations throughout the life of the project. Though not an exhaustive list, this section details some of the logistical decisions that ADU project managers must make when creating and implementing an ADU project. While many considerations are unforeseeable until a project is implemented and may be specific to a location or community, some common considerations include: how the project will be staffed and funded; whether the project will require the involvement of outside agencies; and how the project will choose and match homeowners and residents.

A. Staffing and Funding

Preliminary decisions about staffing and funding differ depending on whether the project is government sponsored. Government-led project organizers are generally hired or appointed from pre-existing staffing structures. For example, the L.A. County Homeless Initiative designed its Second Dwelling Unit Pilot Project as a joint effort between the Community Development Commission, the Chief Executive Office, and the Department of Public Works. Under models similar to L.A. County's, key staff positions are hired internally from other departments. Government-led ADU projects may, in some cir-

---

83. Denver Zon. Code 5.2.2.2(H)
84. *Id.*
85. *Id.* at 11.8.2.1(B).

cumstances, need to hire new employees to staff various positions. To fund the overall project costs, government-led projects secure financial support through ballot initiatives or existing tax funds.

Non-government led projects will likely need to hire employees or seek volunteers to fill necessary staff positions. Often, these projects are led by a board of directors. For example, Facing Homelessness is overseen by a board of directors, an executive director, community director, BLOCK Project manager, and the founder/creative director.[86] Non-government projects should consider crowdfunding and applying for both public and private grants to pay for program costs. Initially, crowdfunding can provide money for individual ADUs, however, as the project grows in size, it will likely need private and public grants or appropriated government funding to assist with long-term expansion and sustainability.

B. Engagement With Outside Entities

ADU projects often rely on engagement with community members and professional partners. During early stages of development, ADU projects often rely on community members like architects, designers, planners, and construction personnel, to volunteer their time and expertise. These relationships not only reduce costs associated with an ADU project, they also promote the program within the community and develop lasting relationships for the program and participants. In turn, there are also concrete benefits for professional partners, project managers and participants, outside organizations, and other engaged community members, including the social benefit of coming together to achieve the common goal of providing stable housing for individuals experiencing homelessness.

C. Eligibility & Matching Processes

ADU project managers must consider the process for interviewing and matching prospective homeowners with residents. These processes determine both parties' eligibility under program guidelines and general fit within program's goals. For homeowners, eligibility may be contingent on ownership of a single-family home, minimum square-foot requirements, and adequate drain-

---

86. FACING HOMELESSNESS, Our Team, https://www.facinghomelessness.org/about (last visited Apr. 29, 2018).

age systems in the backyard. ADU project managers can choose any number of additional eligibility criteria based on individualized interests and goals unique to that particular project. For example, some ADU projects require that neither the homeowner nor the ADU resident have a violent criminal history, and others require the homeowners' lot be located close to public amenities and transportation.

Importantly, when pairing a homeowner and resident, project managers must evaluate the needs of both parties. Given the intimate nature associated with living near the primary home, it is important that the homeowner and resident are comfortable with one another. ADU project managers can help to facilitate amicable relationships by encouraging potential homeowners and residents to communicate and specify additional requirements as part of their ADU agreement, such as limiting alcohol consumption and other concerns.

D. Logistical Takeaways

Governments and organizations wishing to implement an ADU project must consider and plan for various logistical hurdles that will arise throughout the project. In the preliminary stages, ADU project managers must determine how to fund and staff the project, how they plan on engaging with community members and entities to lower costs and build support for the project, and how to determine eligibility requirements and matchmaking processes to create a cohesive fit between the homeowner and the resident. Although many other logistical considerations will arise throughout the project, the above considerations are a good start for getting an ADU project up and running.

ADU Project Logistical Checklist

- ❑ Determine how to fund the project.
  - ❑ Crowdfunding and other fundraising efforts.
  - ❑ Public and private grants.
- ❑ Determine staffing options
  - ❑ Identify responsibilities for all paid staff and volunteers
  - ❑ Identify how many staff members are required to fulfill the project

❑ Engage with community partners and professional entities.

    ❑ Find local partners will to donate time, money, or helping hands in furtherance of the project.

❑ Determine the target homeowners and residents.

❑ Establish a matching/application process for prospective residents.

IV. Legal Considerations

In addition to the logistical decisions successful ADU programs must identify and make, ADU project managers and interested homeowners must also consider and address relevant legal questions. This section does not aim to analyze each legal consideration in depth, but rather provides a basic overview and identify legal concerns to consider when implementing an ADU project. First, ADU project participants must research and determine whether local zoning laws permit ADUs on the targeted home lot, and identify the physical restrictions pertaining to ADUs in their zone district. Next, ADU project participants should understand the development fees, tax and market value implications, and ownership incentives associated with an ADU addition. Finally, ADU participants must consider the various contractual relationships and accompanying rights, responsibilities, and liabilities that are likely to arise throughout the life of the project.

A. Zoning Regulations

Before an ADU project commences, interested participants must identify whether local land use regulations allow construction of an ADU on their property. Traditionally, ADU restrictions and requirements are governed by zoning laws promulgated by local governments. As creatures of local enactment, these regulations will vary widely by jurisdiction. Whereas some municipalities have or are considering favorable ADU regulations, project managers and interested participants may face additional procedural hurdles in localities with more stringent regulations. This section gives background on the different zoning practices, outlines general regulations that traditionally govern ADUs, and provides a checklist of zoning considerations when implementing an ADU project.

1. Historical Development and Current
Forms of Zoning Regulations

Land use regulations, and zoning laws in particular, were born from increasing complexity associated with growing concentrated urban populations.[87]
In 1926, the U.S. Supreme Court in *Euclid v. Ambler* explicitly recognized a
local government's ability to regulate private land uses and segregate those
uses with zoning laws, noting that "segregation of residential, business and
industrial buildings will make it easier to provide fire apparatus . . . increase the
safety and security of home life . . . tend to prevent street accidents . . . decrease
noise . . . [and] preserve a more favorable environment."[88] In this sense, zoning
laws are a tool for local governments to regulate private land use decisions to
promote desirable social outcomes, like managing density. The Court in *Euclid*
determined that zoning regulations were a valid method of limiting urban density by segregating multi-family from single-family residential districts.[89] For
ADU purposes, however, Euclidean zoning regulations do allow for increased
urban density by encouraging development of ADUs.

Most local governments across the country still use zoning codes resem-
bling and rooted in the structure of the Euclidian zoning model.[90] Consistently,
Euclidean zoning codes divide each parcel in the municipality into individual
zone lots and designate those lots as residential, commercial, industrial, or
mixed Use Districts.[91] Many codes then divide those four general categories of
Use Districts into sub-classifications, with additional unique use restrictions
and physical limitations.[92] Importantly, "[t]he system of Use Districts is the
structural core of Euclidean zoning," and those Use Districts are exclusive and
prescriptive.[93] This means that Use Districts are founded in absolute prohibitions that are "applied uniformly in all similar situations without exception."[94]
Because cities differ physically and socially, cities that adopt Euclidean zon-

---

87. *Village of Euclid v. Ambler Realty, Co.*, 272 U.S. 365 (1926).

88. *Id.* at 394.

89. *Id.*

90. Charles Harr, *Zoning and the American Dream: Promises Still to Keep*, American
Planning Association, p. 195 (1990); *Types of Zoning Codes*, re:code LA, Jan. 21, 2014,
https://recode.la/updates/news/types-zoning-codes (last visited Apr. 29, 2018).

91. § 10:2 Euclidean zoning, 1 Rathkopf's The Law of Zoning and Planning § 10:2 (4th
ed.).

92. *Id.*

93. Harr, *supra* note 110.

94. *Id.*

ing codes follow structural similarities of the Euclidean model while adding substantive variations on the types of Use Districts, and physical regulations within those Districts.[95]

Two other common zoning variations include "Form-based" zoning, and Hybrid zoning. Form-based zoning codes are "based upon a shared vision of the kind of place the community desires, [rather than] separating a community into different use areas."[96] Where form-based codes are similar to traditional zoning in the way they proscribe physical and use restrictions within a community, "[t]hey also regulate things that are not typically part of zoning, such as the design of streets, sidewalks, and other public spaces."[97] These codes provide a more comprehensive and cohesive view of land use regulations by regulating private and public land uses under a common vision.[98]

Finally, some localities use "hybrid codes" that borrow aspects from multiple forms of land use regulations. Most commonly, hybrid codes utilize elements of Euclidean zoning and form-based zoning. For example, Denver's Zoning Code follows traditional Euclidean zoning codes by creating identifiable Use Districts. However, like form-based codes, Denver's Code maintains those Use Districts while placing greater emphasis on directed and detailed physical restrictions based on Denver's Comprehensive Plan.

By understanding how zoning laws evolve and why they exist, one also gains a better understanding of why ADU regulations exist in their forms. Although ADU project managers and prospective participants need not be familiar with the intricacies of zoning laws, the form and substance of land use laws in a locality will govern whether and how an ADU can be constructed.

2. Common ADU Regulations and Restrictions

While the substance of ADU regulations varies widely across jurisdictions, some common trends emerge. Generally, Use Districts will delineate both primary and secondary uses for a lot. ADUs are typically only permitted in residential Use Districts. Considering residential Use Districts are the most exclusive, an ADU can only be built on a residential lot when it is expressly permitted as a primary or secondary use. Other use restrictions may include

---

95. *Id.*

96. Mary Madden & Joel Russell, *Part 1: What Is a Form-Based Code?*, Planners Web, Dec. 5, 2014, http://plannersweb.com/2014/12/fbc1/.

97. *Id.*

98. *See id.*

occupancy, familial relationship, and parking requirements.[99] For physical regulations, land use laws typically govern height and bulk restrictions, set-back requirements, lot coverage, and minimum space for habitation.[100] These regulations will substantially impact the building form of an ADU and the location of the ADU on the home lot. Where some jurisdictions outline ADU requirements independently and thoroughly, others do not contain specific ADU requirements or rely instead on regulatory mechanisms outside the zoning code. Ultimately, the first step of an ADU project is to read and understand the zoning code and other applicable land use regulations.

3. Zoning Checklist: Identify Your Zone District

To find the applicable zone district for any given lot, one should first find a city's zoning map on the internet by using key words such as the name of your city and "zoning map." For Seattle, Multnomah County, Los Angeles, and Denver, zoning maps are readily accessible on the various city or county websites.[101] Next, enter or look-up a specific address within each zoning map platform. Zoning maps are typically color coded with a key identifying particular colors for various zone districts. The applicable zone district will likely appear in as a series of three to four letters separated by hyphens and may contain a number at the end. For example, an urban single unit zone may appear as "U-SU-C1."

4. Zoning Checklist: Identify Applicable Regulations

After identifying the applicable zone district, find your local zoning code by using search terms: your city and "zoning code." Within the zoning code, use the index or table of contents to find the code section addressing your zone district. Zoning codes are often hundreds of pages long, so the index is a useful tool for finding the applicable regulations. Once you have found the section relating to your zone district, read through the code sections to determine whether ADUs are a permitted use. If ADUs are permitted, you will also find physical restrictions for ADUs in the same place. If that section does not contain regulations on ADUs, your code may contain a separate and independent section governing ADUs. Again, refer to the index to determine if there is an independent section on ADUs.

---

99. *See e.g.*, SEATTLE MUN. CODE 23.44.041(C)(1).

100. *Id.*

101. Seattle—http://www.seattle.gov/dpd/Research/gis/webplots/smallzonemap.pdf; Multnomah County—http://www4.multco.us/lup/; Los Angeles—http://zimas.lacity.org/; Denver—https://www.denvergov.org/Maps/map/zoning.

5. Zoning Checklist: My Zone District Permits ADUs

If ADUs are permitted on your property, the next step is to contact the local planning office and speak with a planner about permitting and other procedural requirements. Generally, the local planning office must review and approve building plans for the ADU to ensure that the structure meets the physical requirements of the zoning district. Permitting processes may also include additional procedural hurdles like public hearings. Sometimes, the permitting process can be time consuming and expensive. In localities that have not tried to make ADU development more affordable, ADU project managers should work to curtail or minimize these costs for prospective homeowners.

6. Zoning Checklist: My Zone District Does Not Permit ADUs

Although it is unlikely, an ADU project may still be viable if the zoning code indicates that ADUs are not permitted on the targeted property. Prospective homeowners can file what is commonly called a "map amendment," which is the procedure and process that homeowners use to change their zoning district. By filing a map amendment, a prospective homeowner may change their zone district from one that does not permit ADUs to one that does. Although this may sound simple, map amendments are highly uncommon on residential lots, are tedious, time consuming, and expensive, and do not have a high likelihood of approval. Zoning codes lay out the process and timeline associated with map amendments, and planning department websites may contain graphic timelines explaining the process.

Although not a short-term solution, ADU project managers and prospective homeowners should consider campaigning or petitioning their local government to adopt ADU regulations that encourage ADU development and permit ADUs on a greater number of lots in a municipality. In places like Portland, which permits ADUs in all residential and commercial zone districts, ADU projects housing individuals experiencing homelessness will likely be more successful and easier to implement.

7. Zoning Takeaways

Variations in ADU regulations highlight the localized nature of land use and zoning laws. Where the general character of physical and use restrictions is largely similar, local differences require ADU project managers to research and know ADU regulations prior to undertaking a project. Importantly, zoning regulations will determine whether an ADU can be built on a homeowner's lot at all, and if it is permitted, those regulations will set specific physical restrictions that will dictate the dimensions of the ADU. In many cities, local governments recognizing the benefit of ADUs to combat affordable housing and homelessness are amending or passing new laws to encourage ADU construction.[102] Until generous ADU regulations take hold everywhere, project developers may continue to face additional zoning hurdles to further ADU projects.

ADU Project Zoning Checklist

- ❑ Google "your city" + zoning map.
    - ❑ Search for your address.
- ❑ Find your zoning code.
    - ❑ Google "your city" + zoning code.
    - ❑ Find your zone district.
- ❑ Find ADA Regulations for your zone district.
    - ❑ Using the code, find ADU Regulations for your zone district.
- ❑ Does your zone district allow ADUs? If yes…
    - ❑ Contact a planner to discuss ADU permitting process. Contact info for the planning can be found with zoning code.
- ❑ If your zone district doesn't allow for ADUs…
    - ❑ Contact a planner and experienced land use attorney to discuss your options.

B. Initial Financial Considerations

Interested program managers and participants should also consider the initial financial obligations and impacts of an ADU project. These considerations include, but are not limited to, the extensive development permit process and

---

102. Mimi Kirk, *The Granny Flats Are Coming*, CITYLAB, Jan. 16, 2018, https://www.citylab.com/design/2018/01/the-granny-flats-are-coming/550388/; Laura Bliss, *Portland's 'Granny Flats' Get an Affordable Boost*, CITYLAB, Mar. 12, 2018, https://www.citylab.com/equity/2018/03/portlands-granny-flats-get-an-affordable-boost/555083/.

fees, which are required for ADU construction in most jurisdictions, the tax implications associated with increased living space, and examples of potential incentives for property owners, which could offset some of the financial obligations, such as fee waivers, tax abatement, and increased home market value. This section provides a brief overview of these financial considerations and a checklist for interested homeowners and project managers to use as a reference.

1. Development Permits and Fees

ADU project managers and homeowners must receive zoning and building permits prior to and throughout the construction process. To do so, ADU developers must acquire and provide extensive documentation, such as: a zoning review; wastewater and sewage permits; air-conditioning and gas pipe permits; plumbing permits; electrical permits; roofing permits; and right of way construction permits, among others.[103] Further, municipalities may also require other review processes, such as requiring the homeowner to notify adjacent neighbors of the proposed ADU construction by certified mail.[104]

In addition to receiving necessary permits, many municipalities impose fees, sometimes called System Development Fees, which ADU developers and owners must pay to hook the ADU up to sewer, water, and other municipal services. Permits and review processes require independent inspections, which increases the costs of ADU development.

ADU project managers should plan for the administrative burdens and costs associated development permits and fees. For example, the WDRC plans on providing five pre-fabricated ADUs that will be pre-permitted with the City of Denver. The BLOCK project's off-grid ADU design will likely limit System Development Fees, like those for sewer and water. Finally, cities wishing to encourage ADU development may waive permitting fees and processes for ADU development. For example, in Portland, ADUs were historically untenable by high fees including at least $10,000 in Systems Development Charges.[105]

---

103. *See e.g.*, Denver Development Services, *Project Guide for Detached Dwelling Units*, City & County of Denver, https://www.denvergov.org/content/denvergov/en/denver-development-services/home-projects/building-expanding-a-home/detached-dwelling-carriage-house.html (last visited Apr. 29, 2018).

104. *Id.*

105. Portland Bureau of Development Services, System Development Charges (SDCs), https://www.portlandoregon.gov/bds/article/166412 (last visited Apr. 29, 2018).

However, in 2010, the local government reduced municipal fees and adjusted its zoning codes to make it easier for homeowners to add ADUs.[106]

2. Tax Implications

Homeowners should also research potential tax implications when considering the addition of an ADU to their property. Unfortunately, there is no "one-size fits all" model for assessing potential tax implications because taxes associated with ADUs depend on many factors, including the specific jurisdiction and the nature and purpose of the add-on. Most state and local tax authorities calculate property taxes based on the value of the homes within their areas.[107] Because all property taxes are state imposed, there is also little uniformity in how those property taxes are assessed, and jurisdictions include different types of property in their tax assessment. In some states, personal property taxes apply to all tangible property that produces income, such as the furniture inside rental homes.[108]

Generally, any addition (attached or detached) that increases the total living space on the property will cause an increase to property taxes. Conversely, if the ADU is the result of converted existing space (*e.g.*, a finished basement), property taxes will not likely increase without an increase to total living space.[109] Remember, several factors impact property values and taxes, including the type of ADU, its amenities, the property's location, the current housing market, and whether the ADU triggers a reassessment of the property.[110] Even if a reassessment of the property value is not required, homeowners

106. PORTLAND BUREAU OF DEVELOPMENT SERVICES, Waiver of System Development Charges (SDC) for Accessory Dwelling Units (ADU) Extended until July 2018, https://www.portlandoregon.gov/bds/article/575523 (last visited Apr. 29, 2018).

107. Martin John Brown, *How do ADUs affect property values?*, ACCESSORY DWELLINGS, Jul. 2, 2014, https://accessorydwellings.org/2014/07/02/how-do-adus-affect-property-values/ (last visited Apr. 29, 2018).

108. Intuit TurboTax, *What Are Personal Property Taxes?*, https://turbotax.intuit.com/tax-tips/home-ownership/what-are-personal-property-taxes/L2KFeovaB (last visited Apr. 29, 2018).

109. A Regional Coalition for Housing, *Renting Out An ADU*, http://www.archhousing.org/current-residents/adu-renting-out.html (last visited Apr. 29, 2018).

110. Brian Martucci, *What Is an Accessory Dwelling Unit (Granny Flat)—ADU Costs & Benefits*, MoneyCrashers, https://www.moneycrashers.com/accessory-dwelling-unit-granny-flat-costs/ (last visited Apr. 29, 2018).

can still expect to pay increased property taxes, especially if the ADU provides any additional income from rent.[111]

The good news for homeowners is that state and local property taxes for both personal property and owned real estate, including construction costs, inspection fees, and payments made to contractors, have traditionally been deductible from federal income taxes.[112] Governments in some jurisdictions may even abate any increased taxes associated with the ADU if the homeowner agrees to house low-income residents in the unit.[113] However, the recently passed Tax Cuts and Jobs Act limits state and local tax deductions to $10,000 for both individuals and couples.[114]

3. Property Owner Incentives

The costs and taxes associated with ADU construction are mitigated, in part, by incentives offered to property owners for participating in ADU projects. Incentives range from fee waivers, access to low-interest loans, government subsidies covering the cost of construction, to complete ownership of the ADU.

ADU ownership may be the most effective incentive for homeowners to share their backyard. For government-led projects ADU ownership is one of the main incentives offered to homeowners for joining the program. For Multnomah County participants, homeowners can purchase the ADU at fair market value upon completion of the five-year commitment.

Property owners may also benefit from an increase in their home's market value. Real estate values are derived from the structures on the land,

---

111. Red Oak Realty, *Home Truths: Should you add an Accessory Dwelling Unit to your home?*, BERKELEYSIDE, Feb. 8, 2017,

http://www.berkeleyside.com/2017/02/08/home-truths-add-accessory-dwelling-unit-home/; Martin John Brown, *How appraisals and "GSEs" make financing an ADU challenging*, ACCESSORY DWELLINGS, Nov. 21, 2011, https://accessorydwellings.org/2011/11/21/appraisals-and-gses-critical-issues-in-adu-financing-and-development/.

112. Intuit TurboTax, *I'm going to build an ADU on my rental property*, https://ttlc.intuit.com/questions/3997143-i-m-going-to-build-an-adu-accessory-dwelling-unit-on-my-rental-property-it-will-be-a-detached-separated-unit-how-do-i-deduct-the-costs-of-construction (last visited Apr. 29, 2018).

113. MULTNOMAH COUNTY DEPARTMENT OF COUNTY HUMAN SERVICES, *supra* note 55.

114. Samantha Sharf, *How The New Tax Law Will Impact Your Housing Costs*, FORBES, Jan. 9, 2018. https://www.forbes.com/sites/samanthasharf/2018/01/09/what-in-the-final-tax-bill-could-impact-your-housing-costs/.

comparable real estate prices in the area, supply and demand trends in the local economy, whether there are any restrictions or covenants that run with the land, and other factors. [115] Home value is determined by features such as square footage, number of rooms, presence of amenities like pools or garages, upgrades, and the potential for significant rental income.[116] One study found that ADUs contributed, on average, between 25 percent and 34 percent of each property's assessed value and that adding an ADU to a single-unit property "could reasonably add 51 percent to longer-term measures of value or return."[117]

4. Takeaways

Homeowners considering the addition of an ADU to their property must understand the development permit process and fees, associated tax implications, and potential property owner incentives, such as the effect on a home's market value. Real and personal property taxes are calculated by jurisdiction, so it is imperative that the homeowner check with a tax specialist or with their local tax office. Even if a reassessment is not automatically triggered, the homeowner is still likely to see an increase to the owner's annual property taxes. Property owners may be able to deduct increased property taxes and expenses associated with the ADU construction from their federal tax returns.[118] Many community or government sponsored ADU projects offer incentives for homeowners including ownership of the ADU, fee waivers, access to low-interest loans, government subsidies covering the cost of construction, and even tax abatement.

115. Anna Johansson, *6 factors that influence a home's value,* INMAN, Aug. 7, 2017, https://www.inman.com/2017/08/07/6-factors-that-influence-a-homes-value/.

116. *Id.*

117. Martin John Brown & Taylor Watkins, *Understanding and Appraising Properties with Accessory Dwelling Units,* The Appraisal Journal (2012), https://accessorydwellings.files.wordpress.com/2012/12/appraisingpropertieswithadusbrownwatkinsnov2012.pdf.

118. The recently passed Tax Cuts and Jobs Act limits the deductions available for state and local property, sales, and income taxes to $10,000 for both individuals and married couples. Samantha Sharf, *How The New Tax Law Will Impact Your Housing Costs,* FORBES, Jan. 9, 2018, https://www.forbes.com/sites/samanthasharf/2018/01/09/what-in-the-final-tax-bill-could-impact-your-housing-costs/.

ADU Project Initial Financial Considerations Checklist

☐ Identify development permits required in your municipality and fees associated with those permits.

  ☐ To do this, contact your local municipality's planning department either over the phone or in person.

☐ Determine if the ADU increases living space.

☐ Determine if the ADU will trigger an assessment.

  ☐ If it does, contact you local County Tax Assessor's Offuce or Tax Collector's Office and request a "reassessment request" form.

  ☐ Alternatively, contact a tax consultant to reassess the home.

☐ Find out how your jurisdiction calculates property taxes.

  ☐ Google "estimated property taxes" or "property tax calculator."

  ☐ Enter relevant information (e.g., zip code, assessed home value, median home value in neighborhood)

☐ Determine potential property owner incentives, such as any tax deductions, permit fee waivers, or increases to the home's market value.

  ☐ Contact local tax authority or consult a tax attorney.

C. Contractual Relationships

Another key consideration for ADU projects is the contractual relationships formed throughout the project. Parties should consult an attorney, preferably one who specializes in real estate and land use law, because contractual relationships will differ in duration and complexity based on the unique set of associated responsibilities, rights, and liabilities. To determine which relationships are created, all parties involved in the design, creation, and occupancy of the ADU must be identified. Potential parties include, but are not limited to: the leasing party, unit occupant, ADU owner, land/property owner, project sponsor, project manager, contractors, and social service agencies. ADU projects may not involve each of these parties, and many parties can have overlapping roles. For instance, the relationship between the project sponsor and contractors might only exist during the construction period, but the duration of the contractual relationship between the homeowner and unit occupant will vary depending on the specific structure of the project. As an example, Multnomah County's APFY project has a five-year limit for family occupants, while Seattle's BLOCK Project specifies a five-year period but with a potential for renewal.

1. Types of Contractual Relationships

The most common contractual relationships that arise in the context of property rentals are the landlord-tenant and lessor-lessee relationships. With ADUs, the homeowner is not always the *unit* owner. For example, Seattle's BLOCK Project remains the legal owner of the ADU, even after construction of the unit is complete; the unit occupant leases directly from the partnering non-profit, Facing Homelessness. The BLOCK Project addresses the relationship between the unit occupant and homeowner through the terms of a "use attachment" within the lease. In Multnomah County, the non-profit Enhabit, which oversees the design and installation of the ADUs, leases the unit to the homeowners *and* the unit occupants. After five years in the program, the homeowner will gain legal ownership of the unit, and only then would they become the lessor or landlord. In contrast, L.A. County's Second Dwelling Unit Pilot project will establish a landlord-tenant relationship between homeowners and unit occupants. These distinctions are important, and project managers, unit occupants, and homeowners should identify the key differences because they impact which laws govern the ADU projects.

a. Lessor-Lessee

As the name suggests, the lessor-lessee relationship forms when the legal owner of property leases the use of that property to another party, the lessee. This contractual relationship has significant impacts on the rights and responsibilities assigned to each party. Generally, the lessor has fewer obligations to the lessee than a landlord would. For example, the lessor has a duty to repair any *existing* damages to the property but, unlike a landlord, has no continuing duty to maintain the property after the lessee has moved in.[119] Even though a lease typically offers fewer rights, it also offers increased stability because it is

---

119. LawShelf Educational Media, *Lessors*, https://lawshelf.com/courseware/entry/lessors (last visited Apr. 29, 2018).

generally longer in duration and cannot be altered month-to-month, even if the market experiences a spike in rental rates.[120]

b. Landlord-Tenant

Landlord-Tenant laws are governed by state, local, and municipal ordinances, which typically govern health and safety standards, noise and nuisance regulations, and antidiscrimination laws. [121] Although the laws vary by jurisdiction, many states have modeled their landlord-tenant laws after the Uniform Residential Landlord and Tenant Act (URLTA).[122] Guidelines in URLTA include standards for adherence to building and housing codes, property maintenance to ensure safe and habitable conditions, which include electrical, heating, cooling, and plumbing facilities, trash disposal, and tenant rights, such as the right to quiet enjoyment of the property. It is important to understand the general guidelines for landlord-tenant law and make necessary modifications to comply with specific state statutes.

Landlord rights generally include the right of entry, ending a tenancy for nonpayment of rent, material violations of lease, or illegal conduct. Landlord responsibilities include the duty to repair and maintain the premises, return deposit, and provide safe and secure housing to the tenant. Tenant rights generally include the right to safe and habitable conditions, the right to have repairs and maintenance requests be resolved in a timely manner, the right of quiet enjoyment of the premises, the right of privacy and safety, and the right to withhold rent if landlord fails to adhere to duties.[123] Besides rights and responsibilities mandated by statute, leases and rental agreements can be tailored to meet the needs of the parties involved, which is why it is crucial to consult an attorney who specializes in property law.

---

120. LegalNature, *Lease Agreement vs. Rental Agreement,* http://help.legalnature .com/41891-articles/lease-agreement-vs-rental-agreement (last visited Apr. 29, 2018).

121. To find applicable local laws visit these pages: http://www.statelocalgov.net/; http://www.municode.com/.

122. Nat'l Conference of Comm'rs on Unif. State Laws, *Revised Uniform Residential Landlord and Tenant Act* (2015), http://www.uniformlaws.org/shared/docs/res- idential%20landlord%20and%20tenant/RURLTA%202015_Final%20Act_2017mar30.pdf (last visited Apr. 29, 2018).

123. NOLO.com, *Renters' & Tenants' Rights,* https://www.nolo.com/legal-encyclopedia /renters-rights (last visited Apr. 29, 2018).

c. Potential Liabilities

Regardless of the contractual relationships formed, all parties should be aware of all potential liabilities. Landowners, landlords, and lessors have a special duty of care to tenants, lessees, and even to individuals invited onto the property for business or social purposes. Most states have "Premises Liability" statutes that determine a landowner's duty of care in a specific jurisdiction. Landowners (or the party legally responsible for maintaining the condition of the premises) can generally be held liable for injuries resulting from dangerous conditions if the condition resulted from negligence, failure to disclose the danger, or a failure to protect against dangers of which the landowner actually knew or should have known about.[124]

Landlords have a higher duty of care because they are responsible for maintaining a safe, habitable, and hazard-free property. Further, landlords can be held liable for injuries to tenants, criminal activity on the premises, environmental hazards, injuries resulting from a tenant's animal, or failure to adhere to the tenant's right to quiet enjoyment and habitability.[125] To ameliorate these liabilities, landlords can, and should, invest in landowner-occupant homeowners' insurance and hybrid policies for an owner-occupied rental property. There are also rare exceptions when a tenant's conduct will assume liability, for example if a tenant refuses to allow the landlord entry, the tenant assumes all liability for damages and repairs to the rental unit, and consequential damage to other units.

As with any contractual relationship, there are associated consequences for breaching, or violating, the contract.[126] Landlords generally have a duty to mitigate damages if the lease is terminated early and tenants may be able to sue for any financial damages incurred because of an illegal eviction.[127] If ten-

---

124. FINDLAW.com, *Premises Liability: Who Is Responsible?* http://injury.findlaw.com/accident-injury-law/premises-liability-who-is-responsible.html (last visited Apr. 29, 2018).

125. NOLO.com, *Landlord Liability,* https://www.nolo.com/legal-encyclopedia/landlord-liability (last visited Apr.29, 2018).

126. Marcia Stewart, *Breaking a Lease and Leaving Early,* NOLO.com, https://www.nolo.com/legal-encyclopedia/free-books/renters-rights-book/chapter9-5.html (last visited Apr. 29, 2018).

127. Van Thompson, *Consequences of Landlords Breaking a Lease Agreement,* S.F. GATE, http://homeguides.sfgate.com/consequences-landlords-breaking-lease-agreement-49165.html (last visited Apr. 29, 2018); Marcia Stewart, *How Evictions Work: What Renters Need to Know,* NOLO.com, https://www.nolo.com/legal-encyclopedia/evictions-renters-tenants-rights-29824.html (last visited Apr. 29, 2018).

ants break the lease or rental agreement, they are generally obligated to fulfill for the duration of the lease and could have to pay the rent for the remaining months on the lease or cover expenses that the landlord has associated with re-renting (*e.g.*, advertising expenditures). A tenant's credit report could also be negatively affected.[128]

d. Takeaways

All parties considering involvement in an ADU project should consult an attorney due to the complex nature of the contractual rights and responsibilities that may arise throughout the life of the project. Lessor-lessee and landlord-tenant laws are derived from both federal and local law, and the parties involved should contact an attorney with knowledge of those contractual relationships in the specific jurisdiction where an ADU project is to be implemented. Further, ADU project participants should be made aware that all terms of program involvement are specified in contracts between the program or organization, homeowner, and resident. As new contractual relationships arise throughout the life of the project, participating parties should maintain awareness of relevant contract laws and contact an attorney with questions.

ADU Project Contractual Relationship Checklist

- ❑ Identify all parties.
- ❑ Determine who has legal ownership of the ADU.
- ❑ Determine which party is taking on responsibilities of landlord (e.g., repairs, maintenance, and guaranteeing warranty of habitability).
- ❑ Discuss what happens in case of breach; how do parties want worst-case scenario to be resolved?
- ❑ Consult attorneys to ensure all parties understand the clauses and legal ramifications of each contract.

---

128. Christy Rakoczy, *How to break a lease: Pros and cons of breaking your rental contract—and tenants legal rights*, MIC.COM, Jul. 14, 2017, https://mic.com/articles/182068/break-a-lease-the-smart-way-pros-and-cons-of-breaking-your-contract-and-tenants-legal-rights#.JNSWyUkqB.

V. Conclusion

U.S. cities are facing increasing rates of homelessness largely due to a severe lack of affordable housing. When cities and organizations utilize ADUs to house unhoused individuals, those small living spaces help combat rising homelessness. ADUs can be viable, cost-effective alternatives to traditional shelters that provide stable housing and community ties for individuals and families experiencing homelessness. As proven in municipalities like Seattle, Multnomah County, L.A. County, and Denver, cities and organizations across the country can use ADUs to help combat homelessness if they strategically consider the logistical and legal considerations that accompany a homeless-oriented ADU program.

Table of Cases

Index